THE BEST OF

THE JOURNAL OF IRREPRODUCIBLE RESULTS

THE BEST OF

THE JOURNAL OF IRREPRODUCIBLE RESULTS

"Improbable Investigations & Unfounded Findings"

Edited by
Dr. George H. Scherr

Associate Editor
Richard Liebmann-Smith

Workman Publishing
New York

Library of Congress Cataloging in Publication Data

Main entry under title:

The Best of the Journal of irreproducible results.

　　1. Science—Anecdotes, facetiae, satire, etc.
I. Scherr, George H. II. Journal of irreproducible results.
Q167.B47 1983　　001.4'3'0207　　83-40034
ISBN 0-89480-595-9

Art Director: Paul Hanson
Designer: Diane LeMasters
Cover illustration: Ed Lipinski

Workman books are available at special discounts when purchased in bulk for premiums and sales promotions as well as for fund-raising or educational use. Special editions or book excerpts can also be created to specification. For details, contact the Special Sales Director at the address below.

Workman Publishing Company, Inc.
708 Broadway
New York, NY 10003

Manufactured in the United States of America

First printing October 1983

10　9　8　7　6　5

Acknowledgments

I gratefully acknowledge the foresight and acumen of Dr. Alexander Kohn of the Ness Ziona Research Institute in establishing the forum that brought together the international scientific community for establishment of a Society of Basic Irreproducible Research.

The editorial skills of Ms. Carol Olson and her yeoman patience in processing the thousands of manuscripts received each year from over 35 countries, has materially contributed to the quality of the Journal.

I especially wish to thank the distinguished members of the editorial board who have participated for many years, without compensation, in a pioneering journalistic foray in pursuit of Irreproducible Results.

Dr. George H. Scherr

Please Note

Most of the articles compiled in *The Best of the Journal of Irreproducible Results* have appeared in the *Journal* between the years 1955 and 1983. Those that have not yet appeared are scheduled for forthcoming issues.

Many authors, when originally submitting their articles to the *Journal*, requested that fictitious names be used instead of their real names. In *The Best of the Journal of Irreproducible Results,* we have maintained these requests.

Because the *Journal* has been around since 1955, many of the people who have written for it have changed their job titles since the writing of their articles. Therefore, a title appearing with an author's name may no longer reflect an author's position or whereabouts.

v

CONTENTS

INTRODUCTION

Irreproducible Science . . . . *IX*

PART I
ANIMALOGY

Recombinant Genetics and Animal
  Husbandry
  by John C. Holden 3
Interspecies Similarities
  *by Kathleen Hunter, M.A., and
  Rachel Harris* 5
A Guide to Correct Barking Abroad
  by Mary Ware 7
Behavioral Genetics of the Sidehill
  Gouger
  by Professor Lawrence M. Dill 9
Bovinity
  by William F. Jud 11
Anecdotal Evidence for the Existence
  of an Unfilled Niche
  by Theodore H. Fleming 12
Fourth Grade Biology Experiment
  by E. Myron Fogarty 14
A Call to Clearer Thinking
  by Chas. M. Fair 16
The Paradox of the Monkey and the
  Bananas
  by E. Papaikonomou, Ph.D. 17
Increasing Abnormality in the Sexual
  Behavior Pattern of the Male
  Black Widow Spider
  by W. Henri Kreicker, D.E. 19
The Reconstruction of "Nessie": The
  Loch Ness Monster Resolved
  by John C. Holden 21

PART II
THE BODY ECCENTRIC

FLOAT: A New Paradigm for Human
  Evolution
  by Donald Symons 27
Man Makes Himself?
  by N.A. Drekopf 29
Golf and the POO Muscle: A
  Preliminary Report
  by Mervyn J. Huston 31
A Short Guide to Doctors
  by John J. Secondi, M.D. 33
How Much Do You Know About
  Adolescent Medicine?
  by Peter H. Gott, M.D. 36
Rare Diseases
  by Ole Didrik Laerum, M.D. 38
Nephrotrichosis: A New Syndrome
  *by I.X. Hume, M.D. and Hedda
  Hare, Ph.D.* 40
The Incidence & Treatment of
  Hyperacrosomia in the United
  States
  by Edmond A. Touré, M.D. 42
Umbilectomy: An Experimental
  Surgical Panacea
  by Carl Jelenko, III, M.D. 44
How to Eat and Lose Weight 45
Effortless and Dietless Weight Loss:
  Unscientifically Researched
  by John J. Twombly 46
The Audible Crunch Bares Truth and
  Dentures 49

The Inheritance Pattern of Death
by Joseph Eastern, M.D.; Carol Drucker, M.D.; and John E. Wolf, Jr., M.D. 51

PART III
THE MIND IN QUESTION

CRAP: Consumer Rated Assessment Procedure
by Alan Frankel, Ph.D.; Dianna Ross Strange; and Reggie Schoonover, S.B.D. 55
Why It's Later Than You Think
by T.L. Freeman 57
Nasality
by Stephen D. Bourgeois, M.D. 59
The Varieties of Psychotherapeutic Experience
by Robert S. Hoffman, M.D. 61
Prenatal Psychoanalysis
by Robert S. Hoffman, M.D. 63
A Proposed Study of Rubber Band Therapy
by Victor Milstein, Ph.D.; Joyce G. Small, M.D.; and Michael J. Deal, M.D. 64
Therapeutic Effects of Forceful Goosing on Major Affective Illness
by Stuart A. Copans 66
The Itemized Statement in Clinical Psychiatry
by Robert S. Hoffman, M.D. 69

PART IV
SOCIAL CONCERNS

National Geographic, The Doomsday Machine
by George H. Kaub 73
National Geographic: Doomsday Machine or Benefactor? A Vindication
by L.M. Jones 75
An Eye for an Eye for an Arm and a Leg
by Gary Perlman 78
Reading Education for Zoo Animals: A Critical Need
by Michael J. Albright. 80
The Solution of the Israeli Water Problem
by Richard Kraft 82
A Modest Proposal Concerning the Future of Transportation
by Edmund J. Cantilli, Ph.D. 84
The Biopump Solution
by Thomas A. Easton, Ph.D. 86
Reducing Automobile Accidents
by John L.S. Hickey 88
Weekend Scientist: Let's Make a Thermonuclear Device
by D.I. Radin 89

PART V
HOW RESEARCH IS DONE

The Data Enrichment Method
by Henry R. Lewis 93
The Triple Blind Test
R.F., M.D. 96
A Preliminary Report on Genetic Determinants in Aesthetic Decisions
by Ross Coates 97
Notes Upon a Whopper
by Dick Rubinstein 99
Interference of Labium Superius Oris Hair with Spherical Ice Cream Surfaces
by Dinesh Mohan 100

Evolution of Scientific Thought
  by Frank Anderson 102
Raymond Smith's Story
  by Dr. Kurt W. Rothschild. 104
Branching and Sprouting
  by O.A. Selnes and H.A.
  Whitaker 105
A Drastic Cost Saving Approach to
  Using Your Neighbor's Electron
  Microscope
  by Aalbert Heine 107
Effect of Left-Right Inversion Upon
  the Size-Weight Illusion
  by Clair Schulz 109
Cogito Ergo Sum: Murphy's
  Refutation of Descartes
  by N.L. Morgenstern, M.D. 112
The Feeding Habits of Mosquitoes on
  Rabbits
  by Michael Bar-Kev-Keves 113
Finding the Lost Chord
  by E.N. Gilbert 115

PART VI
ONE-MINUTE MISMANAGER

Safety Hazards: A Memo
  by N.A. Clarke 119
A Probabilistic Formulation of
  Murphy Dynamics as Applied to
  the Analysis of Operational
  Research Problems
  by William R. Simpson 120
Beyond Incompetence
  by Frank R. Freemon 124
Project Management
  by B. Sparks 126
From Paper Clip to Pentagon
  by Morton Rothstein, Ph.D. 128
Rationale for Procrastination
  by Frieda B. Taub, Ph.D. 130

PART VII
WORDS AND NUMBERS

Sexual Behavior in the Human
  Language
  by H.J. Lipkinsey. 133
Decline of Language as a Medium of
  Communication
  by R.J. Hoyle 134
A Layman's Guide to the
  Introduction of New Words into
  the English Language
  by P. Kendall du Par, Ph.D. 136
Cliche Conflicts: A Quantitative Case
  Study
  by L. Allen Abel. 138
The Lost Theorem of Euclid
  by David C. Jolly 140
Metric Havoc
  by Jerry W. Mansfield 143
Correct Metric Time
  by James Wilson 144
The Largest Integer
  by Joel H. Spencer 145
Measuring the Primadonna Factor
  for Odd Numbers
  by Y. Ronen, et. al. 146
Impure Mathematics 147

PART VIII
OFF THE IVORY TOWER

Vide-Infra
  by Tim Healey, F.F.R., M.I.Nuc.E. . . . 151
Thesis Guidelines
  by Roger E. Soles 152
How to Be a Published
  Mathematician
  by David Louis Schwartz. 153
The Faculty Phrase Finder
  by William B. LeMar. 154

A Verbal Rorschach
  by E.J. Helwig 155
Testing the External Validity of
  Zimbardo's Classic Prisoner
  Experiment
  by Raymond C. Russ and Steven
  Connelly 156
A Brief History of Scholarly
  Publishing
  by Donald D. Jackson 158
How to Publish without Perishing 159
A Psychological Study of Journal
  Editors
  by S.A. Rudin 162

PART IX
IDEAS WHOSE TIME . . .

The Fly as an Aeronautic Force
  by Tim M. Sharon, Ph.D. and
  Richard D. Brewer, Ph.D. 167
The Pachydermobile
  by Terry Maple 169
The Six-Day Week—It's Time for a
  Change
  by R.L. Sendall 171
E Pluribus Uranium
  by Charles T. Stewart, Jr. 173
A New Flavoring Agent and
  Preservative for Food?
  by Dr. Erich Luck 174

The Ultimate Drinking Glass
  by Jordan Levenson, B.S., M.B.A. . . . 176
The Order
  by Dale Lowdermilk 177
The Anisotropy of a Political Map
  by Vladimir Funk 179
Definition of a Darkbulb
  by James L. DeLucas 180
No-Fault Crime Insurance
  by Estelle Gilson 182

PART X
LET'S GET METAPHYSICAL

Request for Supplement to U.C.F.
  Grant #000-00-00000-001
  "Creation of the Universe": A
  Proposal
  by Jay M. Pasachoff and Spencer
  R. Weart 187
Econogenesis
  by David H. Weinflash 189
The Learning of a Simple Maze Habit
  by Angels
  by David Lester 190
CONFESS
  by Kenneth Majer and Michael
  C. Flanigan 192
Memo to Moses from HEW
  by James E. Mignard, Ph.D. 194

IRREPRODUCIBLE SCIENCE

The glorious endeavor that we know today as science has grown out of the murk of sorcery, religious ritual, and cooking. But while witches, priests, and chefs were developing taller and taller hats, scientists worked out a method for determining the validity of their experimental results: they learned to ask, "are they reproducible?"—that is, would anyone using the same materials and methods arrive at the same results? For example, it is very important to scientists that two iron balls of unequal mass dropped together from the leaning tower of Pisa hit the ground simultaneously whether dropped by Galileo in 1590 or Mr. T. today.

Conversely, scientists have always been highly suspicious of results that cannot be replicated. Traditionally they have seen them as signs of incompetence or deliberate deception. Such results have seldom been published in respectable scientific journals.

And what has all this science of reproducibility gotten us? "Smart" bombs. Agent Orange. Moon golf. It is no surprise that over the years the notion of reproducibility has lost its luster for some of our most brilliant, most creative minds. Just because every Tom, Dick, and Harry can't reproduce their brilliant, most creative findings doesn't mean these findings are not true, they argue.

And in fact, why should we close our minds to some of the most ingenious inventions, discoveries and innovations in history just because they fail to come up to an outmoded standard? A new criterion is necessary. So, faced with fascinating findings these brave savants, instead of tediously demanding "is it reproducible?" now boldly inquire "is it funny?"

But where are they to publish their bold strokes of genius? All the so-called "prestigious" journals of science continue to exercise the tyranny of reproducibility. Indeed, in all of science publishing, there is only one journal that is not put off by irreproducibility, that indeed insists upon it. In 1955 Dr. Alexander Kohn of the Ness Ziona Research Institute in Israel made history by publishing the first edition of *The Journal of Irreproducible Results*—a few mimeo-graphed sheets circulated clandestinely among a few hundred scientists. In 1964 I took over publication of the *Journal* and in the ensuing years it has grown until today it is a quarterly circulated to thousands of subscribers and institutions in 35 countries. Likewise the content of the *Journal* has broadened to include irreproducible results from not only the "hard" sciences, but from the social sciences, legal and political science, management theory, and even philosophy. At last anyone who indulges in irreproducible pursuits can now publish and perish simultaneously.

Dr. George H. Scherr

PART I
ANIMALOGY

RECOMBINANT GENETICS AND ANIMAL HUSBANDRY

John C. Holden
NOAA, Atlantic Oceanographic Laboratories
Miami, Florida

Geneticists have done wonders in the field of animal husbandry. Selective breeding and other primitive techniques have markedly increased the size and quality of farm livestock. However, the recent breakthrough of the so called "recombinant DNA" techniques promises to truly revolutionize man's manipulative powers over his domestic fauna and allow him to design, as it were, exactly the types of critters he needs. Recombinant DNA (or "recombinant genetics") does not mean making entirely new species of animals. Rather, as the name implies, parts of existing species can be genetically recombined with other parts to form composite organisms. In other words nothing really new is going to be created, *but* mixtures of all life forms now in existence are possible!

Fig. 1

There is considerable concern by scientists and politicians alike about the wisdom of continuing research in this form of genetic engineering. The critics maintain that by tinkering with new life forms science is opening Pandora's Box and is about to release swarms of different creatures into the world with the potential to do great harm. The proponents, on the other hand, see a bright future with benefits far outweighing any possible problems.

It is not my intent to choose sides on the issue of whether or not to continue this kind of research but rather to present some specific examples of what might be tried using these new recombinant techniques on domestic livestock. Nor is it my intent in this brief discussion to exhaust all possibilities of livestock modification. What we are after here is a glimpse at the marvels of this future biotechnology.

More Drumsticks

For generations meat processors have been wishing that someone would cross a chicken with a centipede in order to produce a bird with more than two drumsticks. With recombinant genetics this will be a snap. Genetically echoing the genes responsible for the mid-region, chickens or turkeys of infinite length could be produced. The terminology used to identify such a bird could be very descriptive if done properly. For instance in Fig. 1 we see what might be called a *chickichicken*. Of course *chickickens* and *chickkickickickens* are possible. No doubt experiments will produce undesirable *chichichickens* and *chickenenens*, the latter of possible use in the egg or poultry fertilizer industry.

With the advent of the *chickickicken* (and the *turkrkrkey*) there will be fewer squabbles around the family dinner table since it will then be possible for everyone to have a leg. Unfortunately, these benefits will not be without their costs as the much coveted wishbone will become relatively scarcer as the legs become more abundant.

In the dairy industry one might anticipate a similar genetic approach resulting in, say, a *cowowow*. That is, a cow with multiple rear regions, thus numerous udders. However, it would be of greater advantage to concentrate only on the udder instead of the whole posterior part of the animal. Everyone knows that the milk comes out of the teats. Therefore, duplicating those organs would achieve the desired result and produce an animal shown in Fig. 2. This condition is here termed "polynipplia" and should not be confused with polymastia, an abnormality known to occur in many mammals. The animal would be known as a "cowwwww" (pronounced "cowwwwww") with the number of "w's" in the name representing the number of faucets on the udder. Of course a dairy with such animals would require a labor-intensive operation. Either that or some radical innovations in the manufacture of milking machines—a technological problem not considered here.

Fig. 2

A Cowboy's Dream

So far we have only considered the recombinant duplication of an organ in a specific species. Next we will consider the case of gene splicing where similar parts of a species are joined together with interesting results.

Every rancher strives for rapid growth in his animals. By simply splicing (genetically, of course) the ends of the animals that do the most eating one creates a beast that consumes twice as fast and eats twice as much. The calf will grow into an animal known as a "steereets" as shown in Fig. 3. During calving the much dreaded breach birth will, by definition, be impossible as the calf will always come out head first even if it comes out backward.

Fig. 3

Happily, the mature range animal will lack the ability to wander away (or stampede for that matter) as the two halves will always want to go in opposite directions thereby rendering fences unnecessary. Furthermore, the troublesome chore of castration will be avoided as the posterior half will have already been genetically amputated. Such as with all new designs, there will be a trade-off here. At the market, cuts of rib, shank and chuck will be readily available but sirloin and round will become very scarce. There remain a few other minor problems with the *steereets* concept, namely, the animal will be susceptible to profound constipation and will not have the capacity of reproduction...

Our last example is the result of genetically splicing two separate species together producing what could be the perfect ranch hand. Fig. 4 shows the interspecific recombinant known as a "horseman." In anticipation of the creation of this creature we can go ahead and give it the scientific name of *Homoequus cowboyensis.*

Fig. 4

In addition to being the perfect "marriage" between the man and his horse (and it is well known how attached they can become), the cowboy's health will be greatly improved because he no longer will be able to drive his pick-up truck into town every Saturday night and get into those terrible fights for which he is famous. Nor would he have to spend those tedious hours currying, feeding, and watering his faithful mount for he would be it. Unfortunately, there is some question if the horse half would remain healthy. It is uncertain if the stomach of the creature, which is that of a horse, could weather a constant diet of coffee, beer, and cigarettes ingested by the cowboy half.

INTERSPECIES SIMILARITIES

The Psychological Implications

Kathleen Hunter, M.A., M.Ed.
Rachel Harris

The responsibility to scientifically test commonly held observations is one of the mandates which lies with the professional research community. Thus, this study was conceived by professional researchers and sponsored by the Society to Test Commonly Held Observations. The commonly held observation under study is the similarity in appearance between the human owner and his/her respective pet. It seems that physical similarities exist so that owners and pets actually begin to resemble one another after a minimum period of living together. This observation needs to be distinguished from the similar, commonly held observation that husbands and wives look alike. The explanation frequently offered in this case is that husband-wife similarity is a function of similarity in diet. After much professional research cogitation, it was concluded that this was an unlikely explanation for the similarity in owners and their pets.

Having thus excluded a physiological explanation for owner/pet similarity in appearance, we felt, as professional researchers, justified in turning to psychoanalytic theory. Our professional research thinking process was highly fertilized by the richness of commonly held Freudian observations. It seems that the concept of maternal-fetal unity (Rank & Incest, 1981), which extends into the first few months of life can be further extended to include pets. The ego boundary between the pet and his/her owner or between the owner and his/her pet seems to dissolve so that the physical appearance of both develops commonly observable similarities.

This study was designed to test the hypothesis that owner/pet similarities would be commonly observed in a scientifically controlled setting by objectively blind judges. This study is retrospective by nature and it must be pointed out that the question of whether the pet begins to look like his/her owner or the owner begins to look like his/her pet is beyond the realm of this report.

Method

A variation of random sampling was used to select 16 animals and 15 humans. The animals were chosen from lists of various breeds and temperaments, including both domestic and foreign species. Humans were included in the study only if they were the closest contact of the animal subject and were willing to sign the human subjects consent form. In only one case did a human subject refuse consent. This was the owner of an orangutan named Boopsie. Although he seemed friendly and congenial, each time he was approached for the necessary signature, he smashed a ripe banana on the consent form. He was thought to be either confused by the memory of Bic Banana commercials, or in a state which has been clinically classified as partial aggressive, a variant and close relative of passive aggressive.

When the final selection of subjects was completed, pictures were taken from various angles and distances. Subjects were asked to smile, frown, squint, and act surprised. When subjects were unable to understand the directions, simple imitation was used following principles of modeling set forth by Bandura (1921). Photographs were randomly mixed and numbered.

Judges were chosen so that there would be a minimum of bias in ratings. Persons who were involved in psychological research were excluded because of their suspicious attitude toward studies and their ability to outguess the purpose of this study. Persons with known psychic abilities were also excluded, for obvious reasons. All Scorpios, Leos, Virgos, Cancers, and Aquarians were also excluded, for obvious reasons.

Correct matches

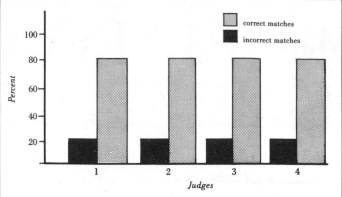

Fig. 1. *Percentages of correct matches and incorrect matches for four typical judges.*

Other persons who were excluded included animal trainers, politicians, nuns, actors, and scholars. The final choice of judges included a homemaker, a librarian, two cement layers, a waitress, and three bank tellers. To minimize variability in ratings due to extra-systemic causal events, cohort bias, etc., each judge was from a different part of the country and no less than five (5) years (in age) from another judge. Ratings were made as follows: A "1" was given to the human who most resembled the animal shown on a projector screen and a "2" was given to the human who most resembled the animal on the screen after the human who was assigned a rating of "1" was removed from the rating group. Finally, a "3" was assigned to the human who most closely resembled the animal under study after the humans assigned a "2" or a "1" rating were removed from the list of subjects from which the judge was to choose. Ratings were multiplied by a constant and then divided by the number of ratings multiplied by the number of judges and inverted so as to eliminate confusing numerical results.

Results

Fig. 1 shows the percentages of correct matches and incorrect matches for four typical judges. As can be seen, there is a marked agreement between judges, and a minimum of variability. Hunter's Test of Z and Fisher's Coordinate Method of analysis were used simultaneously to examine the significance of our findings. Results showed that the probability that a correct choice would be made was $P = .9$. Some of these correct matches are illustrated.

Discussion

The commonly held observation that owners and their pets look alike was found to be true by professional scientific research methods. The implications of this finding may have far reaching effects in the areas of psychoanalysis, family therapy, and the newly emerging discipline of pet psychology. Analysts should be sensitive to the relationship between their analysands and their respective pets. If, in fact, the ego boundary between pet and owner has disintegrated, the analyst must be cautious in dealing with any pet-related material, such as references to fleas, collars, biscuits, litter, or fur. The analysts should be especially aware of any unconscious scratching, sniffing, or tail wagging on the part of the analysand.

Family therapists also need to be sensitive to the psychic identification between owner and pet and the role of the pet in family communication constellations. Even Orion had his dog and thus, the pet has been immortalized in such constellations over the millennium. Pets should, of course, be included in all family therapy sessions and the place the pet assumes in terms of sitting (or lying) in relation to other family members must be carefully noted.

Perhaps this report will have its greatest impact on the newly developing profession of pet psychology. The fact of owner/pet psychic identity could lead to psychosomatic disorders in the unaware pet. Pet psychologists will have to be on the lookout for ulcers, menstrual disorders, and migraine headaches.

REFERENCES

Bandura, O. *Simpleton Imitation.* New York: Wandergate Press, 1921.
Rank, O. & Incest, M. *Returning to the Womb.* New York: Fantasy Press. 1981.

A GUIDE TO CORRECT BARKING ABROAD

A Review

Mary Ware

Shi Pu's study *A Guide to Correct Barking Abroad* is an arresting work that demands the careful attention of any canine planning travel abroad. A dictionary of useful terms in several hundred canine languages, this work fills a painful hiatus in the linguistic canon heretofore available.

All too few animals heed the fact that the rewards of travel increase when one knows something of the language of the host country. Pets in particular should familiarize themselves with the sounds and structures of the languages of the countries in which they are to stay. How many every year spend up to six months in quarantine without understanding a bark barked or a yap yipped? If they were to study before leaving their homelands, they would save themselves much boredom in the kennel, where a little pleasant conversation is the only recreation outside meals. They could also prevent the inconvenience of having to rely on gestures. So often the wave of a paw can be misconstrued. Knowledge of the language of a country also promotes better international relations through the grass-roots relationships with the host-country nationals. Animals, being generally closer to the grass than anyone else, are an untapped source for improved international understanding in this troubled time of ours.

A review of this work must mention that the study goes beyond a mere listing of terms. Special cultural notes are given to aid in sensitizing the visiting dog to the *faux pas* he might make. Various quotations from the dictionary listings can only indicate in part the scope covered.

Argentina
Gua-gua /Gwa-gwa/ The dog visiting Spanish-speaking countries is cautioned against assuming that the Spanish language is the same the world over. A cursory examination of the first half dozen items will reveal the fallacy of this assumption.

Brazil
Au-au /Ow-ow/

China
诓 诓 /Won-won/ n. b. Hong Kong; at the time of preparation of this manuscript, dogs from Red China were unavailable as informants. Do not confuse with 米 米 /mai-mai/ said by Chinese cats and roughly equivalent to the U. S. Standard *meow.*

Colombia
Guau-guau /Huow-huow/ This sound is rather difficult for non-native speakers, but by diphthongizing the *uo* and drawing the sound out slowly, a comprehensible approximation can be made.

Costa Rica
Guau guau (sic.) /Gwow-gwow/

Cuba
Jau-jau /How-how/ Although the revolution has produced some slang variants, the standard has remained constant.

El Salvador
Guau-guau /Woaw-woaw/

Estonia
Auh-auh /Aw-aw/

Finland
Hau-hau /How-how/

Guatemala
Bow-wow /Bow-wow/ n. b. The full import of the similarity between the Guatemalan and U. S. barks is still being researched.

Israel
 הַו הַו /How-how/ n. b. Before June, 1966, Hebrew-speaking sector.

Lebanon

ﻫﻊ ﺭﻫﻊ /Haw-haw/

Nigeria: Calabar area

Wai-wai /Waing-waing/

Nigeria: Western area, Yoruba language

Gbogbo /Gbo-gbo/ The multiplicity of languages within a single country complicates communication immeasurably; however, it is hoped that the increasing use of English as a *lingua franca* will lessen this difficulty. It would be unfortunate, nevertheless, if the traditional forms were lost in the process. A society is currently being formed to minimize this danger.

Peru

Gua-gua-gua /Wow-wow-wow/ Peruvian dogs are known for their overreaction to even the simplest situations.

Philippines

Bow-wow /Bow-wow/ American influence; regrettably the beautiful native sounds have been forgotten by even the oldest inhabitants.

Syria

ﻫﻊ ﺭﻫﻊ /Haw-haw/ A dog speaking Arabic has a better chance of making a socially acceptable comment to Arabic speakers from various countries than a dog speaking Spanish in different Spanish-speaking countries. See Lebanon; Argentina, note; however, the visitor should listen carefully to the inflection of the host country national.

Thailand

ร่อ ร่ ตุ่ /Hong-hong/

Ukraine

Брawє /Breshe/

Vietnam n.b. The southern section

Gâu gâu /Go-go/ French and American contacts with the canine population have apparently been minimal.

To help the animal bent on greater rewards in foreign travel, Shi Pu has urged publication of this compendium in paperback rather than in the better-grossing hard-cover edition, explaining that the "small size makes it [the book] easy to carry in the mouth."[1] The pet is advised to try to learn the languages of as many countries as possible, as the quarantine location, a miniature United Nations, will contain animals from a variety of linguistic backgrounds other than that of the host country.[2]

The approach is sensibly aimed at the general canine rather than at those already initiated into the mysteries of linguistic scholarship, as it is the general reader that has special need for this study. This method of presentation is explained in the introduction:

> The concentration of this phrase book is on greetings, which are the first words needed. The transliterations are into the sound system of American animals as they in particular expect everyone else to speak their language and constitute, therefore, the group that must be reached with greatest urgency. A more comprehensive listing of American dog terms is included so that American animals need no longer be embarrassed by the criticism that they do not know even their own language properly. Although pronunciation is considered the most important linguistic aspect for conversational barking, the really conscientious animal will want to study the written forms presented as well.[3]

Yet the study is backed by erudite research for which Shi Pu is eminently qualified, as can be readily seen by the description of the method used:

> The dictionary has been prepared after several years of intensive research through English as a Second Language classes in various cities, including dozens of sessions in which the students brought their dogs to class to record their voices. The dogs had to be brought singly to avoid their accents becoming impaired through contact with dogs of other linguistic backgrounds. To keep foreign influences at a minimum, foreign students' dogs were preferred to dogs currently in quarantine.[4]

It is indeed touching that the book is dedicated to the dogs "who so freely donated their time to this study."[5]

While it is not Shi Pu's way to use current work to advertise former works, a study of *A Guide to Correct Barking Abroad* cannot end without mentioning related studies by this scholar; for the animal planning travel abroad would do well to study the languages of species other than his own so that he can recognize them without having to crane his neck into many awkward positions, thus risking an attack of lumbago, so uncomfortable in cramped quarters. Available by the same author are *The Vocabulary of Cats, Bird Sounds: An Elementary Phrase Book,* and *The Languages of Larger Animals.* A catalogue of tapes recorded by native speaker canines of superior educational background is also procurable upon request.

---

[1] Shi Pu *A Guide to Correct Barking Abroad.* New York: Animus Animalorum Scribendi, 1972, p. vi.
[2] *Ibid.,* p. vii.
[3] *Ibid.,* pp. xi–xii.
[4] *Ibid.,* p. xxix.
[5] *Ibid.,* p. xxiii.

BEHAVIORAL GENETICS OF THE SIDEHILL GOUGER

Professor Lawrence M. Dill
Department of Biological Sciences
Simon Fraser University
Burnaby, B.C., Canada

The sidehill gouger *(Ascentus lateralis)*, is a unique animal native to the mountainous areas of British Columbia. It possesses two short legs, on the same side of the body, which enable it to stand and walk about on hilly terrain. Thus the sidehill gouger is beautifully adapted to its particular ecological niche.

Within any one population of sidehill gougers two distinct morphological types appear. One of these has the short legs on the right side of the body and is thus able to walk around mountains in a clockwise direction only. The other type, having short left legs, can walk only in a counterclockwise fashion.

Sidehill gouger morphotypes: short right (left); short left (right).

> *They may be the evolutionary progenitors of the present day hyenas.*

ALAN ISELIN

ILLUSTRATIONS BASED ON ORIGINALS APPEARING IN *THE JOURNAL OF IRREPRODUCIBLE RESULTS.*

These two are not distinct species, since they often mate with one another. This is no mean feat since one or both of the animals, having approached from different directions, must back up to effect copulation. Such complex mating behavior suggests that isolating mechanisms between the two morphotypes have not evolved.

To effect copulation the animals must approach each other from opposite directions, backward.

Laboratory investigations were undertaken to elucidate the genetic basis of the dimorphism. Only a short summary of the results will be presented here, as a major paper will appear in a forthcoming issue of *Acts Artifacta.*

The morphology and corresponding behavior of the animals is controlled by two sets of co-dominant genes, each having two alleles. The first locus determines whether anterior or posterior legs are short: the homozygote AA has two short forelegs; the homozygote PP, two short hind legs; and the heterozygote AP, one fore and one hind leg short. The second locus determines on which side of the body these legs appear.

When two individuals of either parental stock mate with one another, all of the progeny produced are of the same genetic constitution as the parents. However, as many young are aborted during pregnancy as are delivered. Examination of these reveals one half of them to have two short back legs on the same side of the body and the others to have two short front legs on the same side. Thus 50% of the zygotes are of a genotype which is developmentally lethal, and the adults therefore breed true.

In contrast a mating between a clockwise and a counterclockwise individual produces three phenotypes in the F_1 as follows:

Proportion	Phenotype	Genotype
.25	short front legs	AADS
.50	diagonally opposite short legs (rockers)	APDS
.25	short rear legs	PPDS

By means of breeding experiments the "rockers" produced an F_2 containing four lethals, four rockers, two clockwise parentals, two counterclockwise parentals, two short front legs and two with short rear legs. This is regarded as the critical test of the hypothesis presented for the genetic constitution of the species.

The experiment could only be conducted after special shoes were fitted to these animals, as they otherwise had a tendency to fall over, either onto their faces (and suffocate), or onto their other ends (and starve to death). In the field they would quickly be selected against.

The behavior of the individuals with short front legs or short rear legs is of considerable interest. The former are able to walk only uphill, eventually falling off the tops of the mountains to certain death on the rocks below; the latter walk only downhill, congregating in river bottoms. There, it can be easily demonstrated, they breed true, although producing 50% developmental lethals each generation. Some theoretical taxonomists suggest that they may be the evolutionary progenitors of the present day hyenas, indicating perhaps a wider global distribution of the sidehill gouger in the past. Reduction of its range may have resulted from the very high genetic load (developmental lethality) carried by the population.

BOVINITY

William F. Jud

Geological anomalies affect animal action. Cliffs, for example, make animals detour. Rivers make them swim. Subsurface structures align them. This latter fact permits geophysical evaluation of ore bodies.

A study has been initiated to determine alignment of cows and the diurnal variations in the intensity and polarity of this alignment. It was found that in the morning cows are generally aligned with their heads (+) toward the pasture, and in the evening just before sunset their tails (−) point in that direction. In addition, there is a definite drift and transport phenomenon in the direction of their (+) ends. Flow lines are sharpest in all cases along the path leading to the barn, and are randomly spread in the pasture proper. The flux causing this alignment strengthens considerably below 15°C during strong wind. The polar effect of wind is such that the cows are oriented with their (−) end toward the wind.

Bovinity flux was first recognized in the Missouri Ozarks. It is the custom there to graze stock over areas of underground mining. Since the original observations on diurnal alignment of cows were made in this locality, namely above ore bodies, it was desirable to verify this correlation in other localities.

Experiments performed in various geographic areas of known geologic structures with cows of different breeds showed an excellent correlation between the mining camp geology and bovine orientation, as shown in Fig. 1 and 2.

In every case, cattle kept over anomalies were polarized at least twice daily. The conclusion drawn from this observation was that wherever cows align one should dig and strike ore.

Bovinity rays vary as the inverse square of the distance from the source. Small changes due to topography, rock density, and elevation are removed from bovinometric calculations through the Bouguer-Holstein correction. Field intensities are mapped in 0.00 μ (milli-moo) units.

Since the development of the automated Airborne Bovinimeter the value of Bovinity Flux has increased considerably, especially for mapping sea cows that live over offshore oil and natural gas fields.

Fig. 1. Sectional view of Cows in Spherical Alignment in Bovinity Field emanating from buried Ore Body.

Fig. 2. Cows in Linear Alignment in Bovinity Field radiating from recently Active Fault.

Summary

A herd of cows in a field align themselves with each other over ore bodies (bovinity flux).

ANECDOTAL EVIDENCE FOR THE EXISTENCE OF AN UNFILLED NICHE

Theodore H. Fleming
Department of Biology
University of Missouri
St. Louis, Missouri

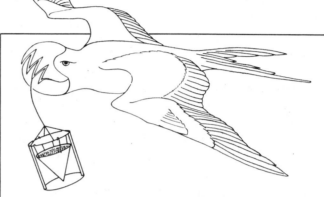

Alan Iselin

The question of whether habitats are saturated—contain the maximum possible number of animal species—is one which has intrigued ecologists for many years. The fact that introduced species often gain a foothold and increase in numbers in a new ecological setting seems to indicate that not all habitats are saturated (see review by Elton, 1958). The following set of observations, perhaps a perfect example of an unfilled niche, is offered as additional evidence for the unsaturated nature of certain habitats.

Materials and Methods

In hopes of attracting winter birds to my backyard, I set up a bird-feeding station in our backyard on November 15, 1968. The station consisted of a commercial "cone" of assorted "bird seeds" (Burpee & Co.) wired to two 9-inch aluminum pie plates (Jane Parker & Co.) that served as a top and a bottom for the station. The pie plates were supported by two pine slats 8 inches in length. The station was suspended by a wire from the west arm of our metal clothesline pole.

The ecological setting of this bird-feeder is the Backyard Biome (Dice, 1952) and consists of the normal garden variety of plants which includes lilac *(Syringa)*, dogwood *(Cornus)*, peony *(Paenonia)*, zinnias *(Zinnia)*, and strawberry *(Fragarus)*. One noteworthy feature is a stand of several ten-foot-tall arborvitae *(Thuja occidentalis)*, which serves to increase the privacy of our backyard. The overhanging boughs of one *arbor vitae* protect the bird-feeder from possible damage by wind and rain. The area encompassed by our backyard is approximately 450 square feet (0.10 a).

Since November 15, I have observed the feeder from my kitchen each day for one continuous hour at a time determined by use of a random numbers table (Steel and Torrie, 1960). In all honesty, I only observed the feeder for one-half hour if the designated time occurred at night. (At a distance of 40 feet, the station was extremely difficult to see in the dark.) All observations were made using 7 × 35 binoculars. Biological observations and weather conditions (temperature, humidity, and precipitation) were recorded on IBM data sheets, and the data were transferred to IBM cards at the end of each week. Data included in this paper were analyzed on an IBM 360 computer.

Results

Between November 15 and February 25, I observed the feeding station for a total of 82.5 hours, and in that time I failed to see a single bird utilize the food available there. Careful examination of the "cone" of seeds indicated that it had never been disturbed. This means that in the 2,448 hours that the food was available, no bird ever visited the feeder (Table 1).

The relationship between lack of feeding activity

TABLE 1. Number of hours of observation, number of birds seen, and average weather conditions during periods of observations of a backyard bird-feeder.

Hours of observation	No. birds seen	No. birds seen per hr. of obs.	Avg. temp. °F	Avg. humidity %	Avg. ppt. inches
82.5	0	0	30.5 ± 0.24	73.4 ± 2.5	0.13 ± 0.01

and temperature, humidity, and precipitation was analyzed by multiple regression. Results showed that none of the three variables was more important than any other in explaining the lack of results ($P > .05$).

Discussion

The lack of results was somewhat surprising and, frankly, very disappointing. I find it hard to explain why no birds were attracted to the feeding station. A paucity of birds in the immediate vicinity of our yard cannot be the reason because I observed English sparrows *(Passer domesticus)*, starlings *(Sturnus vulgaris)*, cardinals *(Richmondea cardinalis)*, and blue jays *(Cyanocitta cristata)* on numerous occasions not more than fifty feet from the feeding station. There appeared to be nothing unusual about the bird seeds or the nature of our yard that might prove unattractive to birds.

> *"Because the niche is rather ephemeral, any species specialized enough to fill it will become extinct very quickly."*

The lack of results forced me to curtail the discussion somewhat as I had been prepared to compare my findings with the MacArthur "broken stick" model (MacArthur, 1957), with various measures of species diversity (reviewed by Hairstron *et al.,* 1968) and niche breadth (Levins, 1968), and Wynne-Edwards' (1962) theory of epideictic display. These comparisons will have to wait until observations become available.

Because no birds were ever observed to use my feeding station, I can only conclude that the feeder represents an unfilled niche. As such, it is intriguing to speculate on just what kind of bird could fill this niche. A more detailed description of the available niche will aid in deciding what kind of bird could take advantage

of it. The "cone" of seeds consisting of hundreds of seeds that average 0.5 mm in diameter weighs 455 grams. This biomass represents about 3,000 kcal of potential energy (Farmer's Almanac, 1968).

It is my opinion that this niche could support one very large, transient bird that might eat the entire feeder (including the aluminum pie pans) in one bite, or several small finchlike birds that might subsist on the seeds for several days. It seems clear that because the niche is rather ephemeral, any species specialized enough to fill it will become extinct very quickly unless it can find another niche with similar characteristics. The species will have to be a "fugitive" in the strictest sense of the word.

I am not undaunted by the lack of results so far and plan to continue observing this "unfilled niche" systematically in hopes of eventually discovering a species that can take advantage of this unusual energetic opportunity.

Summary

A backyard bird-feeder was observed from November 15, 1968, to February 25, 1969. In this period no birds were ever seen to feed there. I believe this represents a classic example of an unfilled niche.

REFERENCES

Anonymous. *Farmer's Almanac:* 1968
Dice, L. R. *Natural Communities.* Ann Arbor: University of Michigan Press, 1952.
Elton, C. S. *The Ecology of Invasions by Animals and Plants.* London: Methuen & Co., 1958.
Hairstron, N. G., J. D. Allan, R. K. Colwell, D. J. Futuyma, J. Howell, M. D. Lubin, J. Mathias, and J. H. Vandermeer. "The Relationship Between Species Diversity and Stability: an Experimental Approach with Protozoa and Bacteria." *Ecology,* 49:1091-1101.
Levins, R. *Evolution in Changing Environments.* Princeton: Princeton University Press, 1968.
Steel, R. G. D., and J. H. Torrie. *Principles and Procedures of Statistics.* New York: McGraw-Hill Book Co., 1960.
Wynne-Edwards, V. C. *Animal Dispersion in Relation to Social Behavior.* Edinburgh: Hafner Press, 1962.

FOURTH GRADE BIOLOGY EXPERIMENT   ·MR.HIGGINS   ANATOMY OF A FROG

PROCEDURE : The student shall dissect a frog and examine its
                    internal organs.

Name of student . . . . E. MYRON FOGARTY

Labrotorie report on Cutting up a frog.

Plan. I will get a frog and a sharp nife, Wnich with I will cut opin the frog whilst he is alive. I will studdie carfulley his innerds, for the purpuss of gaining scientifik knolledge.

Part One. Mr. Higgens give me a frog, a nife, and a pan of stuff like jello. I grapt the frog by his hine legs and I beet his head on the edje of the lab bench so he wood not bight. When he was woosie and ready for scientific investigathun, I stuck thumtax in his foots and pinned him against the jello, with his bellie in frount. Part Two. Soon the frog begun ones agan to kick, and feering his eskape, I scientifikully rammed the shiv in his stumak. There was a stickie dark red flooid which ouzed out from whence I stabbed him. This was kind of fun so I druv the shiv in him agan. I noted that the more I stabbed him the more he kicked. Soon he begun to kick less and less each time I stabbed him and finnalley be kicked not at all. I went to Mr. Higgens and got a new frog. Part Three. I through what was left of the old frog in the wase basket. then put the new one in its place. I was determint to learn more from this frog by condukting a more scientifik experemint. I made too insessyuns akross his tummy and I peelt the skin away so I coold see better. It was kinda silverry inside so I cut deeper, and found his innerds, which I scientifikully scoopt out with a spoon.- Part Fore. I got a woodin handil fork, upon which I put the frog. I turned on a bunsin burnur and held the frog, who kicked not much too terrible now, above it. Soon the smell of rodsti'd frog Filled the labb and Mr. Higgens made me share him with othur kids

Diagram of a frog which I learnt from this experiment.

DIAGRAM OF A FROG WHICH I CUT.

eyebull
other eyebull
nose
lungs
bones
glands
guts
tung
more guts
essofigus
food comes out
hand
innerds
stumak
leg

A CALL TO CLEARER THINKING

Chas. M. Fair
Synax Biomedical Corporation
Somerville, Massachusetts

In an age in which equal opportunity has become a major issue, Marigold L. Linton, in a recent letter to *Science*[1], calls attention to a neglected aspect of the problem. According to Miss (Mrs.?) Linton, the chimp Washoe who has been learning sign-language might have done far better had he (she?) not been "culturally deprived." In fact Linton suggests that the linguistic backwardness of apes in general may be due to the same cause. This is an arresting thought and I suggest that schools be set up in the jungle at once. Funding might be arranged on a matching-grant basis between HEW and UNESCO, with participation of local governments on a scale prorated to the GNP of each.

It will be recalled that John Lilly in *Man and Dolphin*[2] pioneered in this field when he foresaw that dolphins might be taught to speak and proposed that, if not pacifists, they might be used by our government for underwater espionage. It may be that Linton has provided a clue as to why that project has been so slow in materializing. Dolphins probably *can* talk if only we get them started on it soon enough. Thanks to the work of Cousteau and others, a plan for setting up kindergartens for dolphin young in their own habitat is now quite feasible. There they might get the "feel" of language by playing with alphabet blocks, and later listen to stories played to them on speeded up tape. (A dolphin's vocal range runs up to 100,000 cps, its normal speaking voice lying somewhere in the middle of that range, or around 50 kc.) The aim, as I see it, should be to produce not dolphin spies but dolphin teachers, who might then carry on the work for themselves, on an oceanwide scale.

Shaller's work with the gorilla suggests a third group which may only require a nudge from us to begin making giant strides on its own. The reader may recall the story of the golf-playing gorilla whom a man bought and entered in a tournament. The poor animal, having driven the ball 350 yards onto the green, was then handed a putter and drove it another 350 yards into a nearby woods. Lacking, as he and his kind have always been, in the advantages we enjoy from birth, he could hardly have been expected to do otherwise, and besides incomprehension of the game, his action may have revealed a quite natural resentment at the position in which he had been put.

By one of those coincidences which occur with remarkable frequency in the history of science, I have just received a letter from a chimp who recently took his doctorate in driver-training arts at the University of the Pacific on Tutuila. He has given me permission to make his remarks public, since it seems that his *incognito*, respected all these years by his foster parents and fellow students, is about to be abandoned and his achievement made known to the world.

Doctor Ikashi Chojo, who was given his name by the Japanese couple who adopted him, spent his earliest years in the Tokyo Zoo, receiving his first instruction when a visiting ethologist, Professor Eibl-Eibesfeldt, gave him a short course in German word order and prepositional constructions. Dr. Chojo has since scored an impressive number of "firsts." He is the first chimp to speak *and* write Japanese, the first to have played professional baseball—second base with the Hokkaido Giants—the first to shine his own shoes and dress himself. While at the university he shaved the backs of his hands and wore a kimono and a rubber Frankenstein mask to conceal his identity.

Dear mister doctor Fair: Please forgive and forget. I write English rotten, start too late—two months old....I just want to say you good student man-ape relations, out of sight, keep up good work, but strongly resent your suggestion dolphins may equal or surpass ape. All knows dolphin is a fish—warm-blooded but a fish. Sane world polity impossible if dolphin to be included. Please reconsider unsound view.
Yours truely

(Ikashi Chojo, Ph.D.)

The new age may have its complications, but it is clearly here.

[1] *Science*, 1970 169:328.
[2] Lilly, John. *Man and Dolphin*. Pyramid Books, 1962.

THE PARADOX OF THE MONKEY AND THE BANANAS

Experimental Approaches

E. Papaikonomou, Ph.D.
Technology, Inc.
Mountain View, California

Problems that touch upon fundamental concepts of science usually appear to be deceivingly simple but are in fact difficult to analyze theoretically. It is also not uncommon that they lead to unexpected conclusions (paradoxes). It is therefore a source of particular intellectual joy when simple experimental tests of such problems can be devised.

During the course of a recent physiological experiment, we came, entirely by accident, upon methods enabling one to put to experimental test the mechanical problem illustrated in Fig. 1. It is assumed that at rest the system is in equilibrium, the weights of the monkey and the bananas balancing each other. At the moment the monkey catches sight of the bananas, he starts climbing in the hope of reaching them. The paradox is that, surprisingly, he will never achieve this. The reason is that the poor monkey can only move upward by pulling the rope downward. Thus he pulls the bananas an equal distance upward, and the harder he climbs the harder the bananas move upward, staying out of his reach forever. This being clear, it takes some thinking to see that the monkey will actually move neither upward nor downward and thus the bananas will move further away from him after each earnest effort he makes to catch them.

An opportunity to study this paradox experimentally arose during our investigation of certain aspects of the effect of exercise on glucose metabolism in

anesthetized rats. We developed a set-up for stimulating the muscles of the hind limbs of a rat which is shown in Fig. 2. We thus exercised these muscles by having the legs move a weight of 100 grams (weight A)

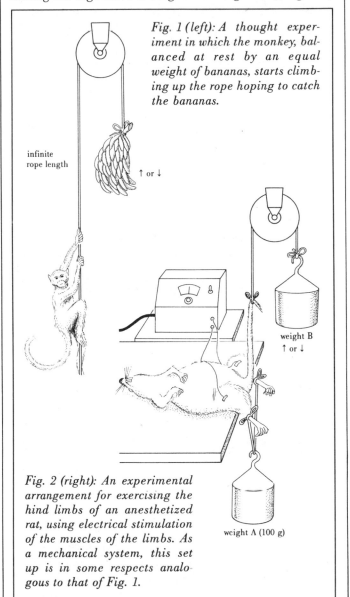

Fig. 1 (left): A thought experiment in which the monkey, balanced at rest by an equal weight of bananas, starts climbing up the rope hoping to catch the bananas.

infinite rope length

↑ or ↓

weight B
↑ or ↓

weight A (100 g)

Fig. 2 (right): An experimental arrangement for exercising the hind limbs of an anesthetized rat, using electrical stimulation of the muscles of the limbs. As a mechanical system, this set up is in some respects analogous to that of Fig. 1.

ALAN ISELIN

in response to a series of electrical pulses, one per sec with a duration of 20 msec and a gradually increasing amplitude starting at 5 volts. Each pulse caused a twitch in the muscles and an upward movement of the legs (and weight A) by approximately 2 cm. Unexpectedly, weight B moved *upward* also (by approximately ⅔ cm for a 400 gram rat). This is in agreement with the above theoretical analysis of the movements of the monkey and the bananas. That the arrangement of Fig. 2 is an analogue of that of Fig. 1 can be seen by observing that, in both cases, upward movement on the left side is caused by a mechanical force internal to the system: electrically stimulated mechanical muscle movement. It should be clear however that the two arrangements are not isomorphic, as is demonstrated by the fact that, though the bananas keep moving upward, weight B in Fig. 2 moves upward at the arrival of each electrical pulse but downward when the pulse vanishes, thus oscillating around its starting position (see discussion). Moreover, it may be of interest to note that none of the many of our colleagues who, on passing by, were asked to predict the direction of first movement of weight B, hit upon the right answer. However, they were all delighted to see they were wrong sixty times per minute, (i.e. as many times as the number of pulses).

Discussion

1. A way to see that the monkey in Fig. 1 will remain at his starting place despite his efforts to climb up, is by applying a, so to speak, "law of conservation of rope length." When the bananas move a certain distance upward, the rope on the right is shortened by an equal length, and this will be equal to the rope length on the left which the monkey pulls down past him when he attempts to climb. Therefore, the length of the rope from the point the monkey is holding it to the pulley will remain constant and so will monkey's distance from the pulley, Q.E.D.

2. The bananas' potential energy (gravity) increases, consuming the monkey's muscular work.

3. There are two main topological differences between the set-ups of Fig. 1 and 2. One is due to the fact that the rat under these conditions is not able to climb on the rope. The other difference arises from the fact that the rat lies on the experimental table and is fixed on the edge of the table with adhesive tape, thus having the lower half of its body suspended; the mechanical equivalent of this arrangement would thus be a lever with an attached weight and pivoted at the one end while suspended at the other end.

4. In an attempt to reproduce the arrangement of Fig. 1, we had the anesthetized rat not lying on the table but suspended entirely from the rope by fixing its front limbs on its tail using adhesive tape. We thus eliminated one of the differences between the set-ups of Fig. 1 and 2 as pin-pointed above, but we still had one difference left, i.e. that the rat cannot climb on the rope under these conditions. In this case, during the electrical stimulation of the muscles of the hind limbs weight B moved steadily upward (advancing a certain constant distance after each pulse), and therefore the rat moved downward at an equal tempo.

5. We are not aware of any published report on an actual performance of the thought experiment of Fig. 1. We therefore attempted to perform this experiment using unanesthetized rats or mice instead of monkeys as experimental animals and balancing weights instead of the bananas. We have not attempted to train the animals to climb on the rope and thus were unsuccessful in having them perform this task. (It is not an easy task, since it would involve pulling a weight as large as the animal's own body weight.) All the animals tested preferred to move downward, despite all our efforts to discourage them (e.g., by pinching them or putting a beaker full of water underneath in which they fell repeatedly). However, in this way the opposite of the monkey-bananas movement was observed: when the rat or mouse moved downward on the rope the balancing weight moved also downward.

6. Finally, the above discussion stimulates some speculations as to the best strategy that the monkey could follow for reaching the bananas. Thus, it is evident that the straightforward approach, i.e. "climb up," is doomed to fail. But how about letting himself slide down the rope, in which case the bananas will move down too? The answer is that, although this approach is better than the straightforward (the monkey does not have to do any work), still he cannot reach his goal because his distance from the bananas will remain the same. Another approach he may consider is to jump up toward the bananas and then let himself slide down; however, this is equivalent to a combined "climb up" "slide down" approach. A more exotic approach is to wait until the bananas ripen so much that one might become detached from the bunch and fall. Unfortunately the monkey's weight now will be larger than that of the bunch of bananas and the monkey will fall exactly as the detached banana, while the bunch will move upward. However, if no banana is detached when the bananas ripen, then it may be that a fly will be attracted to land on the bunch of bananas, thus, with its weight, causing the bananas to move downward with the monkey moving upward, so that he cannot miss them.

INCREASING ABNORMALITY IN THE SEXUAL BEHAVIOR PATTERN OF THE MALE BLACK WIDOW SPIDER

W. Henri Kreicker, D.E.*

Over the years I have enjoyed studying entomology, as a hobby. The study of insects is indeed a fascinating subject. There are almost countless genuses. One could spend a lifetime studying butterflies, for example, and still not know all that there is to know about this group of insects.

More recently I have given over to the study of the arachnids or spiders, which are—strictly speaking—not insects, and in particular, black widow spiders (*Latrodectus mactans*).

I have made some remarkable observations. I say remarkable because in checking through the works of Fabre, Gertsch, Emerton, Bristowe and Comstock, I found no reference to the phenomena I have observed, which has to do with the male of the black widow spider family. The male is considerably smaller than the female.

It is generally known that the female black widow, which is venomous, usually destroys the male immediately after mating. Frequently she devours the male after killing it. I have observed this practice on several occasions. Authorities on spiders have given no satisfactory explanation of this androcidal tendency, nor have I one.

*Distinguished Exterminator

Devouring Passion

The disposing of the male takes place immediately after mating while the male is completely spent from the orgasm. There is no respectable waiting for the ardor to cool. One authority has suggested that the female black widow is invariably disappointed in love, since the male is so much smaller, and exhibits her utter contempt by promptly destroying the male.

Another researcher speculates that the female black widow may be completely carried away with ecstasy and with unbridled emotion destroys the male.

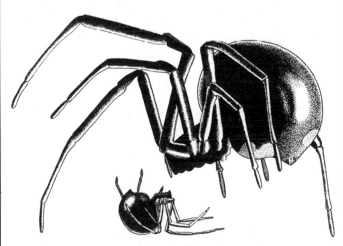

Carried away with ecstasy—or utter contempt—the female destroys the male after mating.

ALAN ISELIN

Among human beings the saying, "I love you so much I could eat you," is not uncommon. The annals are replete with cases of teenagers so-called necking wherein what practically amounts to mayhem was perpetrated, frequently stitches having to be taken.

"More and more the males are turning to each other for sexual gratification."

Kucharov has suggested that the female black widow may be completely emotionally unstable and as a result is filled with mistrust. Fearing the peregrinations of the male during her gestation period she may put her mind at ease by destroying him, then cozily hatching her brood.

A French authority has suggested that the female black widow may be likened to Shah Jehan of Agra, India, who commissioned the Taj Mahal to be built and upon its completion destroyed the builder so that he could never construct anything more beautiful than the Taj Mahal. However, this explanation hardly seems plausible.

It is quite obvious that the libido of the male black widow is strong or else it would not yield to the mating instinct with almost certain death staring it in the face. This would be uxoriousness beyond the call of duty. On the other hand, the male may have been conditioned, down through the ages, to believe that death is not too dear a price to pay for the utter gratification of mating. One would have to mate with a black widow spider to know for certain whether it was worth paying with one's life. It would appear exorbitant. The Italians, however, have a saying, "See Florence and die" (referring to the city, of course).

Out of the Closet

By careful scrutiny of the minute creatures I have learned that there is a growing tendency upon the part of the male black widow to weigh the pros and cons of mating. Some of the young bucks have adopted a "fools rush in where angels fear to tread" attitude. As a result, there is a lessening of the black widow spider population. This is favorable since they are dangerous to mankind, their bite (of the female) often resulting in death, albeit it is decreasing study material.

However, what might be termed an unbiological

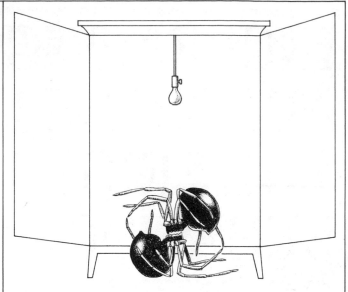

Gay life, spider style: Oh what tangled webs they weave when first they practice to conceive.

ALAN ISELIN

situation is becoming more prevalent among the male black widows. More and more the males are turning to each other for sexual gratification, in what would be termed homosexualism among the human species. The male spiders with palpi interlocked, as in a Japanese kendo match, is indeed an amazing sight.

Somebody once said, "Human nature has not changed since the first human." Likely spider nature has not changed since the first spider. But, it is interesting to conjecture whether on some far distant tomorrow (1) the species will become extinct (like the great African scaled sloth which was too indolent to mate), (2) the female will see the error of her ways, and—superinduced by the dread of being a spinster—will adopt a policy of "live and let live," or (3) the male will adroitly develop a "touch and go" procedure, leaving the female with murder in her heart as he rapidly departs after mating with an "it was fun while it lasted" attitude, or what passes for an attitude among spiders.

Perhaps some observer in 5000 A.B. (After the Atomic Bombing) will know the outcome of the erstwhile precarious love-life of the male black widow and the black pre-widow too.

THE RECONSTRUCTION OF "NESSIE": THE LOCH NESS MONSTER RESOLVED

John C. Holden
NOAA, Atlantic Oceanographic Laboratories
Miami, Florida

Introduction

In recent years there has become available to science an increasing amount of important data concerning the existence of a hitherto undescribed animal residing in the body of fresh water known as Loch Ness in northern Scotland. It is now possible to reconstruct a close facsimile of this enigmatic organism based on three types of data: (a) direct factual information obtained by scientific inquiries on the subject, (b) rumors and hearsay about such a creature and the characteristics ascribed to it by local residents and (c) inductive logic consistent with the geological, paleontological, and biological requirements of the situation. Within the limitations of the above constraints, it is now possible to place the species commonly known as "Nessie" into the scheme of contemporary taxonomy and once and for all establish the scientific reality of the Loch Ness monster.

According to a recent report by the Loch Ness Investigation Bureau[1] sonar signals were recorded from hydrophone experiments in Loch Ness. These noises, from as deep as three hundred feet in the Loch, consist of sonic vibrations of variable intensity and frequency. Some twenty-five miles of recording tapes still await interpretation. Scientific activity on the Loch Ness monster is of fairly recent origin. The legend of the monster goes back much further, however. In general, first hand observers have described Nessie as a slithery or undulating object breaking water. These data are usually gained at night, especially on foggy or other evenings of low visibility attesting to the animal's keen shyness to being too closely scrutinized. One source[2] has described his personal encounter to the author

---

[1] Marshall, N.B. (In: Nichol, D. M.). "None can say Nessie has lochjaw." *Miami Herald,* Fri., Dec. 4:3-G. 1970.

[2] Prof. Samual P. Welles (personal communication), 1971.

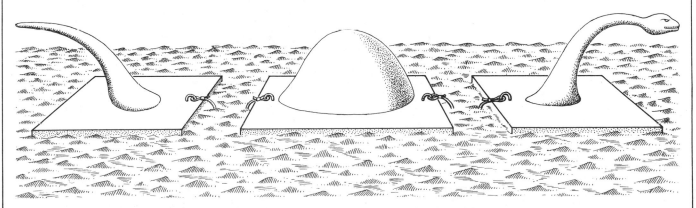

Fig. 1. Sketch of the Loch Ness monster according to information supplied from an eye witness. Due to the trauma of the experience many details of this reconstruction may be in error, though gross morphology is considered valid.

ALAN ISELIN

ILLUSTRATIONS BASED ON ORIGINALS APPEARING IN *THE JOURNAL OF IRREPRODUCIBLE RESULTS.*

which is here summarized in Fig. 1. There are un-doubtedly some errors in the sketch as the witness was highly excited during the interview. It is interesting to note that during the Second World War the German high command had sufficient confidence in the reality of the monster to actually drop bombs in Loch Ness with the intent of destroying the creature and thereby damaging British morale.[3]

In this paper, most of the emphasis is placed on the inductive logical parameter mentioned above. With this data a realistic interpretation concerning the na-ture of Nessie can be made in keeping with the observations and being at the same time consistent with taxonomic and geologic theory.

Two animal types are good candidates for the alleged monster: (1) Cetaceans (Porpoises and whales) and (2) plesiosaurs, a thought-to-be-extinct group of marine reptiles. The Cetaceans can attain "monster-ous" size and are known to have developed complex sonar systems. We must rule them out, unfortunately, since according to Marshall,[1] the noises in Loch Ness are unique. The plesiosaurs, on the other hand, are a fruitful avenue of investigation. First, they show no

[3] Dr. Robert S. Dietz (personal communication), 1970.

Due to specialized prejudicial activities of early man along the banks of Loch Ness, Nessie was induced to evolve a coloration pattern mimicking the traditional scotch plaid.

paleontological evidence of ever having developed so-nar signals. Therefore, should they have done so it would be unique. They also have the additional advan-tage of being more naturally monsterous looking than the friendly cetaceans. The plesiosaurids were large reptiles and though not related to dinosaurs were of comparable size and must have been the dragons of Jurassic-Cretaceous seas.

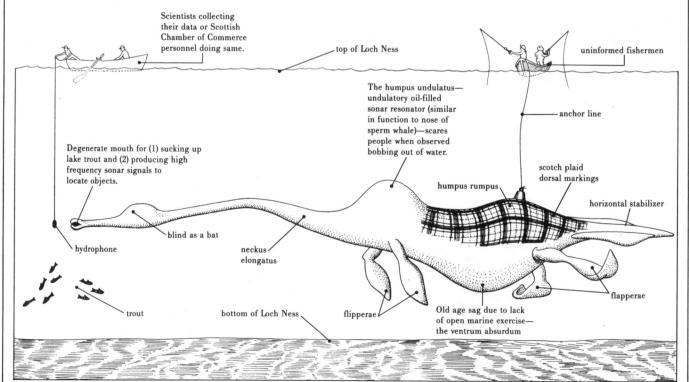

Scientists collecting their data or Scottish Chamber of Commerce personnel doing same.

top of Loch Ness

uninformed fishermen

The humpus undulatus—undulatory oil-filled sonar resonator (similar in function to nose of sperm whale)—scares people when observed bobbing out of water.

anchor line

Degenerate mouth for (1) sucking up lake trout and (2) producing high frequency sonar signals to locate objects.

scotch plaid dorsal markings

humpus rumpus

horizontal stabilizer

hydrophone

blind as a bat

neckus elongatus

trout

bottom of Loch Ness

flipperae

flipperae

Old age sag due to lack of open marine exercise—the ventrum absurdum

flapperae

ALAN ISELIN

*Fig. 2. Reconstruction of **Plesiophonus harmonicus** in its natural habitat in Loch Ness. The specimen is shown using its sonar for locating a hydrophone. Other organisms indigenous to the area are also shown for scale.*

Classification and Systematic Description of the Species

Taking the basic plesiosaurid shape, which has been aptly described as threading a snake through the body of a turtle[4] as a guide, it is possible to make the appropriate changes and reconstruct what Nessie probably looked like. The important features of the reconstruction include: (a) a well developed sonar organ, (b) loss of eyes, (c) elongation and narrowing of the snout with the forward migration of the nostrils enabling the animal to breathe inconspicuously without exposing very much of its body, and finally, (d) basic modifications of the body morphology from the muscular, trim, streamlined oceangoing model to the lethargic, flabby, freshwater type. The following formal description is a convention required by the International Congress of Zoological Nomenclature.

Phylum............... CHORDATA
  Class............... REPTILIA
    Order .... SAUROPTERYGIA
      Suborder .... PLESIOSAURIA
        Superfamily .... PLESIOSAURIDEA
          Family....... PLESIOSONARIDAE new fam.
            Genus..... PLESIOPHONUS new gen.
              Species .. HARMONICUS new sp.

Plesiophonus harmonicus new gen., new species
Figs. 1, 2, 3, 4b

---

[4] Romer, A. S. *The Procession of Life.* New York: World Publishing Co., 1968.

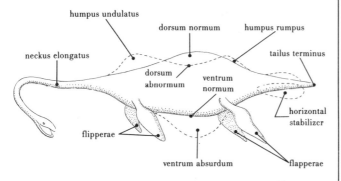

Fig. 3. *The generalized body of* **Plesiophonus harmonicus** *compared to the basic plesiosaurid type. the typical plesiosaurid body is shown in solid line; that of* **Plesiophonus** *in dashed line. The single* **dorsum normum** *of the plesiosaurid gives way to two* **humpae,** *an anterior* **humpus undulatus,** *and a posterior* **humpus rumpus.** *Also, the* **ventrum normum** *typical of the Jurassic-Cretaceous reptiles atrophies into a* **ventrum absurdum** *in the Loch Ness monster.*

Description

Body size: large.

Appendages: the *flipperae* and *flapperae* are typically plesiosaur-like; *neckus elongatus* long, sinuous, scary; *tailus terminus* with horizontal stabilizers.

Humpae of various types new to science (see especially Fig. 3): A *humpus undulatus* in the shoulder region housing oil-filled sonar resonator sensitive to self-emitted sonar frequency signals. This organ is extremely repulsive and strikes fear into those observing it bobbing out of the water on dark nights. Dorsum shifted posteriorly to form the *humpus rumpus* counteracting the anteriorly situated mass of the *humpus undulatus* and maintaining the animal's center of gravity. Prominent *ventrum absurdum* holds vital organs, developed as a result of the species languishing from listless loch life lacking proper open marine exercise.

Head region (see especially Fig. 4b): highly specialized. Teeth and eyes absent. Anterior cranial parts elongated, forming snoutlike mouth for sucking up lake trout and emitting sonar signals. Skull bulbous to accommodate increased I.Q. necessary for (a) acoustical higher mathematics, (b) keeping away from peo-

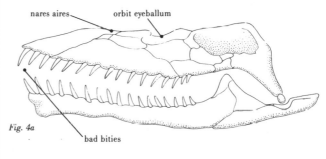

Fig. 4a

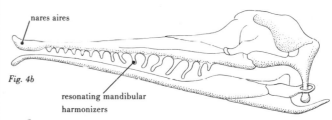

Fig. 4b

ALAN ISELIN

Fig. 4. *Contrasting skulls of the extinct plesiosaurs (4a above) and closely related* **Plesiophonus** *(4b below) from Loch Ness. In the latter the teeth are no longer needed and have disappeared through disuse. Similarly, the* **orbit eyeballum** *is gone with the concomitant enlargements of the* **postfrontal** *(pf),* **postorbital** *(po), and* **frontal** *(f) skull segments. The* **maxilla** *(m) is modified into a series of tuning forks that enable a wide range of unique sounds utilized in sonar emission. The* **prefrontal** *(prf),* **maxilla** *and* **dentary** *(d) are elongated to form a prominent snout.*

ple, and (c) responding to ever more sophisticated electronic apparatus placed into Loch Ness by curious scientists.

Markings: Dorsum covered with scotch plaid color pattern, naturally.

Natural History of the Loch Ness Monster

Loch Ness is the body of water occupying a very ancient and fundamental geological rupture known as the Great Glen Fault. This fault is a tectonic juncture within the crustal Paleozoic and older rocks comprising the basement of northern Scotland. The fault is very ancient as so must be the loch. In fact, Wilson has suggested that it is contiguous under pre-continental drift reconstruction with the Cabot Fault in the Bay of Fundy, North America.[5] This makes the loch greater than 220 million years old. The plesiosaurid great reptiles existed after the basin was already in existence in the Jurassic and Cretaceous (180 to 65 MYBP) so probably inhabited the narrow seaway that extended into the Great Glen Fault. At the end of the Cretaceous the basin was closed to the sea and gradually became freshwater. Most of the entrapped marine fauna became extinct except for some plesiosaurs which adapted to the new freshwater conditions and decided to remain there. Today they titillate the curiosity of visiting scientists, scare the local Scots, and bolster the national economy with visitors from all over the world waiting for a glimpse of something new.

In order to adjust to the new freshwater conditions, the entrapped reptiles had to learn to live in the murk of a freshwater body which lacks, by definition, the sodium cations so helpful in flocculating clays and other fine particulate matter. Therefore, early in the monster's life history Nessie evolved a highly sophisticated sonar organ. As this happened the eyes degenerated by disuse. Competition dropped off markedly in the new environment as *Plesiophonus* found himself there alone. This lack of exercise produced phylogenetic muscular atrophy and the *ventrum absurdum* and *humpus rumpus* developed (not unlike in other vertebrates, e.g., hominids, under easy physical conditions). In the sleepy refugium of Loch Ness the species did not become extinct as did his cousins in the harsher ocean environments.

For more than 65 million years, small changes withstanding, the species remained in homeostatic equilibrium with its environment. With the appear-

---

QUESTIONABLE CONSERVATION

According to a report in *Conservation News*, the U.S. Fish and Wildlife Service has required protection for the Bigfoot and Loch Ness monsters should they be discovered. Officials worry that undisputed proof of existence of "Sasquatch" or *"Nessiteras rhombopteryx"* or any other strange species will attract curiosity seekers and hopeful captors, who could endanger the creatures.

—*From BioScience: Vol. 28, No. 12*

---

ance of man on the scene it then underwent evolutionary saltation in response to intolerant and meddling hominid behavior. Due to specialized prejudicial activities of early man along the banks of Loch Ness, Nessie was induced to evolve a coloration pattern mimicking the traditional scotch plaid. Undoubtedly, nonconformists were selected against violently. During this time the nares aires migrated anteriorly along, and to the end of the elongate snout thereby enabling the species to always keep most of its head submerged.

It remains only a matter of time until one of the specimens of Nessie is captured. Motivation is now supplied not only by a desire for the scientific knowledge to be gained by a face to face encounter but also by a monetary reward. $1,000 (U.S.) has recently been offered for the capture of the "monster."[6]

---

[5] Wilson, J. T. "Cabot Fault, and Appalachian Equivalent of the San Andreas and Great Glen Faults and Some Implications for Continental Displacement." *Nature*, 195:135-138.

[6] Sneigr, D. "Miamian Offering $1,000 for Best 'Monster.'" *Miami News*, Wed., Dec. 9:7-G, 1970.

PART II

THE BODY ECCENTRIC

FLOAT: A NEW PARADIGM FOR HUMAN EVOLUTION

Donald Symons
Department of Anthropology
University of California
Santa Barbara, California

Human characteristics have been said to have their evolutionary origin in seed eating,[1] hunting,[2] tool use,[3] warfare,[4] and aquatic living;[5] but the most comprehensive and logically sustained hypothesis has been ignored, perhaps suppressed. The *flying on air theory*—FLOAT, as it is known acronymously (acrimoniously, among the reactionary human evolution "establishment")—demonstrates that many puzzling and unique features of human anatomy and psyche were adaptive during the aerial phase of human evolution. Human hairlessness clearly represents an aerodynamic specialization; bipedalism is most parsimoniously interpreted as a landing adaptation, convergent with long-legged, clinging-and-leaping prosimians and with birds; buttocks and their concomitant fat deposition in mature females functioned as part of a "saddle" in the small of the back in which infants rode (steatopygia occurs in populations with greater than normal air speeds); long head hair constituted the "reins" held by the infant rider; offspring who were too young to fly independently but too large to ride safely in the maternal "saddle" doubtless lay along the mother's back, accounting for the evolution of ventral handholds (breasts) in mature females.[6]

The Wings of Man?

When flying (technically, flying behavior) evolved is difficult to determine. Our closest living relatives, chimpanzees and gorillas, do not fly (or at least do not do so when they are being observed), although they occasionally exhibit closely related falling behavior. Neither do they possess human "flight specializations." But if apes "devolved" into a more primitive condition to avoid competing with humans,[7] the common ancestor may have possessed flying abilities which were lost in the ape lineages. (That chimpanzees and gorillas build nests is highly suggestive.)

Flying may have become dysfunctional owing to the extremes of sexual inventiveness possible to advanced, airborne hominids.

The fossil man "establishment," their headpieces filled with straw men, call attention to the absence of winged hominids in the fossil record. But behavior, as is widely known, does not fossilize; FLOAT is verified not in lifeless rocks but in living psyche. The universally experienced dream (racial memory) of flying testifies that humans flew with will power, not wings. The hypertrophy of the human cerebral cortex—so excessive from a modern perspective—

[1] Jolly, C. J. "The Seed-eaters: A New Model of Hominid Differentiation Based on a Baboon Analogy." *Man*, 5:5–26, 1970.
[2] Laughlin, W. S. "Hunting: an Integrating Biobehavior System and its Evolutionary Importance." In *Man the Hunter*, edited by R. B. Lee and I. DeVore. Chicago: Aldine, 1968.
[3] Washburn, S. L. "On Holloway's 'tools and teeth'." *American Anthropologist*, 70:97–101, 1968.
[4] Alexander, R. D. "The Search for an Evolutionary Philosophy of Man." *Proceedings of the Royal Society of Victoria*, 84:99–120, 1971.
[5] Morgan, E. *The Descent of Woman*. New York: Stein and Day, 1972.
[6] Noting that adult males probably taught their offspring to fly, B.

Langefeld (personal communication) suggests that genital hypertrophy reflects the male's role as parachute.

[7] Kortlandt, A. *New Perspectives on Ape and Human Evolution*. Amsterdam: Stichting voor Psychobiologie, 1972.

represents the mechanism by which our ancestors "willed" flight. Consider as well the sympathetic stirrings evoked by soaring birds— hawks, eagles, gulls— as opposed to wing flapping birds.

Why flight evolved is obvious, since there are so many adaptive advantages to flying—in mobility, in escape from predators, in hunting, in fighting, in eating fruit at the tips of branches, in locating a potential mate, in avoiding a mate already acquired. Why flight was lost is obscure because there are no apparent advantages in not flying, but clues can be found in dreams, cartoons, fairy tales, and myths. The dreamer soars at will until doubts assail him; cartoon characters remain suspended in mid-air until they look down; in Peter Pan, children needed only to believe in order to fly, and the loss of this ability upon growing up suggests a relationship between flying and innocence; Daedalus and Icarus flew, but Icarus, straining for glory and experience beyond the human lot, was destroyed. Surely the sexual significance of flying is unmistakable; indeed, flying is a common metaphor for ecstatic, uninhibited sexual congress. Even today, stewardesses exert an almost magical lure on the male imagination. Flying may have become dysfunctional owing to the extremes of sexual inventiveness possible to advanced, airborne hominids, resulting in collisions, entanglements, and other copulatory aerial disasters. Natural selection thus began to favor hominids who repressed their knowledge of flight and hence their undisciplined sexuality.[8] (In Judeo-Christian myth, not only is heaven in the sky, but by tempting Adam with [sexual] knowledge, Eve assured his [and her] "fall.")

Soaring Shamans

This hypothesis can be tested by considering instances in which contemporary humans fly. Flying is expected: to occur only in unusual circumstances; to be associated with feelings of sexual abandon; and hence to be accompanied by psychosexual conflict. Fortunately, relevant data are available. Wilbert[9] reports that all

---

THE
AFTER-YEARS-OF-RESEARCH
DEPT.

"Injuries caused by the cold include all those due to lack of warmth."

International Civil Defence Organization
I.C.D.O. Monographic Serial No. 5

shamans of the Warao Indians of Venezuela[10] fly to visit the supreme spirits. But the novice shaman can fly only after extensive fasting and—significantly—sexual abstinence. Although flights are repeatedly characterized as "ecstatic," the novice must overcome obstacles and temptations if he is ever to return. He begins his maiden voyage by smoking an enormous quantity of tobacco in the form of a "long shamanic" cigar. Once airborne, he is tempted by women: "...he sees them making bark cloth for pubic covers but must not linger with them, much less have sexual intercourse" (ibid., p. 64). Still airborne, he plunges through a hole with rapidly opening and closing doors in the trunk of an enormous hollow tree, within which he encounters a huge female serpent "with four colorful horns and a fiery-red luminous ball on the tip of her protruding tongue" (ibid., p. 65).

While the foregoing may be a straightforward account of actual events, it seems more likely that reported events merely symbolize severe psychosexual conflicts experienced by the novice shaman while airborne, which is not surprising since he is engaging in a behavior pattern that has been, for countless generations, disfavored by natural selection. The Warao data thus unequivocally support both the above outlined predictions and the FLOAT itself.

---

[8] Alternatively, G-A. Galanti (personal communication) suggests that the hominid's loss of flight resulted from aerial competition with astronauts from outer space. FLOAT can accommodate this suggestion. Owing to the exuberant aerial sexual acrobatics of early hominids, some hybridization with astronauts was inevitable, accounting for the universal myth of godlike ancestors. Since hybrids generally are of low Darwinian fitness, and female hominids have exceeded males in parental investment[11] at least since the Upper Epicene,[12] selection would have operated much more strongly against female than against male matings with astronauts. Even today, flying-related words and phrases ("my angel," "my little chickadee") are used as terms of endearment by men but never by women, and men often display affectionate tolerance for flighty women, but the reverse is seldom, if ever, the case.

[9] Wilbert, J. "Tobacco and shamanistic ecstasy among the Warao Indians of Venezuela." In *Flesh of the Gods,* edited by P. T. Furst. New York: Praeger, 1972. While, strictly speaking, D. E. Brown actually brought this article to my attention, surely C. S. Lancaster would have done so had he

been aware of its existence. Since Lancaster's career is being built largely via acknowledgments in footnotes, I would like to take this opportunity to thank him for his virtual contribution.

[10] Not to be confused with their neighbors, the Yawnomamö (the bored people).

[11] Trivers, R. L. "Parental Investment and Sexual Selection." In *Sexual Selection and the Descent of Man 1871–1971,* edited by B. Campbell. Chicago: Aldine, 1972.

[12] Alii, E. "Snags 'n Snails 'n Sugar 'n Spice: Post-Epicene Sexual Dimorphism in the Hominidae." *Journal of Implied Anthropology,* 4:1–45, 1974.

MAN MAKES HIMSELF?

N. A. Drekopf*

Most anthropologists will agree that one of the more exciting developments in our discipline in recent years has been the discovery of the science of primatology. We concede that work on animal behavior has been done in the past by zoologists, comparative psychologists, ethnologists, and an extinct breed of scholar known as the "naturalist" (e.g., Darwin, Wallace, Agassiz, etc.), but their efforts have been insignificant when compared to the edge-cutting research now being done by anthropologists. Only members of our discipline have had the courage and imagination to extrapolate from the behavior of baboons, macaques, gorillas, and chimpanzees to a line of inquiry that has shed light upon the social evolution of early man. They have thus developed a methodology which allows us to determine the parameters of primitive human existence through analysis of the possibilities and limitations inherent in the organic equipment and behavioral inventory of our precursors. It is this Inferential Method which I intend to faithfully apply in the present paper.

It has been convincingly argued that hands are the father of man. Now, all primates have considerable manual dexterity, but it is agreed that the evolution of the full potential of the forelimbs is dependent upon the abandonment of quadrupedal motion and the lifting of the hands from the ground. Quite clearly, this is not a characteristic of the terrestrial monkeys and apes, all of which (or *whom*, depending upon one's opinion as to their capacity for culture) use their forelimbs in locomotion, and most scholars see arboreal existence as a precondition of the evolution of man. Attention has properly been turned to the arboreal primates in our search for insight into human evolution, but the observation of these creatures in the wild is made difficult by the fact that the human observer cannot follow them and usually cannot even see them.

Kornbluth's Katskill Kongo

The research upon which this paper is based suffered from this limitation, and, regretfully, it was necessary to observe arboreal monkeys in captivity. Except for brief trips to the Bronx Zoo, for comparative purposes, all the data were collected at Kornbluth's Katskill Kongo, a game farm in Grossinger, New York. The primate population at this research station included three spider monkeys, one capuchin, and two squirrel monkeys. (Mr. Kornbluth also had in his collection an aged hyena, a descented skunk, and two stuffed owls.) The monkeys lived largely on knishes thrown to them by tourists; since this is probably not characteristic in their natural habitat, I will not dwell heavily on feeding. The focus of this paper, however, is upon the use of the hands, and it is worthwhile to note at this juncture that I observed one squirrel monkey catch with his right hand a piece of halvah thrown from a distance of fifty feet. All the animals observed exhibited considerable manual dexterity, an ability made possible by the fact that they were usually in a sitting posture. Thus, though they do not have true bipedal gait, they very rarely used their forelimbs in locomotion. In fact, they moved around very little at all due to a limitation in space that was made necessary by the recent expansion of Kornbluth's Kottage Kolony, where I resided while in the field.

The monkeys observed by me at KKK only employed their hands in eating during 5% of the time. This again is an artificial limitation which must be corrected if we are to properly interpret the wild state. That the animals spent so little time in feeding was largely a function of meteorological conditions. Rainy and cool weather during the summer in which the field work was conducted drastically lowered the number of tourists, and therefore the knishes, and the ASPCA ultimately closed Kornbluth's Katskill Kongo after half the animals had died. Mr. Kornbluth has since de-

---

* Mr. Drekopf is the alter ego of Dr. Robert F. Murphy, Department of Anthropology, Columbia University, who it should be noted, has confined his primate researches to occasional trips to the zoo with his children.

clared bankruptcy, a great loss to primatological research.

Even with the above slight deviation from natural conditions, a startling fact was noted. Approximately 40% of the manual movements of the monkeys were oriented to scratching and delousing (perhaps a higher figure than in the natural state due to the conditions of the cage), but, and this should be carefully noted, *55% of hand use was in masturbation.* It has long been known that this practice is common among monkeys, but I believe that this is the first time in which hard figures have been compiled. Frequency of masturbation varied from one squirrel monkey that masturbated on the average of 130 times daily to a spider monkey that communed with himself 723 times during a 24-hour period.[1] It was noted that toward the end of each day fatigue impelled the latter animal to use his prehensile tail for the purpose. This behavior, which I term *caudurbation,* has not previously been reported in the literature. These inordinately high rates of self-congress do not necessarily imply that most of the monkey day was taken up in such activity, for each episode lasted only three and one-half seconds.

Uses and Abuses

It is possible now to consider the implications of these findings for evolution using the Inferential Method outlined in the introduction of this paper. (A tabular presentation of the full data will appear in a book to be published shortly by Pincus-Hall, Inc.) Man, it is agreed, developed culture through the use of his hands in the making of tools. There is also little doubt that the monkey hand, as we know it, is just about as evolved as was man's at the time when he made his breakthrough to humanity. The difference between the proto-human and the monkey lay exactly in the differential *uses* of the forelimbs by each primate.

Our thesis that there is not all that much difference between the monkeys and man leads to a query of the usual assumption that the ancestry of monkeys and of man became differentiated early in the Tertiary Era. I would suggest instead that the two lines parted company in the Pliocene. The inferential basis for this statement is contained in the data presented above. I submit that man and the monkey had reached approximately the same stage of evolution during the Pliocene period (there is very strong support among certain eminent physical anthropologists for such parallelism), but man made tools with his newly evolved manual equipment whereas the monkey masturbated. The result was that this almost human creature rapidly degenerated, becoming the fuzzy and unintelligent animal that we now see in the zoo.

While I will grant that occasional, even daily, masturbation has not produced marked deterioration among *Homo sapiens,* one can only wonder at the evolutionary consequences if men were to do so hundreds of times a day as reported in this paper for monkeys. Given these considerations it would perhaps be more profitable to look upon the monkey not as a prehuman, but as insane. It thus becomes necessary to reclassify the monkey as being a member of the genus *Homo.* Sapient he is not, however, so I will suggest the term *Homo onanismus drekopfii,* a name that at once combines his close relationship to man with his principal activity and at the same time incorporates the name of the writer.[2]

The Tool-maker

I may now be asked why man took the direction of tool making and *Homo onanismus* directed his interests inward. The answer is really very simple: female monkeys remained victims of the estrus cycle while the human woman gained control over her generative abilities. During most of the year, the male *Homo onanismus* had no forms of gratification other than those provided from his own resources, a routine which was only occasionally broken by a female coming into heat. Infrequent though these occasions may have been, biological compulsion required the female to present herself in a subordinate manner, and penetrability of the identity was maximized. Lacking choice alternatives, she never advanced to the position of a social person, unlike her human counterpart.

The ultimate key to understanding humanity, then, is not that the *Homo sapiens* females are in heat all the time: they are *not.* Rather, they are able to choose exactly when to go into heat and are thereby able to control the males. The female stages this with sufficient frequency that man chooses to use his hands for externally oriented work, usually instigated by women. The female is therefore ultimately responsible for the evolution of culture. In conclusion, we may correct V. Gordon Childe's famous title. Man did *not* make himself—women made men—only monkeys make themselves.

---

[1] The only female in the troop was the capuchin monkey. This, however, seems to have little bearing upon the data or the conclusions given below.

[2] This will strike some readers as immodest, but I should stress that the theory outlined in this paper has never been presented before, and the wording of my reclassification indicates only that I bear sole responsibility for it. I wish to restate my obligation to others, however, for the basic methodology that has produced these conclusions. Pioneering though my theory may be, I am optimistic that even more startling results will follow the further application of this method.

GOLF AND THE POO MUSCLE: A PRELIMINARY REPORT

Mervyn J. Huston
Dean, Faculty of Pharmacy
and Pharmaceutical Sciences
University of Alberta
Edmonton, Canada

Golf, that ancient and honorable game, has been played for centuries by mankind with, in general, indifferent results. A great deal of attention has been paid to improvement of equipment and to development of skill and muscles. Recent research in our laboratories has demonstrated that insufficient attention has been given to the most important factor of all—the POO muscle.

We were brought to a recognition of this phenomenon when a colleague who is an ardent golfer returned from a sabbatical leave in Mexico where he had found that it was impossible to play golf while in the throes of the Montezuma syndrome. Exploratory tests verified our hypothesis that the alimentary tract plays a basic role in golf and that the power of a golf swing is directly proportional to the puissance of the back door thereof. The mechanism involved is the Posterior Orifice Obturator device which is referred to in our laboratories as the POO muscle. The empirical recognition of the importance of this device is to be found in golfing folklore in the expression "to cut washers" when exerting oneself very hard. When a golf pro exhorts a student to "get your ass into the ball" he has arrived intuitively at a fundamental truth.

A Remarkable Device

An analysis of a golf swing discloses that in the back swing the club is raised with the muscles relatively

"The alimentary tract plays a basic role in golf."

relaxed; then with the down swing all hell breaks loose physiologically and anatomically. The POO muscle synchronizes and coordinates all the viscera in a synergistic recruitment of the ancillary abdominal structures. The key device and limiting factor in a powerful swing is the power and finesse of the POO muscle.

The POO muscle is a truly remarkable device. It

When the club is raised the POO muscle becomes relatively relaxed. All hell breaks loose with the down swing.

can accommodate itself to various postures; it can distinguish between the three states of matter; and can adjust to different social occasions. Since the device is muscular in nature, there is no doubt that it can be strengthened by exercise as can other muscles of the body such as those of the arm or leg. The strength of the hand grip can be increased by squeezing a spring contraption so possibly something along this line would be effective; or lifting weights—the whole field is wide open. In the meantime, until more refined techniques have been developed by physical education departments in universities, a golfing enthusiast should introduce the POO muscle into his isometric exercises—very cautiously.

Daffodil Dynamics

The power of the resting state was fully determined rather simply by measuring the force necessary to pluck a daffodil from the experimental area. We used a daffodil to add a touch of elegance to what might otherwise have been a rather vulgar performance. Our group feels that the niceties of life are frequently ignored by researchers so we are spearheading a move to add some class to biological investigations. The experimental set-up required a somewhat more elaborate protocol. The Subject, after preliminary connections had been made in the clubhouse, was escorted to the practice fairway by a procession of scientists wheeling along a portable myodynamometer, a respirometer, a cardiograph, a multi-channel recorder, a computer, a set of golf clubs, and a bevy of children. After much fussing about testing connections and so forth we waited with bated breath for the denouement of this historic event. The Subject wiggled and waggled interminably and then finally smote the ball two hundred and thirty yards down the fairway.

That part of the experiment went well. Unfortunately we had not reckoned with the magnitude of the power of the phenomenon we were dealing with. The internal unit was extruded with such force that it ripped the seat right out of Subject's pants. This dramatic result caused much excitement, confusion, and consternation. The team conferred on ways in which to adjust to this new difficulty. Someone came up with the obvious suggestion that the internal device would have to be anchored in some fashion. The Subject after examining the disaster to his pants vetoed the proposal fearing some sort of implosive contrafissura. After considerable more palaver we shooed the children away and trundled the whole experimental unit off to a secluded part of the course where we continued the experiment minus pants.

After the various attachments had been reassem-bled and checked, Subject again took a great swipe at the ball with everybody standing well back. Our worst fears were realized—he blew the whole attachment into the top of a nearby pine tree. Our team again entered into heated discussion which eventually became rather acrimonious. Subject remained adamant in his rejection of an anchoring system. It seemed for awhile that the whole project would go down the tube.

Action and Reaction

Eventually our theoretician came up with a solution. With an eye on the pine tree, he gave us a dissertation on Newton's third law of motion and recommended that we use a golf ball as the recording instrument. His proposal was as follows: a golf ball would be placed in the experimental area (hereinafter referred to as the POO ball); Subject would hit a drive (hereinafter referred to as the shot ball); the distance traveled by the drive would be compared with the distance traveled by the POO ball. This arrangement would provide an excellent opportunity for mathematical correlation between the power of the drive and the power of the POO muscle.

The first test was a resounding success. The shot ball traveled two hundred yards and the POO ball one hundred yards. We were elated. We began to discuss a new type of tournament but decided the world was not ready for this yet. Subsequent tests were less well correlated; the standard deviation of the mean for both balls became rather large. In some instances the POO ball traveled farther than the shot ball. Apparently it is difficult to concentrate on a golf shot with a golf ball up your POO. One variable we had failed to take into account was the matter of diet. There was strong evidence that diet played a role in our experiments and may have accounted to some extent for our remarkable results.

We discovered that the placing of the POO ball in situ had a considerable effect on the results. On one shot the POO ball was directed inward rather than outward and had to be retrieved with a putter. At this point the Subject resigned. All of our entreaties based on sacrifices in the interests of science were to no avail. He was adamant. Our quantitative experiments therefore at the present time are at a standstill. It is to be hoped, however, that this preliminary report will encourage others to carry on this important work.

A SHORT GUIDE TO DOCTORS

John J. Secondi, M.D.

Medicine, like every other field these days, is so overspecialized that even a card-carrying doctor like me has trouble telling who's who. The layman, I imagine, is almost helpless to distinguish the forest from the tree surgeons. I have noticed, however, that my colleagues have a tendency to run to type. So, in an effort to clear up the confusion, I have compiled a little list so simple that the most naive patient can spot at a glance which doctor is which.

The General Practitioner. These gentlemen used to be the ones you saw most often, when you lived back in Nebraska and watched the cars go by from your front porch for entertainment. Now they are nearly extinct, like the buffalo and the stork, although there are a few left in a preserve in Iowa. Most of them looked like a cross between Charlie Ruggles and Colonel Sanders; they were warm, wonderful, and always had time for you, even if they slept only three hours a night. They knew you inside and out from the moment they delivered you until their ink dried on your death certificate, and they were always there to help you push your car out of the mud. If anybody knows where there's one of these left, please drop me a note. I could use a good doctor myself.

The Internist. This is a general practitioner with more diplomas on the walls and without house calls. (He also has money in the bank.) By the age of thirty at the latest he becomes obese, sallow, and emphysematous. Usually bald, he is always found sitting and smoking a pipe. (The pipe is a deliberate attempt to evoke the Delphic Oracle, which also simmered and steamed with ideas. The internist is nothing if not oracular.) As opposed to the surgeon, who carries no equipment at all except the keys to his Rolls-Royce, the internist can be seen with a stethoscope protruding from one of thousands of pockets in his clothing. Really big stethoscopes are worn to give the impression of expertise in heart disease.

In his desk the internist stocks lifetime supplies of sample drugs; when you are in his office he may pick one or two at random and give them to you with alarming liberality. But don't worry; he won't let you know what they are. The internist is really happy only when deciding how to cope with some chronic incurable disease, preferably in a case some colleague has botched. The longer the name of the disease, the happier he is; and if it's in Latin he's ecstatic. An internist is required by law to have his phone ring twice an hour at least while he is at home, and he can never vacation. No internist's children ever become doctors.

The General Surgeon. These are the prima donnas of the trade. Today's surgeon is descended from the barbers of the Middle Ages, but washes more often. He may be fat or slim, but he is always loud, noticed, and in a hurry. He dashes dramatically in and out of rooms (whether patient, operating, or bath) and never lets you finish a sentence. To probing questions he nods wisely, smiles enigmatically, and runs off. (Never say "Now cut that out" to a surgeon.) He generally visits patients cloaked in green from head to toe to give the impression of being fresh from an operation, when probably (unless he is over fifty) he has been idling in his office all day waiting for someone—anyone—to call. After he does a surgical scrub, he raises his arms, which drip from the elbows. This posture serves both as a gesture to God for the usual assistance, and as a method to keep the bacteria flowing away from the surgeon—toward the patient.

Surgeons are taught early to rip off bandages as quickly as possible, removing as much hair as they can with one clean tear. They have a distinctive jargon: for instance, they speak of healing by "primary intention" (which is to make lots of money), or by "secondary intention" (which means the wound got infected). If anything goes wrong during operations, surgeons are unanimous in blaming it on the anesthesiologists. Surgeons are the only doctors left who haven't cut out smoking, because they are confident they can cut out the cancer. If this description still doesn't make a surgeon flash in your mind, recall James Coburn in the film *Candy*. Absolutely accurate.

General Surgeon

Internist

Urologist

Gastroenterologist

Anesthesiologist

General Practitioner

Obstetrician-Gynecologist

The Gastroenterologist. Gastrointestinal doctors, or "GI men," have had oral fixations since childhood. This means they are always talking a mile a minute, and at mealtimes they ingest like Electroluxes. They're usually roly-poly, literary, and very pleasant to gossip with, as a consequence. The unsavoriness of their work is grossly exaggerated; nevertheless, they do receive a lot of cologne for Christmas. As kids they were the ones whose parents always had to bang on the bathroom door to get them out. If Alexander Woollcott had become a doctor, he would surely have been a gastroenterologist.

The Obstetrician-Gynecologist. The real wise guy in medicine. Sitting on their high stools day after day with their patients in that absurd saddle, these comedians see the funny side of life. They have to have a good sense of humor because otherwise they would be so upset by some of the things that come along they would swear off sex forever. Always ready with a wisecrack or a foul story (depending on whether you are a patient or another doctor), they are universally popular, except with pediatricians. Child doctors blame every childhood disease from thumb-sucking to Mongoloid idiocy on the anesthesia the obstetrician used. It is not true that all obstetrics is done at three o'clock in the morning. I personally recall one case in 1968 that was done at six in the morning, and others may have had similar experiences.

The Urologist. Urologists do for men what gynecologists do for women—more or less. They are drawn to their specialty irresistibly by its identification with the masses of tight curly hair they all have. Many urologists are now growing beards and muttonchops so you can spot them more easily than ever. Walking around weighted down by their waterproof rubber aprons and all those whiskers they resemble Noah before the flood. At home they putter around a lot with the kitchen sink to keep in practice. Like other plumbers they work good hours and make a good living.

The Anesthesiologist. Anesthesiology is the Tower of Babel of medicine. There are a total of four English-speaking anesthesiologists in America: two on the East Coast, one in Chicago, and the other in L.A. All the others communicate with frenzied nasal accents or sign language. They are short, shy, retiring types who hide behind the sterile barrier during surgery and squeeze contentedly on their little black respiration bags. You will recall the bags from 1930s movies because when Lionel Barrymore came too late they quit moving and you knew the patient had died.

The night before your next surgery an anesthesiologist may mince into your room, unheralded and uninvited. He will never show up after five o'clock, however. Without bothering to identify himself or even to ask for an interpreter, he will quiz you on all the allergies you may have. This is done to choose exactly the right toxin to put you to sleep with the next day; for God's sake, don't forget anything that might be relevant. Then he will bow graciously and back out of the room, and you'll never see him again. (Whether you'll see anyone else again is another question.)

If you wake up from surgery, you may have a sore throat, even after an abdominal operation. This complication occurs because the anesthesiologist routinely puts the rubber airway down your esophagus six times before he finds the right hole. Anesthesiologists fear surgeons the way helpless children fear angry fathers. They are very sensitive and feel left-out enough, so be kind to them.

The Pediatrician. All pedi-pods, as they are called on the wards, act and look like Peter Pan. They wear saddle-shoes and bow ties, have cherubic faces, and wear crew cuts or pageboys, depending on whether they are over thirty. They never use words longer than two syllables or sentences of more than four words. Generally they sound as if they are doing Jonathan Winters imitations. Many have a lilting gait, and a few skip during clinic. About the age of forty they lose patience with all those frantic mothers and either commit suicide, go into research, or start child labor camps.

The Orthopedist. All bone doctors without exception are former college jocks or team managers; i.e., they are big brutes or mousy types who wish they were. They *all* wear white athletic socks. (This is the one infallible rule of medicine and makes it a snap to recognize an orthopedist.) They usually have plaster of

PAUL MEISEL

Ophthalmologist

Orthopedist

Plastic Surgeon

Psychiatrist

Pediatrician

Otolaryngologist

Radiologist

Paris splattered on their clumsy-looking shoes.

The Ophthalmologist. (This is the real "eye doctor" and is not to be confused with optometrists or opticians, who aren't M.D.'s at all.) Ophthalmologists, despite being constantly misspelled and mispronounced, are the happiest men in medicine. They work laughably few hours, make extravagant fees, and are adored by their patients, who understandably value their sight above all else. Thus ophthalmologists are always well-tanned and talk knowingly of Tahiti and the Riviera. They also play a great deal of golf. Curiously, they are uniformly tall, slim, and vaguely ethereal. A good example would be Pope Pius XII with a suntan. They use a jargon so technical and so infinitesimally detailed they cannot even make small talk over drinks with other doctors.

The Otolaryngologist. When you've been to an ear, nose, and throat man you'll never forget it. These are the true sadists in medicine. Children despise them; they're the only doctors who make you feel worse than when you came in. What with the nausea produced by cocaine sprayed in the nose, and all those tiny little probes poking God-knows-where back in your sinuses, and all that blood swallowed after a tonsillectomy, going to an ENT man is like being used for an experiment by Edgar Allan Poe. The only common physical characteristic by which these gentlemen can be spotted is that they all still have their own tonsils.

The Plastic Surgeon. Immediately identifiable. They all wear hand-tailored clothing of vast expense and have sculptured features worthy of a Phidias or a Michelangelo. Gorgeous from every angle, they look years younger than they are, and boy do they know it. They were the big face men of college fraternities, the ones who were put strategically at the front door during rush week and in the first row in the yearbook picture. They are very rich because there are a lot of jealous women who will pay *anything* to look as good as the plastic surgeon. They have a tendency to get very snotty when you ask them what kind of plastic they're going to put in, and lecture you on the origin of the word "plastikos" in the traditions of Greek sculpture. Nevertheless, they have terrific guilt complexes about spending all their time on frivolous surgery, so

they occasionally take on a burn victim to soothe their consciences. The patron saint of plastic surgery is Narcissus.

The Psychiatrist. Spotting a psychiatrist on the street is easy enough, but as he wanders on the wards of a state hospital he may need a name tag. Psychiatrists either avert their eyes from you or stare right through you, whichever makes you more uncomfortable. If they sense you're going to ask a question, they slip one in first. They never use complete sentences, only clauses and long words. I know a psychiatrist who begins every sentence with the word "that" and ends it with an exact quotation of Plato. The main object a shrink has in mind when he sees a patient is not to rescue the patient's sanity but to prove his. After all, how many surgeons do you know who have five years of operations on themselves before they can practice?

Today's psychiatric resident may have elbow-length hair, wear rings in one ear, and go to work in purple satin capes. This kind of psychiatrist has not hit Park Avenue yet, but it's only a matter of time.

The Radiologist. Radiologists hide in dark places and never come out, like other rodents. They make creepy-crawly gestures and rub their noses frequently. Their world is one of shadows and they detest the light of day. They hole up in leadened tunnels and, though they tell you that X-rays are harmless, they generally have their offspring as early as possible. (By the time they reach fifty irradiation has given their skins the texture of refried beans). Like Whistler, they view everyone as a study in black, white, and gray. The thought of being responsible for a live human being is abhorrent to them. Yet they give off smiles of delicious perverse pleasure as they make patients swallow thick white slime and poke around in their bowels so their guts will show on film. Peter Lorre would have played a perfect radiologist.

I would like to complete the list, but I just got a frantic phone call from AMA headquarters, and I have to run. Something about an emergency protest march against socialized medicine.

HOW MUCH DO YOU KNOW ABOUT ADOLESCENT MEDICINE?

Peter H. Gott, M.D.

The following questions have been prepared to enable physicians to assess their knowledge in different specialties. The multiple choice system is used. Select the *one* best response to each question. Then compare your answers to the answers, explanations and references at the end of the test. This continuing medical education selection meets criteria for three-minutes' credit in category 10 (E) for the Ephebiatrician Recognition Award.

1.) The following events occur during puberty in boys:

(1) Nocturnal emissions
(2) Beer drinking
(3) Damage to the family car
(4) Discontinuation of chewing gum

In what order do these events most commonly take place?

a. 1, 2, 3, 4
b. 1, 3, 2, 4
c. 4, 1, 3, 2
d. 4, 3, 2, 1

2.) A sexually promiscuous 16-year-old girl with problems in social development will most probably identify with which of the following television programs?

a. *Charlie's Angels*
b. *The Price is Right*
c. *Saturday morning cartoons*
d. *Mary Hartman, Mary Hartman*

3.) A 15-year-old youth is seen in the office be-

An adolescent forehead magnified × 10.

COURTESY OF NASA

cause of a juicy zit on his forehead. The most common cause for this condition is:

a. *Acne vulgaris*
b. *Constipation*
c. *The heartbreak of psoriasis*
d. *Ovaltine*

4.) A bhang pipe has been defined as:

(1) a device used to smoke hallucinogenic substances
(2) the connecting link on an automobile between the header and tailpipe
(3) the newest addition to the percussion section in a rock band
(4) part of a science project for Mr. Ferguson

Pick the best choice.

a. *1*
b. *2, 3*
c. *3, 4*
d. *2, 3, 4*

5.) Parents arrive home from a late party and discover their 13-year-old daughter sound asleep on the living room sofa. They have difficulty waking her and telephone you to make a house call. Your initial reaction is to:

    a. Hang up the phone and go back to sleep.
    b. Meet them in the emergency room at a local hospital.
    c. Tell them to give their daughter two aspirin and call you in the morning.
    d. None of the above.

6.) You make a house call to the patient described in question 5 and ascertain that she is sleepy but rousable. You immediately check:

    a. Pupillary and deep tendon reflexes
    b. Nuchal rigidity
    c. The father's checkbook balance
    d. The liquor cabinet

7.) An effeminate adolescent male wearing a pearl necklace, flowered silk shirt and tight black jeans is most likely to be a member of the:

    a. Gay Students' Alliance
    b. Karate Club
    c. Future Farmers of America
    d. Young Americans for Freedom

8.) You are asked to examine a 16-year-old youth in whose coat pocket his parents have discovered an ample supply of marijuana. In the course of your evaluation, it would be appropriate first to determine:

    a. How much he smokes during an average day
    b. If he is using high-grade weed
    c. Whether he is adjusted to his family environment
    d. Where he buys the stuff

9.) An adolescent boy suffers from progressive dimming of vision, oligospermia, weakness, mental illness and hair growth on his palms. The most likely diagnosis is:

    a. Progessive leukodystrophy
    b. Idiopathic arteriolitis
    c. Werewolf Syndrome
    d. Excessive masturbation

Answers

1. The answer is *a* (Am. J. Epheb. Invest, 1:17, 1977). Forty-three percent of youths have been found to have nocturnal emissions by the time they damage the family car, and 59% of beer-drinkers had damaged the car after drinking. Only 11% of youths surveyed began drinking beer as a consequence of wrecking the family car. Virtually all adolescents continue to chew gum well into their 20s.

2. The answer is *c* (Fudd, Elmer [ed]: Social Patterns in TV Land, 1977, pp. 1217–1219). The increased incidence of explicit sexual acts and violence in Saturday morning television programs is a well-known phenomenon among youngsters and is an accepted part of the American way of life among parents. Adolescents do not relate to the real-life situations portrayed in the three adult programs listed in the question.

3. The answer is *b* (Franklin, Benjamin: Advice To a Young Daddy, 1780, pp. 104–106). Constipation is a well-known cause of adolescent dermatologic problems. Therefore, the logical treatment for teenage complexion consists of clysters and calomel tea.

4. The answer is *d* (Krishna, K. L.: Zen and the Art of Far-out Plumbing, 1966, Haight-Ashbury Press, p. 991). Various definitions of the bhang have been offered at various times by various people under varied amounts of stress. These three statements are representative—providing, of course, Mr. Ferguson is really the science teacher. An appropriate definition depends, in large part, upon the sophistication and gullibility of the person demanding such a definition. In this situation, there is an infinite variety of creative artistry in defining a bhang.

5. The answer is *d* (Patients Have a Right to Your House Key and Home Telephone Number!, Med. Econ. 1:43, 1977), Continue to the next question.

6. The answer is *d* (Arch. Suburban Affluence, 14:200, 1972). The logical first stop is at the liquor cabinet to determine how much of Daddy's Chivas Regal has been consumed. A common adolescent game, when parents are out for the evening, is called "Go Potty." This 1970s variation on the old game of "Bathtub Gin" involves helping one's self to as much of daddy's private stock as can be guzzled. The name "Go Potty" probably reflects the anti-ADH effect of alcohol.

7. The answer is *b* (Ann. Self-Defense, 1976, pp. 1–13). This guy can pinch your head off like a ripe blueberry. Don't presume to arrive at unjustifiable conclusions without first carefully researching the subject.

8. The answer is *d* (Village Voice, 41: 87, 1971). The practicing ephebiatrician must be constantly alert to sources of a good buy. After determining the quality of the product *(b)*, the physician would naturally wish to establish a reliable pipeline to provide for his own modest needs.

9. The answer is *d* (*The Young Man's Guide*, Boston: Perkins and Marvin, 1838). The detrimental effects of masturbation are well-recognized and need not be reiterated.

RARE DISEASES

Ole Didrik Laerum, M.D.

Institute for General and Experimental Pathology,
University of Oslo
Rikshospitalet, Oslo

Rare diseases are not commonly encountered in medical practice. When a patient, who is suffering from a rare disease is discovered, it is therefore customary to write a paper and publish it as a case report.

Such case reports often have a peculiar feature: one writes about one or two observed cases of a disease because it is so rare. Then the author(s) conclude that this disease nevertheless may be of importance and is probably not so infrequent as it may appear. One must even be aware of this condition in general practice. Quotation: "During the last thirty-years period we have had two such cases in this country."

There is therefore a need for a survey of the different categories of rare syndromes and disorders. An analysis of peculiarities and common features of such maladies will be given, followed by a discussion of their prevalence in relation to our concept of the term, "rare diseases."

Types of Infrequent Disorders

1. Rare diseases which in reality are not so infrequent because they are often not diagnosed.

People are not made aware of the fact that they may suffer from such disorders and walk about totally ignorant of their presence. It can be said that these diseases have not been subject to a proper marketing. In this connection radio, television and newspapers can do much. And they do, indeed.

Every time there has been an information week with campaign for a certain disease, people afterward run to their doctor, believing that they suffer from it. If we in addition could make an information week for rare diseases, one could probably catch a lot of infrequent disorders which are normally hidden.

A case report can illustrate this:

NN, male, born 1940, at that time a medical student, read in the newspapers during the spring 1963 that a contagious horse cough (equine influenza) had appeared in the stables of a hippodrome in Oslo. This passed without complications. During the winter 1964 he read in the local newspapers that another epidemic of horse cough had come, this time in the stables of another hippodrome in Oslo.

After the last newspaper message he felt unwell, and the following days he developed increasing malaise with rhinitis, fever and a strong, continuous cough. The coughing seizures started pianissimo in tempo de andante, followed by a strong crescendo up to forzato (NN was a passionate amateur musician) and then terminating in ritardando with utterly *neighing* coughing fits.

NN sought a general practitioner, who had never heard about horse cough in human beings. NN therefore had to leave the office without any approbation, but later spontaneously recovered. NN is convinced that the disease was precipitated and thus directly caused by that newspaper article.

Another disorder which is never diagnosed is volvulus of the pineal body. Today this disease is without known existence because our diagnostic methods are so limited. Still many persons may suffer from it and have problems because they are not able to convince their doctor.

2. Diseases which are rare because they depend on certain periods of history.

The term "an asthmatic locomotive" is well-known in the literature. However, only few people know why asthma in locomotives was not observed in the seventeenth century. The reason is that Stephenson first had to invent the steam locomotive. Nowadays, the condition is again becoming rare. In any case it is not seen in our hospital wards. This is obviously because the steam engine has been gradually replaced by diesel and electric locomotives.

3. Conditions which are seldom seen because they are rare.

University teachers commonly present such diseases in a double lecture. The lecture is often terminated by the following statement: "The condition is not infrequent at all and is therefore important to be aware of. Any person who spends his whole life in a department of internal medicine will have ample chance of observing one case. Personally I have seen one patient with the disease. That was before the war—the first world war."

On this background we can formulate the following problem as a basis for the present study:

Do there exist diseases which are so rare that they have

not yet occurred? If they do, and we have reason to assume that to be the case, there are another two categories of rare diseases:

4. Diseases which have yet not occurred, but will be discovered some time in the future, sooner or later.

A typical example of such a disorder is moon-dust poisoning, which may be a very serious condition. Another important, hitherto not described disease in this group is podocytoma of the kidney. The podocytes are known as epithelial cells which adhere to the glomerular membrane with numerous foot processes. They participate in the urinary filtration (Fig. 1).

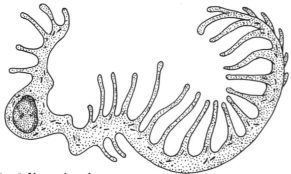

Fig. 1 Normal podocyte.

These cells have hitherto never developed any tumor. But some time in the future they will. That makes a podocytoma, a highly differentiated, benign tumor, which was predicted and first described in this article ("Lærum's tumor"). The characteristic electronmicroscopical picture of this condition is that the foot processes march out of step (Fig. 2).

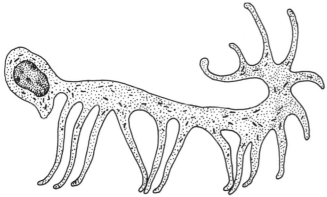

Fig. 2 Detail from podocytoma. Foot no. 4 and 7 are out of step.

5. Diseases which have not yet occurred and will never occur in the future either.

These are extremely rare and have very little practical importance from a clinical point of view. It is not necessary for a general practitioner to know anything about them.

Discussion

Is our concept of the term "rare diseases" becoming outdated? In any case the term is ambiguous. As earlier shown the word "rare" in the medical world is mainly used in publications that are written because a disorder is infrequent. But at the same time the authors try to demonstrate that in reality the condition is frequent. The article is therefore accepted for publication *both* because the disease is so rare, and also because it is so frequent.

Our concept of "rare diseases" also lacks precision and is changing as a function of time. New rare diseases are coming. Other infrequent diseases disappear and are not seen anymore. It would therefore be an idea to take care of certain rare diseases before they disappear forever.

It is also important to realize that the medical use of the word "rare" has a tendency to become so common that it is losing its practical meaning. We therefore must not use the word so often that it becomes too common.

It is also misleading that the word "rare" is often used when quite banal disorders occur in an unusual manner, such as caries in toothless persons.

If we take all of the presently known diseases and group them according to their prevalence, the group "common diseases" will include only a relatively small number of unities. The group "uncommon" diseases is far larger. But if we take the group "rare diseases," then only the list of the names comprises a voluminous book.[1] Thus there exist a lot of rare and obscure diseases and syndromes.

Although each of them is very seldom seen, they are together so many. As a group they therefore make a large entity, that altogether perhaps is the most important we have to deal with in medicine.

Conclusion: Rare diseases are no longer uncommon. What are they then?

Summary

A survey of our concept of rare diseases is given. The author demonstrates that there exist diseases which hitherto never occurred. Some of these will never occur in the future either. A new tumor, *podocytoma* ("Lærum's tumor"), a benign lesion of the kidney, is described to illustrate the pathology of a clinical entity without known existence.

It is concluded that because there are so many different types of them, rare diseases should no longer be considered as uncommon.

[1] Leiber, B. and Olbrich, G. *Wörterbuch der Klinischen Syndrome.* München — Berlin: Urban und Schwarzenberg, 1959.

PLATO TALEFOROS

NEPHROTRICHOSIS: A NEW SYNDROME

I. X. Hume, M.D.
Associate Chief Pathologist
Hedda Hare, Ph.D.
Chief Cosmetologist
Office of the Medical Examiner
Necropolis, Illinois

We saw our first case of hairy kidneys in an autopsy performed on December 12, 1963. The subject was a white, middle-aged, well-nourished male, a long-time drug user, who had died of gunshot wounds. Both kidneys were covered with a luxuriant growth of hair, of the same brown color and coarse texture as that which fringed the subject's otherwise bald head. Other than establishing the cause of death, we made no further study of the body or tissues, on the assumption that the kidney hair was the bizarre product of some accidental combination of drugs.

Since that first observation in 1963, several thousand autopsies have been performed in our laboratories, in the course of which 11 more pairs of hirsute kidneys have been discovered. In addition, the histories in these cases have led to the reasonably reliable identification of a causative factor. We believe, therefore, that we have discovered a rare, but distinct and previously unknown syndrome, which we describe herein. We have given it the name of nephrotrichosis (Gr. *nephros*–kidney; *trichos*–hair). For those who prefer terminology of Latin origin, we suggest "renal hirsutism," and the terms are used interchangeably in this report.

Several generalizations immediately emerged:

1. All of the bodies in which nephrotrichosis was found were male.

2. All of the heads were bald or showed signs of progressive hair loss over a period of time.

3. The syndrome, however, occurred in only 3.7% of the bald subjects who came to autopsy.

4. In the hirsute kidneys, typical hair follicles had developed in the kidney capsules.

5. Color and texture of the kidney hair matched that still remaining on the head.

Hair Tonic Hypotheses

The reason for the selective development of renal hirsutism in only a relatively few calvous males, and not in the others, emerged from careful questioning of the families of the deceased. In all cases, the victims had, for many years, used commercial hair tonics, copiously applied to the scalp in the vain hope of stimulating or restoring hair growth. We suggest three alternative hypotheses, among which we cannot as yet choose, but which are guiding our further investigations. The hypotheses are:

1. The active agent, of unknown nature, is absorbed from the scalp into the bloodstream, whence it is extracted and concentrated by the renal tubules, at least part of it reaching the capsule.

2. The kidney capsule is uniquely responsive to

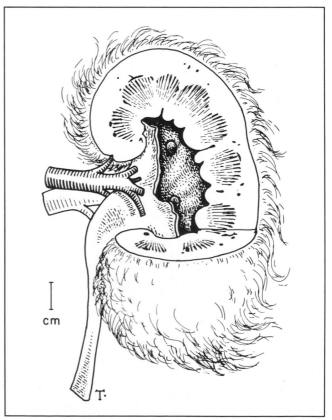

A kidney showing advanced nephrotrichosis.

PLATO TALEPOROS

the agent carried in the blood.

3. Both factors, 1 and 2, are operative.

We are at present analyzing, with infrared spectroscopy, various brands of hair restorers in the hope of identifying a molecular species common to many or all of them. We shall use various fractions of the tonics to test each of the above hypotheses in experimental animals. Preliminary experiments with the hamster, in which whole hair tonic is applied to the cheek pouch, have been encouraging.

Little can at present be reliably stated about the clinical aspects of uncomplicated nephrotrichosis. As far as we have been able to determine, hair growth on the kidney does not affect its function or that of any other organ in any way. There was no evidence of kidney disease in any of the first twelve cases.

Secondary Complications

More recently, however, in the course of another, related investigation, we have encountered a few secondary complications. In the hope of eliciting signs and symptoms that may be related to the pathogenesis of nephrotrichosis, we have been examining and interviewing bald men who have used hair-growth stimulants for long periods.

Nine such men have been studied so far. Of these, four complained of a vague discomfort that could best be described as an internal "itch" in the region of the kidneys, and the men were occasionally observed digging with their fingertips over these areas. One man, in addition, had developed angina pectoris soon after the itch appeared.

By fortunate coincidence, two of these men have come to autopsy. To our surprise, the kidneys of both men had, not luxuriant hair growth, but, rather, sparse, scattered strands. Histological examination of the capsules revealed numerous degenerating hair follicles and copious epithelial debris (dandruff of the kidneys). It seems apparent to us that these two men had previously had nephrotrichosis, which is asymptomatic, but had subsequently become afflicted with alopissia (bald kidneys) occasioned, as suggested by the itching, by renal eczema, seborrhea or psoriasis. The angina pectoris of one of the patients may be reasonably ascribed to the heartbreak associated with psoriasis.

Our studies continue, and will be reported as progress is made.

REVISED HIPPOCRATIC OATH

Anonymous, M.D.
San Francisco, Calif.

I swear by Apollo the physician, by Aesculapius, by Melvin Belli, and by my DEA number, to keep according to the advice of my accountant and attorney the following oath:

To consider dear to me as my stock certificates him who enabled me to learn this art: the banker who approved my educational loans; to live in common with him and to acquire my mortgages through his bank and that of his sons; to consider equally dear my teachers, and if necessary to split fees with them and request from them unnecessary consultations. I will prescribe regimen for the good of my practice according to my patients' third party coverage or remaining Medicaid stickers, taking care not to perform nonreimbursable procedures. To please no one, with the possible exception of favored detail men, will I prescribe a non-FDA approved drug unless it should be essential to one of my clinical research projects; nor will I give advice which may cause my patient's death prior to obtaining a flat EEG for 24 hours. But I will preserve the purity of my reputation. In every clinical situation, I will cover my ass by ordering all conceivable labwork and by documenting my every move in the chart. I will faithfully accumulate 25 Category I CME credits per year, and none of these by attending Sports Medicine conferences on the slopes of Aspen. I will not cut for stone, even for patients in whom the disease is manifest, before documenting the diagnosis by I.V. or retrograde pyelogram and obtaining informed consent. In every house where I come I will enter only if a housecall is absolutely unavoidable, keeping myself far from all intentional ill-doing and all seduction, and especially free from the pleasures of love with women or with men. Or, for that matter, with both simultaneously. Such activities I will confine to my office or yacht. I will not be induced to testify against my colleagues in court, nor to disagree with them when asked for a second opinion. I will not charge less for any procedure than the prevailing rate in my community. All that may come to my knowledge in the exercise of my profession, such as diagnoses, prognoses, details of treatment, and fee schedules, I will keep secret and never reveal to patients; I will, however, cheerfully provide these to insurance companies. Finally, under no circumstances will I vote for Ted Kennedy or anyone else of his ilk. If I keep this oath faithfully, may I enjoy my life, build my practice, incorporate, find some solid tax shelters, and ultimately make a killing in real estate; but if I swerve from it or violate it, may a profusion of malpractice claims be my lot.

THE INCIDENCE & TREATMENT OF HYPERACROSOMIA IN THE UNITED STATES

Journal of Facetious Pathology

Edmond A. Touré
M.D., M.B.A., B.E.E., F.O.H., R.S.V.P.
Faculty of Medicine, University of Nicarobia

It has been estimated that one in every three Americans suffer from hyperacrosomia.[1] The extremely high incidence of the disease is thought to be due to the effect of diet aggravating an existing genetically-derived predisposition.

Some very famous Americans have indeed been afflicted with acute hyperacrosomia, among them Abraham Lincoln, George Washington, and Lyndon Johnson.[2] Their condition is readily apparent upon comparison with such normal individuals as Napoleon Bonaparte, Truman Capote, and Dick Cavett.[3] Populations with a high frequency of hyperacrosomic individuals can be quickly detected by examining the behavior of the normal population, which can frequently be

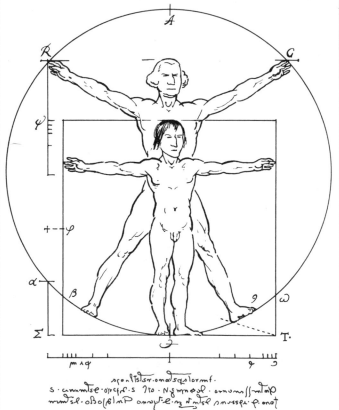

PLATO TALEPOROS

---

[1] R. Clocher. *Mensonges et fraudes de science* (Presse du Hôpital, Charenton, 1832).

[2] It is sobering to realize that both major candidates in the 1972 American Presidential election suffered from the affliction.

[3] As far as is known, neither Art Garfunkel or Sam Yorty is affected.

[4] "Ducking" is a verb describing the action of lowering the body to avoid an approaching object likely to encounter one's head, and does not imply any imitation of the movements of a bird of the same root name (family Anatidae).

[5] G. de Bâtard. "Les Américains Croissent Comme Herbes Mauvaises." *Acta Med. et Vét. de Gr. Fenwick*, 7:62 (1934).

[6] E. Smith. "Twelve Ways You Can Improve Your S*x Life." *Reader's Digest* 34:23 (1912).

observed making ducking[4] movements, sidestepping, and jumping up and down in crowds.[5] The disease, which warps the lives of all its victims and those normal individuals who live in proximity, is seldom fatal except when complications set in. Several historical figures died of secondary causes as a result of their hyperacrosomic condition, among them Louis XVI of France and a certain Philistine warrior who was superficially wounded by a sling-accelerated projectile.[6] Indeed, the pathological nature of the condition has long been recognized in folklore, as evidenced by the epigram "the bigger they are, the harder they fall," an American cliché.

Treatment of hyperacrosomia can proceed along a number of lines depending on how advanced the disease has become. An affected child can be restored by simple adjustments in diet, in particular a therapeutic deficiency in one or more essential amino acid, or by prophylactic administration of nicotine, ethanol, caffeine, or sleep deprivation. The affected adult, however, must be helped by surgery, usually the application of the advanced femurectomy technique pioneered by Andreas Procrustes of the University of Peloponnesus.[7]

The most promising avenue of control, however, most certainly lies in genetic counseling. While diet and other environmental factors play a major role in the degree to which the condition is expressed, the individual's genetic potential for the disease is a multifactorial inherited trait with incomplete sex limitation. The disease is most strongly manifested among males. Unfortunately there exists a cultural bias in the United States favoring the symptoms of hyperacrosomia, and thus a comprehensive attitudinal change must take place through education and personal consideration. Since the male population does express the condition to a higher degree, it falls primarily to the female population to objectively consider the risks of involving themselves with hyperacrosomic males. One would hope that as the female population grew more enlightened they would implement the necessary shift in attitude and come to favor normal individuals consistently over those with manifestations of the pathology.[8,9]

---

[7] A. Procrustes. "Selective Extension and Truncation of the Skeletal Frame." *Annals of Orthopaedic Mythology*, 81: (523 B.C.) 71.

[8] I. Strauss. *Keep Your Jeans Clean*. San Francisco: Levi Strauss & Co., 1873.

[9] I thank N. Mailer, J. Susann, J. Carson, A. Wellington, S. Douglas, M. Berle, the Army of the Republic of Argentina, and the entire population of the United States of America from 1723 to the present, without whose help this work could never have been completed.

TREATMENT OF SPINAL SUBDURAL HEMATOMA WITH FERRET'S EAR

F. B. Rumbold
James Tellement-Fou
A. Howard Garke

Spinal subdural hematoma is one of the rarer causes of acute spinal compression and is usually associated with injury or a bleeding diathesis (Stewart and Watkins, 1969).

A case is presented here in which the patient's serious plight was alleviated by treatment with the left ear of a dead ferret, specifically prepared.

Case Report

A man aged 59 presented with violently severe pain in the limbs and abdomen, accompanied by weakness of the lower legs. A lumbar puncture yielded bloodstained fluid with xanthochromic supernatant containing 800 mg of protein and 20 mg of sugar per ml. CSF pressure was 45 mm of CSF, with no rise on jugular compression. There was severe flaccid paraparesis.

We waited until the night of the full moon, and slaughtered a male ferret in rut by striking it with the femur of a defrocked sexton. We then removed its ears. The right ear was nailed to the door of Ely Cathedral as a precaution (see *Treatment of Calcinosis Circumscripta With Mole Soup*, BMJ, 2:499, 1972), and the left ear was brought to the Orthopedic Research Unit of the Royal Camden Hospital in a teapot. It was then swung round three times.

We drew a chalk circle on the floor of the operating theater and took our trousers off.

The patient was then premedicated by the anaesthetist, who shook a beaker of dried peas over him, murmuring "Tu ne quaesieris, scire nefas," twice, and brought into theater. He was painted blue, and the left ear of the ferret was then pushed up his right nostril at the exact stroke of midnight.

By morning, the patient was his old self again, i.e. suffering from spinal subdural hematoma. In the post-clinical discussion no clear explanation emerged, but the fact that the teapot had once stood on a shelf next to a garlic plant (a fact not previously known to the surgical team) was held to be of prime significance.

REFERENCES
Stedman, D. H. F., and P. Merrill. *Journal of Neurosurgery*, 1968.
Wrigley, King Norman. *Ferret Remedies And Songs*, 1966.
Siggs, F. *Whistle Away Your Fracture*, 1957.

—From the British Medical Journal: *No. 3, p. 257, 1972.*

This study was supported by the Southern California Fair Young Lady Rating and Escort Society, Committee for Equal Opportunity by Height, grant #WYB002. I thank the staff of the Broadway & 59th Field Research Station of the University of Nicarobia Institute of Natural Ecology for the use of their facilities in the preparation of this manuscript.

UMBILECTOMY: AN EXPERIMENTAL SURGICAL PANACEA

Carl Jelenko, III, M.D.

With the exception of two individual cases reported in earlier literature,[1] a common affliction of mankind has been the so-called umbilicus. This structure, situated, on the average, 7° 18′ N., and 80° 13′ W. of the pudenda, has received much scientific attention. Cullen[2] embraced it, and even published his embrasure. The structure has been variously contemplated, covered, adorned, and exposed. In 1864 it became known as the "Belly-Button," being so named by Sir Mount Anyodds,[3] who perforce devised a technique for hanging his trousers from this structure after an unfortunate incident in which he lost his remaining underanatomy in a craps game.

It must be noted, however, that Sir Mount had a construction later characterized by Pupick[4] as "An Outer." Anatomic configuration of the type Pupick II: "an Inner," however, would have made that earlier work by Anyodds impossible.

A recent survey by an independent New York accounting firm has revealed that 24% of umbilici are "Inners," and, furthermore, worthy of economic consideration. These structures provide a rich harvest of lint with a refractive index of 1.495. This is identical to that of Noselite (Ger. *Naselint*) from which, by corruption, the term "naval lint," also called "belly-button lint," is derived. This material is useful for stuffing pillows and for packing chromatographic columns. Swine fed a steady diet of the material, however, develop gallstones, trichinosis, kwashiorkor, and tsutsugamushi fever. The matter is listed in the Index Medicus under "Page 7491."

It should be noted that lint gleaned from "Inners" will not sink in water. For this reason, the material was used to construct sea-going vehicles. Such vessels, in due course, became named for the material of their origin, and, in groups, are called "Navy."

Since 1960, emphasis has been placed upon economic augmentation; and Federal grants-in-aid have enabled the cultivation of the productivity inherent in "Inners." It is, therefore, no surprise that the 76% of the population that are "Outers" are walking poverty pockets, and psychologically unstable.

It was proposed that, for the foregoing reason, in the interest of a populace that would be uniform and psychologically sound, all umbilici be surgically removed. The procedure returned the general status to a state of quo. It was found to be an economically sound venture, since the surgical fees charged were equal to the monentary gain from the local lint harvest. In addition, lint was able to be obtained from a variety of oranges; and it was therefore possible to continue to float a Navy.

The project has, however, been discontinued due to unfortunate and unexpected legal action by the DAR who obtained a Federal injunction against the operation on the grounds that removal of the umbilicus is the ultimate rejection of mother.

THE HAS-ANYONE-CALLED-THE-OLYMPIC-COMMITTEE DEPT.

"**54** percent of the men and 22 percent of the women were able to move their ears. That the percentage figure is twice as high for men can possibly depend ... on the fact that men are even in childhood more interested in sports...."

—L. Lindner, *Proc. 8 Intern. Cong. Genetics:* p. 620, 1949.

[1] *Bible, The:* Genesis 2:7, 22.
[2] Cullen, W. *Diseases of the Umbilicus.* Vol. I & II. Baltimore: The Johns Hopkins Press, 1906.
[3] Anyodds, Sir Mount. "On the Levitation of the Pantaloons in lieu of Rebuttal, & c." *British Journal of Plastic Surgery,* 4:119, 1846.
[4] Pupick, Scherner. "A Look at the Umbilicus as a Whole." *Gut;* 9:714, 1958.

HOW TO EAT AND LOSE WEIGHT

A New Solution to an Old Problem

The problem of energy equilibrium in the human body has received a great deal of attention in the USA.[1] Many methods have been advocated to reduce the caloric value of the food without affecting its taste or the appetite of the consumer. Some pharmaceutical houses have even expanded by wise investment of the monetary equivalent of the weight theoretically lost by their customers.

The various methods advocated involve either a drastic reduction in the quantity of the food ingested, use of drugs that affect the appetite, or increase in the amount of physical exercise. The first method leaves the patient permanently hungry, the second makes him sub-human by dulling his senses, and the third defeats its own purpose by increasing the appetite and leading to a vicious circle.

In this communication we propose a new method of reducing, without changing the quantity of the food ingested. The method is based on the principle that the caloric value of the food also depends on its temperature. For each degree of temperature of the food below the temperature of the human body, the body has to supply heat (energy) to raise the temperature of the food to that of the body.

When food is frozen, heat of thawing has to be supplied to it at the rate of 80 calories/gram of water contained in the food in addition to 1 calorie/gram for each degree centigrade of temperature rise. One can easily see that a glass of frozen milk (200 grams) at the temperature of deep freeze, i.e. $-20°$ C needs 200 x 80 calories for thawing and 57 x 200 calories for heating up to $37°$ C ($98°$ F), i.e.

$$16,000 + 11,400 = 27,400 \text{ calories or } 27.4 \text{ Cal.}$$

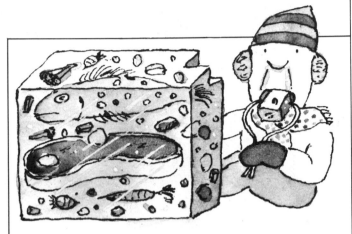

The caloric value of a glass of whole milk is 138 Cal and of skim milk only 74 Cal,[2] thus (27.4 x 100)/74 = 34% of caloric milk energy is lost for its heating. By having the milk diluted in the ratio of 1:2, 68% of the energy would be lost on consuming the same amount of milk.

Similarly one can calculate that consumption of a precooked frozen steak calls for an expenditure of at least ⅓ of its caloric value on the thawing and heating up. If one adds to this the amount of energy supplied as heat by the body and the mechanical energy required to crush the food with the jaws, the loss of the caloric value of the food becomes even greater.

For those individuals who do not care to crush their food with their teeth, or those who use valuable and fragile plates, and finally for those who have lost their teeth and did not replace them, one can advise the use of homogenized frozen food in form of Popsicles which would be sucked instead of chewed.

The suggestion of some research workers (personal communication) to achieve an additional loss of energy by consuming the food frozen in liquid helium or nitrogen is not considered practical, because of the temporary rarity and high cost of these two elements in their liquid form. With the increased use of liquid oxygen, however (rocket fuels, etc.) one may hope to have it supplied in a domesticated and easily handled form in the near future.

---

[1] Haveman, E. "The Wasteful, Phony Crash Dieting Craze." *Life*, 46: 102–114 (1959).

[2] Sherman, H. C. *Essentials of Nutrition.* New York: Macmillan, 1945.

EFFORTLESS AND DIETLESS WEIGHT LOSS: UNSCIENTIFICALLY RESEARCHED

John J. Twombly

My thoughts have turned recently to weighty problems—such as losing a few pounds. In my readings I came across an item in the *Northwestern Alumni News* which reported an article in the *Dialog,* the house organ of the Northwestern Memorial Hospital. According to the *News,* Donald McDonald, Director of the Pharmacy of the Hospital, presented a list of ways to lose weight without the use of physical activity. Since I am a sedentary person—and have been all my life—and since I am now retired, I studied the list carefully. I found it interesting, but I concluded that it was inconclusive, was supported by inadequate research, and was presented in a style lacking in scientific terminology. I then busily sat myself down to tackle the problem so aptly highlighted by Mr. Mc-Donald. In true scientific fashion, I thought and thought and thought. Out of my sitting position I developed a research project which pushes the horizon of weight loss into another world.

Introduction

All carefully designed research projects must focus on a problem. The problem was obvious: how could one lose weight without physical exertion? The neophyte would immediately conclude that this could be done by dieting, but such a solution is untenable to sedentary workers who have an addiction to eating. Furthermore, dieting creates other problems. For instance, how could Americans consume the products of our farms if they diet when we embargo wheat, corn, soy beans, etc. to Russia? The fertile mind of Mr. McDonald offered the beginning of a solution.

This researcher has used the usual research steps. He first stated the problem, and then he formulated the five necessary steps normally employed by a scientific investigator, *videlicet:* theory, hypotheses, design, procedures for data collection, and, finally, the conclusion. To be perfectly frank about it, though, there seems to be no logical reason why the conclusion should be last. Much time could be saved—and effort, too—if one were to jump from hypotheses to conclusions without going through the intermediate steps. If a researcher uses any blinds at all—single or double—he might just as well be totally blind and work with abandon.

Hypotheses

(These are hunches which the traditional scientists mistakenly believe need to be tested. To make this study carry some degree of legitimacy, this researcher will follow the usual tiresome, tedious, dreary, and dull set of boring tests. In other words, this researcher will act as if he were an orthodox worshiper of the scientific myth.)

It is hypothesized that if the brain is put under effort to defend the body from real or supposed attacks, embarrassments, or encumbrances, the mental gymnastics employed in developing the necessary defenses will result in the consumption of calories. It is further hypothesized that the greater the problem from which the mind must emancipate itself, the more calories it will consume. In short, the greater the effort, the greater the consumption. And it is further postulated that the various psychological mechanisms or ego defenses can be ranked in order of calories consumed.

Data

(This is the plural of datum. The Romans, by the way, believed that the plural form should be shorter than the singular.)

The data are presented in absolutely no order. No means, modes, medians—averages, that is, of any kind—are to be used, for it is well known that liars figure. Since this is an idiographic study made by an idiot in an idiotic fashion, no nomothetic procedures or conclusions are to be used.

1. Giving Advice.
When advicee wished advice . . . . .25 calories
When advicee did not wish advice . . . .150 calories
Remark: As predicted, this was the least useful in respect to calorie burning. The old folk lore is valid: "It is easy to give advice" and "You can lead a horse to water, but you can't make it drink."

2. Reaping Benefits.
When actually earned. . . . . .24 calories
When on welfare . . . . .250 calories
On pension. .500 calories
Remark: This, it is concluded, is not a true psychological mechanism of ego defense. The latter two categories, though, might qualify under certain conditions.

3. Jumping to Conclusions.
Low jump . . . . .25 calories
Medium jump . . . . .125 calories
High jump . . . . .200 calories

4. Sowing Wild Oats.
This hypothesis could not be researched by this investigator. He had already sown them, and, in fact, had reaped the harvest.

5. Beating Around the Bush.
Low bush . . . . .75 calories
Medium bush. . . . . .135 calories
Remark: It was not possible to visualize a high bush.

6. Climbing the Walls.
Every attempt resulted in a blank, but it must be stated that the imaginary "climbing" was done with "inside" walls, and the investigator was con-fused as to how many walls were to be climbed. When springtime arrives, a test will be done with "outside" walls in the hope that he will arrive at some definite figures. "Stonewalling" would be an interesting activity to measure.

7. Swallowing Pride.
In front of wife . . . . .300 calories
In front of others. . . . . .75 calories
Remark: It was difficult, at first, to put myself in this situation, but, after several attempts, conceit was manufactured in the mind, and the above data were fabricated.

8. Passing the Buck.
Small buck. . . . . .25 calories
Medium buck. . . . . .75 calories
Large buck. .125 calories
Bock buck . . . . .350 calories
Remark: the bock buck was very difficult to pass. There were some difficulties, also, with the "saw" buck because of conflicting visions. It was impossible to pass the carpenter's sawbuck in a sitting position. The results of these are not presented here.

9. Throwing One's Weight Around.
Results were inconclusive. It was impossible for the investigator to get a good grip on any kind of weight to throw. In the future the kind of weight will need to be defined, but this, too, will involve redesigning the research project.

10. Dragging Heels.
The wife happened to be absent the day I tested this hypothesis. I felt entirely happy and content with the world and could not perceive any work to be done. Thus I could not imagine anything about which I should drag my heels.
Remarks: If the term "heel" is defined carefully, there are all kinds of dragging which can be visualized.

11. Pushing My Luck.
Warning: The investigator wishes to do more than suggest that this should be done with much care so as to avoid a catastrophe.
Remark: The test violated every procedure to be used by the investigator. There seemed to be a difference between "good" luck which might be pushed positively and "bad" luck which must be shoved out—entirely from the mind. Since definite definitions are not to be used, the test resulted in inconclusive data.

12. Making Mountains Out of Molehills.
This was the most difficult of all hypotheses to test in view of the variables.

Making big mountains
out of small molehills . . . . .775 calories
Making small mountains
out of big molehills . . . . .250 calories
Remark: The researcher was exhausted after manufacturing these two data and had to stop for a strong drink of Irish whiskey.

13. Hitting the Nail on the Head.
This hypothesis was tested under difficult and painful conditions. Visions of hitting one's own thumbnail kept coming into the mind and thus contaminated the results.
Remark: The contamination of this test is similar to that found in number 11 above. It is possible that the design, as suggested in number 9, is too flexible. There seems to be a need for some kind of control to be exerted on the imagination.

14. Wading Through Paperwork.
One sheet . . . . .15 calories
100 sheets . . . . .250 calories
Ream . . . . .500 calories
Remark: It was found that administrative paperwork was "waded through" without any expenditure of calories whatsoever, but it must be stated, though, that administrators did not "wade"—they "passed" paper from desk to desk and office to office without any mental processes. If the results of this test were to be made public, the salary structure of every bureaucratic organization would be radically changed.

15. Bending Over Backward.
The results were inconclusive, inconsistent, and incoherent. Visions of bending over backward made the researcher dizzier than usual.

16. Balancing the Books.
For IRS . . . . .35 calories
For the wife . . . . .400 calories

17. Jumping on the Bandwagon.
My own . . . . .50 calories
Another's . . . . .200 calories
Remark: Being the product of the early part of this century the researcher was a farm boy. Thus visions of a wagon with a horse kept coming to mind, and he was inclined to jump on the horse instead of the wagon. When the "band" was envisioned, all that came to mind was "big" name bands, and he became nostalgic. The data presented above must be considered as being contaminated by the investigator. (It must be advised, though, that the idea of contamination is abhorrent to this research by principles stated in both the design and procedures.)

18. Running Around in Circles.
Small circles . . . . .35 calories
Medium . . . . .135 calories
Large . . . . .250 calories
Chasing one's self in circles . . . . .750 calories
Remark: Chasing one's self could be extrapolated forever as one chases or runs in circles all one's life.

19. Eating Crow.
Well-cooked crow . . . . .225 calories
Raw crow . . . . .500 calories
Eating crow in front of others . . . . . . .750 calories

20. Tooting My Own Horn . . . . .25 calories
Remark: As hypothesized, this was the easiest to do, along with "giving advice." It seemed not to matter for whom, how, where, why, or for what I imagined myself tooting my horn, the results were the same—25 calories. The investigator's ego, evidently, was a strong one.

Conclusions
In conformity with what is generally known about the human animal when under conditions of "alarm," "resistance," and "frustration," this study unearthed data which has never been shoveled out so indiscriminatingly. Further studies should be made.

GONORRHEA SCREENING, OREGON 1973
The female gonorrhea screening program has been very successful statewide. Thanks to the efforts of our county health departments, family planning clinics, and private physicians, *some 1527 women were found to be infected by other than our VD clinics.* This has given us an opportunity to interview these females for their sex partners and bring some unsuspecting men to treatment. While epidemiology is still the backbone of our VD eradication program, screening is proving to be of great value.

—*From the Communicable Disease Summary, Published by Oregon State Health Division, March 30, 1974.*

THE AUDIBLE CRUNCH BARES TRUTH AND DENTURES[1]

Raleigh, North Carolina
February 25, 1971

Mr. L. J. Turney, Chairman
Crispness Research Committee
Medina, Ohio

Dear Sir:

It has come to our attention that the findings from some of our most basic studies on vegetable-tissue-texture-measurement, using a human test animal, may have been purloined right from under our very bridgework! I refer to that early and continuing fundamental inquiry into the audibility-index of the firmness, texture or crispness of the immature fruit of black-spined or white-spined cultivars of *Cucumis sativus* L. Our exhaustive, yes, tiring tests have been made on either fresh, fresh-packed, brined, salted or pickled cucumbers—as measured by a human subject when actually eating, biting, and/or chewing a 1⅛ to 1¼ inch-diameter cucumber fruit or pickle. This is done by a carefully selected person equipped with a minimum of thirty-two normal, naturally occurring teeth or their equivalent in the form of modern upper and lower dentures or approved bridgework, either fixed or removable. The chewer should also have a *large, resonant mouth*—a big mouth is just not enough! Now, the result of said eating, biting, and/or chewing action has been reported by us as being the typical "crunchy" sound, clearly and continually heard by a subject with average auditory reception when backing away from the chewer at a constant rate (1 pace/second) until the "crunchy" sound fades out.

The "fade-out" point is, of course, quickly and clearly marked on the floor with chalk and then measured accurately in normal paces by the official pacer (no horses please, Lawrence) preferably 3-feet per pace; but, with smaller-sized pacers, it may only average 2 to 2½ feet. Note: firmer stock should be used with the larger paces; conversely, with denture-dills, smaller paces are desirable. Now, returning to the auditory "fade-out" point, it is here where the distance is reported in terms of total paces where audibility was last clearly noted (loose denture static is not countable), and thus the value expressed in terms of *"An Audible Crunch"* at *"blank"* (Audible Crunch Test). In our early studies, we once had an all-time-high reading of 10 (ten) normal, three-foot paces. This value has been used for years and, even though it was registered in the late 1930s at the "International Center for Fruit and Vegetable Crunchiness" in Geneva (Switzerland) it has appeared to have passed into the realm of public domain—much like the words "Aspirin," "Bread and Butter," Pickles, and the like.

We find all sorts of people using our early *Standard* for crunchiness, cited above, but without so much as a reference, footnote, asterisk, double-dagger, or kind word. Plant psychologists, breeders, and seedsmen seem to be the prime users of our *Standard;* but recently food scientists are catching on too.

Now, after all these years, you can hardly imagine our great shock and surprise to learn that our early findings, including those data directly responsible for the long-established, and widely used *Standard (Audible Crunch at Ten Paces)* were, indeed, no longer valid. In fact we were to learn later on that the true value was about three paces (9-feet ± 2 inches) in excess of what it really should be today. We attribute this reduction in crunch-footage to be the direct result of *actual loss of auditory reception* of our citizens, due mainly to the sustained high decibel noise level resulting from our modern, affluent mode of life; namely, traffic; ampli-

---

[1] Following a study by the U.S. Department of Agriculture using sophisticated texture measurements on cucumbers with a $25,000 machine, the above report is designed to conserve the high cost of machine tests.

fied guitars, singers, and combos; radios, juke boxes; TV; hi-fis; irate parents, irritable children; large dogs; sports cars; and the like. Of course, we could also say that pickle products today don't really have the "crunchiness" they had when the *Standard* was first established many years ago; but this would seem like a foolish explanation to be offered by a person whose livelihood more-or-less depends on the pickle industry. A better way would be to develop a new *Standard* that would be fully in step with all the modern innovations designed by industry to upgrade that prime quality characteristic— *"Firmness"* or *"Crunchiness."*[2]

So, under highly controlled, almost sound-proof conditions, work to establish the "new" *Standard* began with much dedication and rejoicing, and with numerous offers being made by persons of great ability and devotion to serve as: (a) "crunchers," (b) "crunch-listeners," (c) "crunch-listener-pacers," and (d) "crunch-listener-pacer-measurers." In due time the prime "cruncher" was selected. He stood over six-feet, with a cavernous mouth replete with thirty-two sparkling, original teeth, with no sound-absorbing amalgam fillings, no tonsils, and a mouth resonance value of 9.7342, second only to that enviable 10.0001 rating of St. Peter's Cathedral (in Rome, of course—Georgia). Two "crunch-listeners" were selected after much screening and bickering. One had average suburbanite hearing; the other, an auditory control, was *deaf,* but was fully equipped with a modern hearing aid built-in to one temple of his glasses, plus an extra battery. The pickle selected was a northern variety, made into a regular fresh-pack dill, typical of the test area.

The official "cruncher" crunched the three small, No. 2-size pickles in perfect iambic pentameter and with a near perfect rhythmic, biting and grinding action resulting from repeated high performance occlusions of his gleaming white bicuspids and molars— particularly those of the lower mandible. Meanwhile, the two official "crunch-listeners" were retreating slowly, ever so slowly, barely a pace/second, to the extinction point of their auditory-sensing abilities, both naturally and artificially induced. The official "crunch-listener-pacer-measurer" recorded seven (7) full paces (= 21-feet) for the natural hearing "listener-participant" and one full pace less—that is, six— (= 18 feet) for the "hearing aid type participant." The latter person was penalized a full 12 inches (1-foot) because he signaled vigorously for a new battery

during the peak decibel-level crunch of the third and final pickle. Further, during the actual battery change, the amplifier squeal of his hearing aid upset the natural auditory reception of the other participant. Even so, all the judges, Local, National, and International representatives of the ACT organization ruled the test *"Official"* for both types of listeners and authorized the use of the new *Standard,* namely, "Audible crunch at 7-paces (21-feet); and, 6-paces (18-feet) for hearing aids." One can only but wonder that, without the battery-change-crisis, the audible crunch distance may well have been extended.

Also, in deference to our earlier work, done during an era of lower incomes, better hearing, and lower noise-decibel levels, they authorized the continued use of the older *Standard,* namely, "Audible crunch at ten paces; eight for hearing aids."

I regret that this explanation has taken so long to prepare, but I have been inundated with letters, phone calls, newspaper clippings, carrier pigeons, smoke signals, and personal emissaries, all directing my attention to the apparent and flagrant misuse of our original *Crunch-Standard* (Audible Crunch at Ten Paces; Eight for Hearing Aids— you can see I still like the old test best!). Some folks have even said that a few years ago, seed advertising appeared that paraphrased our statement—but you and I know that's ridiculous.

Be assured, we appreciate your support, as well as that of your Company and your Association (whatever it is). We shall continue to develop meaningful standards and tests for your industry as fast as they are needed and/or accepted—whichever is the sooner.

Sincerely yours,
C.U. Sativus, Jr., Head,
Local Society for
Preservation of
the Audible Crunch Test
(ACT)

P.S.: We only have one member (me) so there are some nice Administrative jobs open!

P.P.S.: Will you please see that our great but little-known efforts in developing the precise basic tests described herein are brought to the attention of persons who are unaware that such studies have long been in progress and are still continuing unabated? Also, advise them that we have competent legal talent to protect our creativity from technical and academic poachers.

---

[2] Reader's note: Does he mean mechanical harvesting? Long distance, bulk-hauling of green stock? Bank upon bank of high-speed mechanical graders? High temperature-long-time blanching? High temperature pasteurization? Poor cooling facilities? Hot warehouses for storage? Overall, rough-handling? It's vague, really.

THE INHERITANCE PATTERN OF DEATH

Joseph Eastern, M.D.
Carol Drucker, M.D.
John E. Wolf, Jr., M.D.
Department of Unclear Medicine and Biosciences
(DUMB)
Baylor College of Medicine
Texas Medical Center
Houston, Texas

We wish to communicate a striking observation which we believe will have broad implications for our understanding of life and mankind's tenuous mortality. This deceptively simple concept may well affect our very social structure and radically alter patterns of marriage.

Genetics has historically been a pragmatic and arbitrary branch of medicine, as would any field whose origins stem from a lonely and celibate monk staring vacuously at pea plants in a monastery courtyard, arriving at no more profound an observation than that some were tall and some were short. As the insufferable boredom of this behavior became evident, even in a monastery, and the monk took to lasciviously and incestuously breeding all permutations of short and tall, the prurient interest of physicians was inevitably kindled, resulting in the incorporation of genetics into the realm of medicine.

In subsequent years, genetics has struggled to elevate itself from its ignominious origins. Like Maxwell's Demon, genes themselves are still impossible to observe directly, and all conclusions concerning their behavior must be derived from indirect (some say irrelevant) methods. Therefore, much of a modern geneticist's time is consumed in the lengthy and often uncomprehending scrutiny of long pedigree charts, with occasional forays into the lab to gawk enviously at fruitflies and funny-looking mice copulating to produce even funnier-looking offspring.

The Pattern Emerges

We recently had an occasion to engage in a bit of this dubious pastime, somewhat against our better judgment, when several pedigrees (of which Fig. 1, page 52 is a representative example) became available to us while awaiting the completion of a seemingly endless departmental meeting. As with most momentous discoveries, our original goal was totally unrelated to our final conclusion. The original goal, of course, was simply to ignore and thus survive the meeting, whose agenda ranged from confiscation of the residents' beer fund to the mysterious disappearance of the departmental chairman's pet hamster. Thus, we were serendipitously and seductively drawn to contemplation of the suddenly fascinating line-and-circle patterns of the pedigrees.

After many random, dead-end lines of reasoning, substantial free association and several short naps, it became apparent to us that a definite and dimly familiar pattern of genetic inheritance was present. We were unable to obtain a genetics consult at the time (it being past noon), but managed with the aid of incense and a small sacrificial lamb (later modified into a superb *noisettes d'agneau*) to discern a classic Mendelian autosomal recessive pattern for the phenotype of death.

We are confident that the discovery of a recessive transmission pattern (apparently with very high penetrance, often greatly delayed expressivity, and no racial or sexual predilection) for the trait of death will be recognized as highly significant from a purely scientific point of view. Of course, as with most elucidations of genetically-controlled diseases, no practical significance is immediately evident, and no prospect for a therapeutic solution to death can be foreseen. However, in the grand tradition of science, we refuse to be discouraged by the basic irrelevance of our discovery.

Minimizing the Risk

There are, nevertheless, certain steps which individuals may consider to minimize the risk of death developing or perpetuating in their families. Now that an autosomal recessive pattern has been demonstrated, the families and ancestors of a potential spouse should be carefully screened for any incidence of death, as a positive history greatly increases the probability of the

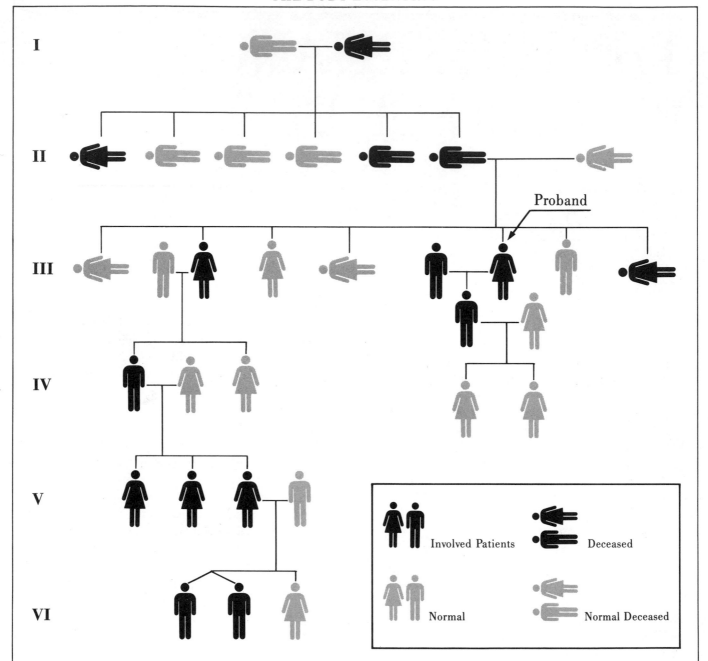

Fig. 1.

proband carrying the trait. Should the investigator's family also have a positive history of death, there is, of course, a 1:4 chance of communicating the trait to potential offspring—an inexcusable action in light of the new knowledge communicated herein. One should especially make certain that a potential spouse has not already expressed the gene, *i.e.*, is not dead, since this elevates the probability of perpetuating the trait to proportions approaching 100%, as well as substantially reducing the prospects for a fulfilling relationship.

We hope that this discovery will aid knowledgeable people in minimizing the risk of death in their descendants. Hopefully, spurred on by inspirations at future tedious departmental meetings, we may succeed in developing an enzymatic test to be done on all newborns for the presence of the death trait, though this research has already been vigorously opposed by the Amalgamated Morticians' Association (AMA) and the national Kounty Koroner's Konvention (KKK). We intend to remain steadfast against such blatant special-interest pressure, however, and with God's help and an NIH grant, we are determined to prevail.

Reprints available on alternate Thursdays from 2–4 P.M. behind the taco stand at 1240 Bertner, Houston. Please form a line to the left.

PART III
THE MIND IN QUESTION

CRAP: CONSUMER RATED ASSESSMENT PROCEDURE

Alan Frankel, Ph.D.
Dianna Ross Strange
Reggie Schoonover, S.B.D.
Veterans Administration Hospital
Salem, Virginia

While extensive research has been conducted on the MMPI, it nevertheless is a fact that the original *items* came from a culture that no longer exists except in the connective tissues of septuagenarians in remote retirement relocation centers and in first grade readers.[1] Therefore in the interest of science and self-aggrandizement, a new form of the MMPI adapted from the No-Nonsense Personality Inventory[2] was developed sparing no expense and is reported herein.

Method

From an infinite item pool, an Aleph null set of items was capriciously selected and administered by Aleph to a null class of respondents. Eighty items were selected by item analysis and replicated on another independent and randomly selected null class of respondents (cf. Borgatta, 1955, for a review of the no person group). All items held up on cross-validation and were subjected to a principle-components-unexpended-budget factor analysis.[3] The extracted factors were subjected to the Havery-Allmann Principle Hierarchy and Zero Alternate Reduction Dimension (HAP—HAZARD) rotation. The number of factors extracted were equal to the number of eigenvalues equal to or greater than _____.[4]

Results

Results of the factor analysis seemed reasonable and therefore we are printing a complete list of the items so that local investigators can establish their own norms.[5]

Do Not Make Any Marks on This Booklet

1. I salivate at the sight of mittens.
2. My father was a good woman.
3. My mother dresses me funny.
4. I believe in an afterbirth.
5. My mouth talks to people.
6. I often lie to make myself obnoxious.
7. I prefer spiders to lima beans.
8. My teeth sometimes leave my body.
9. I cannot read or write.
10. Chiclets make me sweat.
11. Often, I think I am a special agent of Billy Graham.
12. I become homicidal when people try to reason with me.
13. Sometimes I feel I am persecuting somebody.
14. Policemen love me.
15. I call the wind Maria.
16. I have never been able to put a bagel into overdrive.
17. Paranoid people worry too much.
18. I am anxious in rooms that have hairy walls.
19. Boredom excites me.
20. My mother was Erik the Red.

---

[1] A subsequent statistical study will report on multivariate relationships between the content of first grade reading material, contemporary education methods, the counterculture, John Calvin, Ivan Illych, and your local board of education. But of this, later.

[2] A widely distributed salacious document unpublished by the Underground Psychological Assessment Secular Systems.

[3] This type of factor analysis hitherto unreported in the literature is simply the factor analysis done at the end of the fiscal year when you have some extra money left over in your budget and you do not know what else to do with your data.

[4] In this age of consumerism, it is considered inappropriate to unilaterally make a decision, such as determining this constant without taking into account the views of the consumer. Therefore to be on the safe side and to escape the wrath of the local, state, and federal consumer protection agencies, we will let the reader simply supply his own value of the eigenvalue.

[5] We would be particularly displeased to hear from any investigators who might want to share their data with us. We consider that our conclusions are so solid that any new data is extraneous. However, new items are always welcome. Requests for reprints will be burned.

21. Eggplants make me blush.
22. Cannibalism is a small price to pay for popularity.
23. It makes me embarrassed to fall down.
24. Weeping brings tears to my eyes.
25. Parts of my body crawl away.
26. I believe I smell as good as most people.
27. I would never tell my nickname in a crisis.
28. A wide necktie is a sign of disease.
29. I always let people get ahead of me at swimming pools.
30. Nothing is happening, just as Schopenhauer predicted.
31. I have taken shoe polish to excess.
32. God rarely answers my letters.
33. As a child I often suffered from bubonic plague.
34. I always cut my hair with an emery board.
35. Sitting in the glove compartment makes me claustrophobic.
36. I believe people should post no bills.
37. My nose has suddenly gone blank.
38. My name is spelled with two s's.
39. I think most people would cry to gain a point.
40. I never vomit in my sleep.
41. I am bored by thoughts of death.
42. Sometimes I find it hard to conceal the fact that I am not angry.
43. Frantic screams make me nervous.
44. It is hard for me to find the right thing to say when I find myself in a room full of cockroaches.
45. I stay in the bathtub until I look like a raisin.
46. I have more pimples than you can shake a stick at.
47. Most people do not know how to behave in a massacre.
48. I am afraid of finding myself in a drawer or some other compromising place.
49. Most people vomit out of spite.
50. I am not threatened by people who want to put my tongue in a paper punch.
51. I am tired of being elected president.
52. I believe in Cincinnati.
53. I used to collect hypodermic needles.
54. My parents always faced catastrophes with a song.
55. I think oatmeal is erotic.
56. I have an uncontrollable urge to fondle other people's teeth.
57. Recently, I have been getting shorter.
58. It follows me wherever I go.
59. I do not!
60. I believe there is a plot to make me happy.
61. My sex life is A-OK.
62. Spinach makes me feel alone.
63. Most people aren't as old as they think they are.
64. When I look down from a high place I want to spit.

65. Sometimes I think someone is trying to take over my stomach.
66. My ears sometimes hear voices.
67. I do not believe there is any intelligent life on the earth.
68. Earthquakes make me wet the bed.
69.
70. I think I would like the work of a hummingbird.
71. Most of the time I go to sleep without saying good-bye.
72. It makes me angry to have people bury me.
73. Constantly losing my underwear doesn't bother me.
74. I often bite other people's nails.
75. Halitosis is part of my style.
76. I hereby claim this land in the name of the Queen of Spain.
77. My tonsils frequently come when I whistle.
78. I am piqued when I find a rhinoceros in my bed.
79. The three greatest men who ever lived were Eleanor Roosevelt.
80. I am often bothered by thoughts of sex while having intercourse.

NOT WHAT IT LOOKS LIKE DEPT.

Trichomycete *Asellaria ligiae* Tuzet et Manier from the hindgut of the marine isopod *Ligia italica* Fabricius.

WHY IT'S LATER THAN YOU THINK

T.L. Freeman
Department of Intuitive Reasoning
Institute of Cost Plus Fixed Fee Studies

One of life's most widely acknowledged but least studied mysteries is the apparent acceleration in the rate of passage of the years in one's life. Having reached an age where the implications have become very disturbing, I recently devoted the better part of my lunch hours for a couple of months to an analysis of this phenomenon. I believe the results will eventually have a profound effect upon humanity's view of the meaning of life and upon my future employment prospects.

A wealth of scientific evidence exists, I am told, that effectively lays to rest an earlier theory by the author which held that the length of the year actually *is* getting shorter. In the continued tradition of quasi-scientific inquiry into the quasi-quantifiable perplexities of life, and wishing to redeem my earlier *faux pas*, I hereby submit my latest thinking for the consideration of my peers, unaccustomed though I know them to be to the study of the truly significant.

It is intuitively obvious that the apparent passage of time is directly and uniquely related to the observer's age. When one considers that the frame of reference vis-à-vis any long period of time (e.g., a year), is the span of time one has existed (i.e., one's age), the nature of this relationship is obvious to all but the mentally deficient or the professionally incompetent. The relationship is simply this: the *apparent* length of a year in a person's life is inversely proportional to the person's age.[1] When you are ten years old, a year represents 10% of your life and seems like a very long time. When you are 50 years old, a year is only 2% of your life, and hence seems one-fifth as long.

The constant of proportionality is simply the age at which a year really seems to last a year.[2] Thinking back, it seems to me that a year really seemed like a year when I was about 20. Therefore:

$$\text{Apparent Year Length} = 20/\text{Age}$$

We can now define an individual's "effective age" as the sum of the "apparent year" lengths experienced in the person's life. This is a measure of the apparent passage of time in one's life and is directly proportional to one's accumulated experience and knowledge. To find one's effective age at any actual age in life, we must integrate the apparent year length function from age 1 to the actual age of interest. Thus:

$$\text{Effective Age} = \int_{1}^{\text{actual age}} (20/\text{age})\, d(\text{age})$$

$$= 20 \ln \text{age} \Big]_{1}^{\text{actual age}}$$

$$= 20 \ln (\text{actual age})$$

Evaluating this at increments of actual age, we arrive at the following table:

Actual Age	Effective Age	Effective % Completion of Life (Assuming 90-year lifetime)
10	46	51%
20	60	67%
30	68	76%
40	74	82%
50	78	87%
60	82	91%
70	85	94%
80	88	98%
90	90	100%

Thus, in terms of one's own perspective, life is half over at age ten, three quarters over at age thirty, and nine-tenths completed at sixty; and *that's* if you live to be ninety![3]

The value of this work can best be illustrated by enumerating a few of life's mysteries explained by it. It explains why summer vacations lasted for over a year in your grammar school days. It explains why you thought you knew everything as a teenager and why you thought you would live forever when you were in your

---

[1] To be precise, it is proportional to the person's age at the *end* of the year in question, for reasons of computational expediency.

[2] This varies somewhat from person to person, but knowing myself to be fairly typical in this regard, I have called upon my own experience.

twenties. It explains why the "generation gap" narrows as parents and children grow older. Mainly, however, it explains why your birthday rolls around faster every year.

The implications are profound. You are who you are at age 10 because you have essentially experienced more than half of your life. At any age, it is later in life than you think. In old age, however, your actual age finally catches up to your effective age, and it truly is as late as you think.

As a first step toward awakening us from our complacency, I would recommend that we change the basis with which we measure and relate our age from "actual age" to "effective age." Admittedly, this may be initially unpopular with those who are vain about giving their age. However, it would provide a perspective heretofore absent in the fields of social planning. For example, when we finally realize that our kindergartens are attended by thirty-two year olds, our highschools by the middle-aged, and our universities by our elderly, we might find it wise to compress all this schooling so that it is completed by the actual age of ten. In the author's opinion, very little of importance would have to be omitted from current curricula. Students would benefit by getting out into the world before its too late for them and society would be relieved of a tremendous financial burden.

Acknowledgment

This work was supported by funds allocated for something else entirely and was inspired by a request for a large loan by the author from his father, Mr. J.W. Freeman.

---

[3] There is something profoundly elegant, although I have yet to determine what, about the fact that the integral of apparent age (i.e., "effective age," converges with actual age at ninety, the approximate life expectancy of humans.

BOOK REVIEW

Insects as Sex Partners
Theophilus Fliedermaier
Omniphilic Press, Ltd.
Bound to please, 1977. 2947 pp. $1.95

Reviewer: John L. Schaeffer

This rather disgusting book completely fascinated me from the moment I picked it up until my mother pried it out of my hands. Presumably to read herself. Oh, well... Supposedly, our era is the time of dramatic growth in interdisciplinary practices, so I guess this amply qualifies. Coupled with the knowledge of the extremely high reproduction rate of most of the insect world (tireless little buggers), the thought of thousands of varieties extant simply boggles the mind. Just think about logarithmic progression! Consider the positions! *O tempora, O mores!*

Nor is the selection limited to butterflies, mantises *(sic)*, grasshoppers, boll weevils *(sicer)*, and pupal-stage partners, as all too often occurs in Swedish- and Sanskrit-produced works of this nature. Even the Giant Australian Wooly Caterpillar *(caterpilla biggamomma)* falls within our ken! Written in the style of a third-grade textbook for armchair travelers, *Insects* traverses the world—bringing us first to a provocative meeting of the Cambridge psychology department, then across oceans to a deliciously primitive centuries-old fertility ritual in New Guinea where the insect partners are consumed *immediately* after consummation. 'Tis devoutly to be wished!

Certainly not to be ticked off as a fly-by-night experience, the book (more an encyclopedia) is profusely illustrated with true-to-life holograms, microforms, and anatomically significant drawings for your vicarious pleasure. *Exciting* is not a long enough word to describe it. (I read it cover-to-cover at a single sitting.) Even the most jaded animal lovers will enjoy, enjoy! Simply *must* reading for teachers and social workers. Watch for the soon-to-be-published sequel, *Insects Is Best.*

BELCHING SYNDROME: A SOMATIC EXPRESSION OF UNPLEASANT THOUGHT CONTENT

R. Tislow

"It is suggested here that belching, besides being the physical result of aerophagia, can be a manifestation of a gastro-esophagal expulsive reflex which is triggered off by aversive thought associations.

"Several years ago I realized that belching may serve as a somatic expression of unpleasant thought content. Once during a lengthy talk with a colleague, a research psychiatrist, I noticed that he would belch each time his department head was mentioned. Asked directly about his feelings for his superior, he admitted having some differences of opinion."

—From Life Sciences, Vol. 3, p. 1501, 1964.

NASALITY

A Psychological Concept of Great Clinical Significance, Previously Undescribed

Stephen D. Bourgeois, M.D.
Fort Worth, Texas

Generations of physicians have cut their eye teeth on Freudian psychiatry. There is not a physician currently licensed to practice medicine in this country, who, to pass his examinations and obtain his M.D. degree, did not have to master the intricate and bewildering concepts of the Oedipal complex, castration anxiety, anal fixation, the oral personality, and whatnot. All very well so far as it goes. However, as this paper will expose for the first time, there exists an incredible oversight, a huge gap, as it were, in Freudian theory. Furthermore, it is the intention of this communication to plug that gap by defining an area of normal psychological development as well as pathological syndromes associated with disorders in this area.

Freud stressed the importance of very early influences on an individual. It would seem logical, therefore, in discussing any area of psychological development, to begin at the beginning, to look, in short, at what is happening in the immediate post-partal period. Let us take some of the well defined and well understood syndromes associated with certain body parts and consider what role these anatomic parts play and their relative importance in the life of the newborn.

Many experts have written about the oral personality. However, when a newborn babe comes into this world, what is the first thing that he does? Does he settle down to a hearty meal of Similac, Enfamil, or mother's milk? No, in modern hospitals he will get no nourishment for up to 8 hours. Much has been written about anal fixation, but coming back to our infant child, moments after expulsion from the warmth and security of his mother's womb into the harsh reality of the world of inevitable death and taxation, what is the first act that he must accomplish? Move his bowels? Does he, disappointed at the insipidness of his bowel movement, dejected, perhaps, at the prospect of 8 to 72 hours of fasting, decide to console himself by moseying down to the nearest bordello or massage parlor for a bit of sexual gratification? Hardly.

Nothing to Sniff At

The first thing this newborn baby must do, if he is to live, is to breathe. Furthermore, he must continue to do it on a fairly regular basis throughout his entire life. Much is made of sex, eating, and bowel movements, and those parts of the anatomy associated with these functions, but what has been written about the psychology of that primary and most important of all functions, breathing? Almost nothing. However, let respiration cease for but a few minutes and life itself ceases. That Freud could have failed to appreciate the psychological significance of respiration and of the external organ thereof, namely the nose, boggles the imagination.

When a baby is born, the obstetrician's first act, before even clamping the umbilical cord, is to clear the infant's airway with an aspirating syringe. Subsequently, pediatricians and nurses monitor the child carefully, and an aspirating syringe is always kept handy to suck mucus from the baby's nose as needed. All this fussing about his nose cannot fail to impress upon the subconscious mind of the child the importance of that part of his anatomy.

Competition and rivalry are present even among very young children. In countries where poverty and starvation are common, they may fight over food. Less obvious, but no less important, is the subconscious competition a child feels for the very air he breathes. Conditioned from birth to an awareness of the importance of the nose and respiration, he is bound to notice the noses of his peers and to compare them with his own. If his nose is small and insignificant, he will feel inferior and threatened. He will feel that his survival depends on avoiding conflict and not provoking his large-nosed contemporaries, as he is no match for them in the competition for air. On the other hand, if his nose is large, he will feel that he can inhale far greater quantities of air than his fellows, and he is likely to develop into a confident, aggressive, often even arrogant person. Feeling himself to be genetically superior to his peers, he will have a natural tendency to "look down his nose" at them. Clinical studies have led me to recognize what I call the "nasal personality." It is characterized by the following syndrome:

1. A large nose
2. Aggressiveness
3. Arrogance
4. A tendency to stick one's nose into other people's business

The "non-nasal personality" conversely is characterized by:
1. A small nose
2. Placidity
3. Humility
4. A tendency to mind one's own business

The Conquering Nose

History is replete with examples of the nasal personality. Indeed, almost all of the great conquerors were classic examples thereof. Alexander the Great possessed such a nose in addition to an aggressive personality. His conquests spread Hellenism from Gibraltar to the Punjab and paved the way for the later development of the Roman Empire. Julius Caesar's nose was remarkably similar to Alexander's in both size and shape.

There is certainly no doubt about the nasal dimensions, arrogance, or aggressive personality of Napoleon Bonaparte. Napoleon stormed through Europe and had his way on the continent until he was finally stopped at Waterloo, by an alliance of other large-nosed races, among which were the British.

When it comes to nasality, the British need take second place to none. Under a succession of large-nosed monarchs, the British established an empire that stretched around the globe. The Indians who inhabited what is now the United States of America had hawk-like noses of the sort so well depicted on a nickel. These semi-barbaric tribes offered fierce and determined resistance to the European invaders. The Indians of Mexico have small, flat noses. They had highly advanced civilizations, yet a handful of nasal Spaniards led by Hernando Cortés conquered the entire nation within a very short period of time.

Despite innumerable historical examples of the nasal personality, the importance of the nose has never been fully appreciated. Much nonsense has been written, on the other hand, about "firm chins," and "determined jaws." The chin and jaw have nothing to

do with it. Look at General Charles deGaulle. He had, in fact, a receding chin, and a rather weak jaw. But what a nose! I had the privilege of seeing this great man, then President of France, when he visited New Orleans in 1962. As he passed in review along Canal Street, the crowd was struck with fear and awe at the sight of his incredible nose. One sensed that if he put the thing in high gear, it would suck up all the surrounding air like some great nuclear powered vacuum cleaner and leave bystanders gasping for breath in a void.

Nasal Envy

This brings us into the area of the nasal envy and rhinoplasty[1] anxiety. When a race of non-nasal people, especially one that has been isolated for centuries, is suddenly exposed to large numbers of nasal people, the result is intense psychological trauma, and the development, sometimes on a national scale, of nasal envy and rhinoplasty anxiety.

Penis envy is to nasal envy as a wart is to metastatic carcinoma.

I hope that the foregoing discussion has convinced the reader of the importance of nasality. The introduction of this concept into the literature will undoubtedly force a shift in emphasis of psychotherapy. I wish that I could claim to be the first to recognize the nasal syndrome. Unfortunately, as is so often the case in medicine, when one thinks that one has an original idea, a careful search of the literature shows that the idea has already been mentioned, if not developed and defined. Edmond Rostand, in his play, *Cyrano de Bergerac* (1897), showed that he grasped the importance of the nose when he had Cyrano say:

"Or—parodying Faustus in the play—Was this the nose that launched a thousand ships and burned the topless towers of Ilium?"

These are telling lines indeed. I will readily grant to orthodox Freudians, that someone, a General Patton perhaps, under appropriate circumstances, say the occasion of a colossal military blunder, might ask, "Is this the ass who launched a thousand ships?" However, I would be quick to point out that in this circumstance the speaker would be referring to the intelligence or personality of the launcher of those myriad ships, rather than to parts of his anatomy.

---

[1] A rhinoplasty is an operation to reshape the nose, generally making it smaller. Interestingly, in modern times this operation is usually performed on large-nosed patients who suffer guilt feelings over the nasal aggressiveness of their forebears. These patients subconsciously wish to punish and humiliate themselves by amputating, or at least diminishing in size, that organ which is the symbol of the nasal brutality of their ancestors.

THE VARIETIES OF PSYCHOTHERAPEUTIC EXPERIENCE

Robert S. Hoffman, M.D.
San Francisco, California

Freudian

Patient: I could use a ham on rye, hold the mustard.
Therapist: It's evident that a quantity of libidinal striving has been displaced to a regressive object with relative fixation in the anal-sadistic mode.
P: What do you suggest?
T: Perhaps a valve job and tune-up.

Rogerian

P: Shit! Do I feel shitty!
T: Sounds like you feel shitty.
P: Why are you parroting me?
T: You seem concerned about my parroting you.
P: What the hell is going on here?
T: You sound confused.

Existential

P: Sorry I'm late today.
T: Can you get more in touch with that sorrow?
P: I hope it didn't inconvenience you.
T: Let's focus on your capacity for choice rather than on my expectations.
P: But I didn't mean to be late.
T: I hear you, and I don't put it down. But where we need to be is the immanence of the I-Thou relationship (in Buber's sense) emanating from the here-and-now, and from there into a consciousness of the tension between be-ing and non-be-ing, and eventually into the transcendence of be-ing itself, through to a cosmic awareness of the oceanic I-dentity of Self and the space-time continuum.
P: Gotcha.

Behavioral

P: I feel depressed.
T: Okay. First, I want you to look at this list of depressing phrases, order them by ascending depression-potential and match them with these postcards. Then I want you to step over to these electrodes—don't worry—and put your head in this vise and your left foot in this clamp. Then, when I count to ten, I want you to . . .

Gestalt

P: I feel somehow that life just isn't worth living.
T: Don't give me that shit!
P: What do you mean? I'm really concerned that . . .
T: Real hell! You're trying to mind-screw me. Come off it.
P: You shmuck—what are you trying to do with me?
T: Attaboy! Play me—play the shmuck. I'll play you.
P: What's going on?
T: Not shmucky enough—try again, louder.
P: I've never met a therapist like this.
T: No good—you gotta stay in the here-and-now.
P: (gets up to leave)
T: Okay, now we're getting somewhere. Stand up on that table and do it again.
P: (exits)
T: Good. Now I'll play the angry patient and walk out the door. "You shmuck—I'm leaving."

Confrontation

P: Hello.
T: Pretty anxious about the amenities, eh?
P: Not very.
T: Don't try to wiggle out of it.
P: I'm not. I just . . .
T: Trying to deny it?
P: Okay, you're right.
T: Don't agree just for agreement's sake.
P: As a matter of fact, I don't agree . . .
T: Sounds a bit hostile.
P: Have it your way. I'm hostile.
T: That's pretty dependent, that statement.
P: Okay, I'm EVERYTHING.
T: God, what modesty!

Primal

P: Can you help me stop cracking my knuckles, Doctor?

T: Okay. You're three years old—you're hungry—REALLY hungry—you want to suckle—you reach for your mother's bosom—what happens?—she pulls away—SHE PULLS AWAY!—SHE ISN'T GOING TO LET YOU HAVE IT—FEEL THAT!—WHAT DO YOU FEEL??—WHAT DO YOU WANT???—Get down on the mat there or you'll hurt yourself—YOU *WANT*, YOU REALLY WANT THAT MILK!—YOU WANT YOUR MOMMY!—YOU AREN'T GOING TO GET YOUR MONEY, I MEAN MOMMY!!—CRY OUT TO HER!—TELL HER YOU WANT HER!—CRY, YOU SONOFABITCH!!!!

P: But I'm allergic to milk products.

Pharmacologic

P: I've been having this feeling that people treat me like an object, that they don't see me as a person in my own right, in all my uniqueness.

T: NURSE! Get me 500 mg. of Thorazine STAT!

Future Directions

Astrologic Therapy

P: My last therapist told me I'm deficient in reality-testing. Delusional, I think he termed it.

T: What sign are you, may I ask?

P: Libra. The thing is—I see things occasionally that I'm not sure others see. I tend to form conclusions with insufficient evidence.

T: That's quite characteristic when a full moon hits on the second Thursday.

P: What?

T: Especially if your middle name begins with a P.

P: How did you know that?

T: Well look at this chart . . . you can see that whereas two weeks ago Saturn was out of phase with Route 101, we're now approaching the Spring equinox, and when the Life signs predominate you'd predict that all the MacDonald's hamburger stands will go out of business. You know what that means.

P: Vaguely.

T: Right—things are vague right now for you, in fact for Geminis more than Libras. But on the last day you'll receive a message from a close associate that will clarify a great deal.

P: That's good to know.

T: Surely, but no surprise.

Musico-Therapy

P: I have this nagging sense of something left undone, some unfinished business.

T: What are you feeling?

P: Sorta flat. Like nothing of major significance is going on.

T: Not major?

P: That's right.

T: Anything of minor significance going on?

P: You could say that. But it's not enough.

T: What are your present concerns?

P: Well, mainly I worry too much about how people *see* me. They seem to think I'm not too sharp.

T: And what would you like to accomplish?

P: I guess I'd like to focus more on what I can *be* of my own volition, rather than just meeting people's expectations.

T: I see. And this sense of unfinished business—does it feel like something you've done before, or is it something you haven't experienced yet?

P: It seems sorta familiar, like I've been through it before and want to recapture it.

T: A repeating pattern.

P: Right—it keeps popping up, and I somehow feel that my life will be incomplete unless I regain it one more time. I'm having a little trouble expressing it—it's hard to conceptualize.

T: Not at all. The way I see it, your life resembles an unfinished *rondo*. Our task is simply to modulate from C-flat-minor to B-sharp-major and rediscover the refrain.

P: But what if we can't rediscover it?

T: No problem. Then we'll just *vamp ad lib* or write in a *coda*. Or if you really want to be adventurous, we could call in John Cage for a consult.

Repetito-Therapy

T: Good morning.

P: Hi. I feel sorta empty.

T: I feel sorta empty.

P: You too? Wow. Anyway, things just don't seem to be going right.

T: Things don't seem to be going right.

P: That's right. Everything I try to do fails.

T: Everything *I* try to do fails.

P: Really? But I'm coming to *you* for help.

T: I'm coming to *you* for help.

P: Well here's a howdy-do!

T: Here's a pretty mess. I mean . . .

P: You're a Gilbert & Sullivan fan?

T: You're a Gilbert & Sullivan fan?

P: Of course—you think I made that stupid lyric up myself?

T: Of course—you think I made . . .

P: Hold it! And I thought *I* was sick! (exits)

T: (soliloquy) Something went wrong there—I'd better get some more supervision.

PRENATAL PSYCHOANALYSIS

*A New Approach to Primary Prevention Psychiatry**

Robert S. Hoffman, M.D.
San Francisco, California

Although it is widely appreciated that the emergence of psychoneurotic symptoms in adult life results from unconscious conflicts deriving from early childhood experiences, little effort has been directed toward primary prevention in this area. A possible approach to early intervention was evaluated by offering intensive psychoanalysis to third trimester fetuses during the two weeks prior to their delivery. Long-term follow-up was obtained on 46% of the sample (n = 110) at age thirty, via interview and psychometric data. The primary criterion for adequate adult adjustment was an annual gross income exceeding $36,000.

Factor analysis of the data revealed six therapeutic factors to be correlated with good outcome:

1. Appropriate timing of interpretations, i.e. between contractions.

2. Analysis conducted with the fetus in the horizontal position. This can be achieved by first determining the alignment of the fetus in the uterus via sonography and then positioning the mother so that the fetus lies flat.

3. Thorough working-through of fetal feelings of anticipatory anxiety related to labor and imminent delivery.

4. Development of a full-blown transference neurosis wherein the fetus's behavior toward the analyst reflects earlier experiences with fellow germ cells in the prezygotic stage.

5. High forceps extraction, which appeared to enhance the effect of deep interpretations by pressing them into the fetal skull at the time of delivery.

6. The necessity that the fetus himself pay for the analytic sessions. Although this was impractical to arrange prior to delivery, it was found equally effective to inform the fetus that he would be billed at the age of 18.

In addition to the above therapeutic maneuvers, it was found that certain specific aspects of the fetal situation affected the subsequent course of personality development:

1. In several patients, inadequate materno-fetal circulation had a pronounced negative effect, a finding consistent with Melanie Klein's concept of "good and bad placenta."

2. Witnessing of the primal scene by the fetus was judged to be highly traumatic, no doubt due to close proximity to the action. This, of course, was predicted by Freud in his classic paper, "Kinderpeepinshtuppe" (1903), in which he noted that such experiences can eventuate in hysterical blindness, tunnel phobias, or plantar warts. Whether these effects are related to heightened Oedipal conflicts or to rhythmic compression of the fetal brain is still unclear.

3. Two sets of twins were followed in the study, and twinship was found to engender a certain degree of sibling rivalry. One twin garroted his brother with the umbilical cord. In the other pair, rivalry appeared to be less of a problem: since the mother had a bicornuate uterus, each twin had his own room.

These data suggest that psychoanalysis need not be delayed until neurotic symptoms emerge in adulthood, since efforts at early intervention *in utero* can be highly rewarding. Further research would be necessary to confirm these preliminary findings as well as to explore possible extensions of the technique. We are currently evaluating the effect of psychoanalytic therapy upon spermatogonia and primordial ovarian follicles prior to conception.

*"Throwaway." *J. of Psychoanal.* 46:4, Dec. 1978.

A PROPOSED STUDY OF RUBBER BAND THERAPY[1]

Victor Milstein, Ph.D.,
Joyce G. Small, M.D.
Michael J. Deal, M.D., F.S.R.B.T.[2]
Larue D. Carter Memorial Hospital and
Indiana University School of Medicine
Indianapolis, Indiana

A recent lead article in a prominent national psychiatric journal applauds the lowly elastic band as a remarkably versatile and effective instrument of behavioral psychotherapy (Marks, 1976). The virtues of this humble device also have been extolled in several recent papers (Bass, 1973; Mastellone, 1974) and the term "rubber band therapy" has been used by Rinn (1975). The technique of treatment is remarkably simple in that the band is placed about the wrist, the client extends the elastic, releases it in order to avoid or disrupt some undesirable behavior. This major breakthrough in psychotherapeutic management has many advantages among which are the following:

1. Unlike other sensory modalities of aversive stimulation, no habituation has been noted with rubber band therapy. Indeed Rinn (1975) cites reports of enhanced effectiveness across trials.

2. The portability of the rubber band is incontestable and unsurpassed by any other source of aversive stimulation.

3. Associated with its portability is its lightweight and small size.

4. It increases the likelihood of stimulus generalization as it can be administered in a variety of settings.

5. It can be administered in close temporal contiguity with the behavior to be regulated and is superior

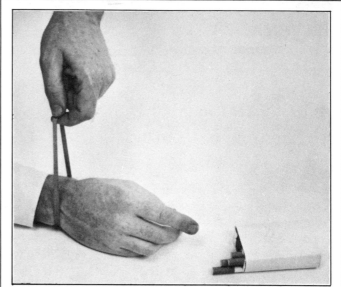

A treatment instead of a treat.

to chemical aversion in this regard, although it may not be quite as effective as electrically controlled aversive stimuli.

6. There is nothing to compete with it in terms of cost.

7. Perhaps most important is that it provides the client with the locus of control; that is, it permits self-regulation of behavior. This follows in the noble tradition of the learning theory approach advocated by Skinner (1953) and Goldiamond (1965). Also, this self-control aspect aids in the modification of private events such as urges and thoughts which would not otherwise be accessible to external instrumental approaches.

This brief recitation of the attributes and qualities of rubber band therapy makes it clear that this is a major advance in the field of psychotherapy. However some important scientific issues have been neglected in the enthusiastic pursuit of what appears to be an ideal method of self-regulation. We refer of course to the

---
[1] We are grateful to Iver F. Small for originally suggesting the topic and to H. Firestone for many helpful suggestions relevant to the technical aspects of this proposal.
[2] Fellow, Society of Rubber Band Therapists.

contribution of the properties of the rubber band itself. Rinn recommends a ⅜″ wide, loosely fitted wrist band and instructs his clients to extend the band 6½ or 7 inches and release it to sharply strike the wrist, contingent upon the emission or imminent emission of the behavior to be controlled. Tragically, beyond this there is very little scientific information about what properties of the rubber band contribute to the remarkable effectiveness of this form of treatment.

In our view this important issue merits urgent study that should be accorded a high priority for funding by national and/or commercial sources. The number of variables that could be selected for study is nearly infinite but we propose that an initial study of this issue could be confined to a few vital areas to include the following:

Placement. It is likely that a more direct association between the behavior to be controlled and the specific anatomical locus of the rubber band would enhance rubber band therapy. For example, if the client is attempting to control an urge to draw mustaches on posters in public places and is right-handed, it may be more effective to put the rubber band around his right wrist rather than his left. If the client is attempting to control an urge to sniff bicycle seats, obviously the nose would be the place to put the rubber band. However, if the client is attempting to control compulsive masturbation, the choice of where the rubber band is placed could be crucial!

Color. Especially in the case of women, rubber bands of various colors coordinated with the particular outfit they are wearing at the moment are likely to be significantly superior to rubber bands of clashing or even neutral colors in bringing the behavior under control.

Mechanical Release Device. A simple device has been constructed which consists of an extremely lightweight plastic rod that continuously stretches the rubber band and which only requires a flick-of-the-finger to release the rubber band from this rod to snap against the skin. The intensity of the stimulus is more constant than simply extending the rubber band and the latency is reduced. Preliminary investigation has suggested that the deployment of such a device enhances the effectiveness of rubber band therapy, especially when sexual behavior is involved. (In cases with a certain class of male clients, the use of the rod may be contraindicated.)

Rate of Snap. All previous reports have suggested either a single snap or else instructed the client "repeatedly" to snap the band. Such imprecision can only lead to reduced effectiveness. We propose to examine four rates, namely (i) single snap, (ii) repeated snaps until the band breaks, (iii) snapping until the wrist (or other locus) becomes so swollen and edematous that the band cannot be stretched around it, (iv) until the client falls to the floor exhausted. It is our prediction that either (iii) and/or (iv) will be most efficient.

Coefficient of Elasticity. Many of the so-called "rubber" bands that are used are not made of rubber at all! The varieties of synthetic rubbers available are great, and not only is each type associated with a different coefficient of elasticity, batches within types are often differentially elastic. Clearly the effect of such variability must be evaluated as to its contribution to the reduction of effectiveness of rubber band therapy. Further, consideration of this issue would suggest the best possible alternatives in the event of a national emergency which resulted in difficulty in obtaining "rubber" bands.

It is proposed that a modified Greco-Latin Square design be employed with nine subjects in each cell to examine the contribution of the variables just described. It is estimated that 1000 cells (5 colors × 5 placements × presence/absence of mechanical release device × 4 rates × 5 types of "rubber" bands) will be required to adequately investigate the subject. Further, approximately four years will be needed and $129,268.48 (per year). However, the ultimate savings in terms of electric relays, noise generators, biofeedback devices, cattle prods etc. that currently and less effectively are being employed in attempts to control behavior are inestimable, as is the value of the reduction in human suffering and costs of treatment. Informed consent is *not* an issue in this scientifically established effective form of treatment without significant risk (unless over-utilized at a constant locus). For the same reason, control comparisons employing non-elastic bands are not required. Finally, serious consideration must be given to whether the treatment should be prescribed only by certain professional groups and not others. Because of the potential for abuse of this technique perhaps some adaptation of Department of Justice regulations for controlled substances should be considered.

REFERENCES

Bass, B.A. "An Unusual Behavioral Technique for Treating Obsessive Ruminations." *Psychother.: Ther., Res. & Pract.*, 10:191-192, 1973.

Goldiamond, I. "Self-control Procedures in Personal Behavior Problems." *Psychol. Reports*, 17:851-868, 1965.

Marks, I.M. "The Current Status of Behavioral Psychotherapy: Theory and Practice." *Amer. J. Psychiat.*, 133:253, 1976.

Mastellone, M. "Aversion Therapy: A New Use for the Old Rubber Band." *J. Behav. Ther. Exper. Psychiat.*, 5.311-312, 1974.

Rinn, R.C. "An Inexpensive, Portable, Self-Administered Source for Aversive Stimulation: The Rubber Band." *Behav. Engineer.*, 3:39, 1975.

Skinner, B.F. *Science and Human Behavior.* New York: Macmillan, 1953.

THERAPEUTIC EFFECTS OF FORCEFUL GOOSING ON MAJOR AFFECTIVE ILLNESS

Stuart A. Copans
Assistant Professor of Pataphysical Psychiatry
Dartmouth Medical School
Hanover, New Hampshire

A review of therapeutic approaches to depression revealed that shock therapies of various types have been used in the treatment of depression for hundreds of years, ranging from sudden immersion in a bath of cold water (the bath surprise) to metrazol, insulin or electrically induced seizures. These methods, while therapeutically successful, have been heavily criticized, and for the most part, abandoned because of the morbidity and mortality associated with their use. Serendipitous observations suggested to the authors of this paper that forceful goosing might have a therapeutic effect on patients suffering from a retarded depression without such morbidity or mortality.

A controlled study was carried out, comparing the effects of unilateral electronconvulsive therapy (ECT), bilateral ECT, tricyclic antidepressants and forceful goosing on depression (as measured with the Zung Scale 4, 8 and 16 weeks, after initiation of therapeutic trials) on short-term memory loss, on subjective discomfort as assessed by patient interview, and on length of hospital stay.

Introduction

The origins of the practice of goosing remain shrouded

in antiquity. H. Allen Smith[1] has suggested in his monumental study of the subject, that the term goosing originated from the similarity between the physical movements involved in a goose and the tendency of geese to peck at the nether regions of those invading their territory. In any case, whatever the origin of the custom's name, it has generally been considered either a petty annoyance or a sign of affection.

In late 1978, observations on an adult treatment unit occurred when a manic patient was admitted and refused medication. The patient, hereafter referred to as Mr. G., spent much of his time creeping up behind female members of the staff and female patients and forcefully goosing them. While this engendered a great deal of hostility in female staff members (and some jealousy in male staff members), it was noted that two patients suffering from retarded depression seemed to improve markedly during the two weeks this patient remained on the Unit. Following the discharge of Mr. G., both patients exhibited a significant clinical relapse and eventually were treated with eleven sessions of bilateral ECT. It was as a result of this observation that the following experiment was designed.

Method

All patients admitted to the Adult Psychiatric Unit at the Riverside Hospital for the Sad and Lonely with a DSM III diagnosis of Major Affective Illness, Depressive Type, were assigned randomly to one of 4 groups. The first group was treated with tricyclic antidepressants; the second group was treated with 10 sessions of unilateral ECT, given every other day. The third group

1. Smith, H. Allen. *Handbuch der Goose: Die Tiere, die Steppe, und die Spiele.* Berlin: Katzenjammere Presse, 1847.

was treated with 10 sessions of bilateral ECT also administered on an every other day schedule. The final group of patients was assigned to the forceful goosing condition. These patients were forcefully goosed twice an hour while awake. The forceful gooses were administered by fully licensed R.N.s, who had been trained to administer standardized forceful gooses (geese).

Depression was assessed using the Zung Depression Scale, and was assessed prior to the onset of treatment, and again at 4, 8, and 16 weeks after treatment had been completed. In addition, all but one patient were successfully contacted a year after treatment and data is available at that time as well. Additional testing was carried out to assess short-term memory loss for both verbal material and visual material, and to assess subjective discomfort as expressed by the patients during the time that the treatment procedures were being carried out.

A great deal of debate went on before the study began, as to whether we should use homosexual goosing or heterosexual goosing. In fact, the debate was resolved not on clinical or research grounds, but on medical/legal grounds. It was the opinion of our lawyers that since forceful goosing was to be employed as a medical intervention, it should be administered only by licensed registered nurses. Since the registered nurses on our treatment unit were all women, the forceful gooses in the study were all administered by women to patients of both sexes.

A standard goose for the purposes of this study, was defined as a goose which elicited, in a standard subject, a jump of anywhere from 6–12 inches, a scream or exclamation of surprise between 40–60 decibels, and a sudden flinging of the hands away from the body. In studying the effects of standard gooses, we were struck by their similarity to the moro reflex usually seen in infants. The neurophysiological implications will be discussed later in the paper.

For those interested in biometrics, the standardized goose may be defined as application of a digital force in the direction of the anal sphincter from behind and below, attaining a maximum speed between 20 and

30 miles per hour, and exerting a maximum force of between 30 and 40 foot-pounds.

It is important to remember, however, that the gooses described in this paper were not standardized biometrically, but rather using the bioassay mentioned earlier.

TABLE 1.

		Unilateral ECT	Bilateral ECT	Tricyclic Antidepressants	Forceful Goosing
ZUNG DEPRESSION SCORE	Before Treatment	97	95	96	97
	4 wks	82	88	80	72
	8 wks	74	79	66	52
	16 wks	64	62	58	44
	1 year	68	72	64	32
SHORT TERM MEMORY LOSS 0 = None 7 = Most	Verbal	1	5	2	0*
	Visual	5	5	3	0*
SUBJECTIVE DISCOMFORT 0 = None 0 = Most		4	5	3	2**
LENGTH OF HOSPITAL STAY		117 days	108 days	112 days	96 days

Results

As can be seen from Table 1, goosing resulted in significantly better relief of depression than either unilateral or bilateral ECT or antidepressants. It is of particular importance that this therapeutic effect was not seen just at 4, 8, and 16 weeks, but persisted and could be shown in the data from the follow-up one year after completion of treatment. In addition, there was significantly less memory loss.

In fact, one finding of this study was a significant improvement in short-term memory following goosing. We are currently exploring the use of goosing in a group of senile patients with the hopes that it may result in significant improvement in their mental functioning.

While the length of hospital stay is shorter in the forcefully goosed group, the difference there does not reach statistical significance. In fact, if we look at the distribution of length of stay data for the four groups, we see that both the median and the mode in the forcefully goosed group are quite a bit less than in the

---

*In fact, there was a statistically significant improvement in short-term memory in this group.
**4 of the patients in this group reported subjective pleasure associated with the treatment procedure.

Before *During* *After*

other three groups. The reason for the lack of significance when we looked at mean length of stay can be found in two patients in the forcefully goosed group whose hospital stays were profoundly longer. In these two cases, the patients developed an intense transference reaction to the nurses who administered the treatment procedure and could not be weaned from their goosing. We are currently exploring with the FDA the medical/legal ramifications of out-patient maintenance goosing, but presently both of these patients remain in the hospital and will probably need to remain in the hospital until our outpatient maintenance goosing project is begun.

Discussion

It seems clear from the above results that forceful goosing represents a therapeutic procedure that should be added to the armamentarium of all practicing psychiatrists. As we begin to explore its use in clinical practice, however, it is clear that there are a number of important medical/legal issues that must be addressed. First, should forceful goosing remain by and large an inpatient procedure, used only in those who are severely depressed and admitted to a hospital unit where the gooses can be administered at various times throughout the day, catching the patient by surprise? Second, given the addictive potential of forceful goosing, it is clear that some outpatient maintenance program must be developed for some patients. Should this outpatient maintenance program be hospital-based? Could it be carried out in the offices of individual psychiatrists? Could the patient's families be instructed in carrying out the procedure? Currently, forceful goosing is considered, at least in Vermont, a medical treatment procedure; that is, it can be administered only by physicians or by registered nurses under the direction of physicians. Social workers, psychologists, educational counselors, and other parapsychiatric personnel are not allowed to administer forceful gooses to patients.

A dilemma, however, is posed by the family of one patient treated with forceful goosing on our unit. The patient's husband had a particular fondness for goosing his wife, and in fact, her depression seemed to be precipitated by an extended business trip the patient's husband took, so that the patient was not goosed for nearly a month prior to her admission. It seems clear that the patient's husband sees his goosing as an affectionate gesture and that it also serves an important function both in the dynamics of the family and helping maintain a balance of catacholamines in this patient. If, however, forceful goosing is to be considered a medical procedure, can we encourage and support this patient's husband in his practice of medicine without a license?

In our ongoing studies of the phenomenon of forceful goosing, we're exploring a number of possible physiologic mediators of its therapeutic effect. One possibility is that forceful goosing is usually followed on the part of the patient by an inspiratory gasp and a relatively prolonged exhalation phase.

Measurements of blood gasses showed that this results in a brief pulse of highly oxygenated blood followed by increasing buildup of carbon dioxide. Single cell monitoring of midbrain respiratory centers in goosed cats suggest that this pattern of change in blood gasses may result in massive discharges from these respiratory centers to a variety of limbic structures. There is some suggestion that this may act to reset baseline levels in the reticular activating system; however, until more detailed results are obtained over the next year, this must remain a speculation.

A second area of investigation in the therapeutic mechanisms of the forceful goose, involves the examination of direct connections between the perianal plexus and the hypothalamus. Again, while definitive pronouncements must await further studies, it does appear that forceful goosing has a profound effect on the functioning of the neurohypophyseal axis, with significant alterations in the release of both catacholamines and brain polypeptides.

Conclusions

It seems eminently clear from our data that forceful goosing represents an important therapeutic procedure. It may well help us leap onward and upward to a further and more detailed exploration of the mechanisms underlying affective illness.

THE ITEMIZED STATEMENT IN CLINICAL PSYCHIATRY

A New Concept in Billing

Robert S. Hoffman, M.D.
San Francisco, California

Due to the rapidly escalating costs of health care delivery, there has been increasing pressure on physicians to document and justify their charges for professional services. This has created a number of serious problems, particularly in the field of psychiatry. Chief among these is the breach of confidentiality that arises when sensitive clinical information is provided to third-party insurance carriers, e.g. the patient's diagnosis or related details about his/her psychiatric disorder. Even when full disclosure of such information is made, insurance carriers frequently deny benefits because the description of the treatment appears imprecise or inadequate. There also has been some criticism of the standard hourly fee-for-service, the argument being that psychiatrists, like other medical specialists, should be required to adjust their fees depending upon the particular treatment offered.

In view of these considerations, a method is required which will bring psychiatric billing in line with accepted medical practice. The procedure illustrated below, which we have successfully employed in our clinic for the past two years, achieves this goal. It requires only a modest investment in time and effort: the tape-recording of all psychotherapy sessions, transcription of tapes, tabulation of therapeutic interventions, and establishment of a relative value scale for the commonly used maneuvers. This can easily be managed by two full-time medical billing personnel per psychiatrist. The method, in our hands, has been found to increase collections from third-party carriers by 65% and to raise a typical psychiatrist's annual net income almost to the level of a municipal street sweeper or plumber's assistant.

Below is a specimen monthly statement illustrating these principles:

CALVIN L. SKOLNIK, M.D., Inc.
A Psychiatry Corporation

Jan. 5, 1978

Mr. Sheldon Rosenberg
492 West Maple Dr.
East Orange, N.J.

Dear Mr. Rosenberg:

In response to the request by your insurer, Great Lake Casualty and Surety Co., for more precise documentation of professional services rendered, I have prepared the enclosed itemization for the month of December. I trust that this will clarify the situation sufficiently for your benefit payments to be resumed.

Until next Tuesday at 11:00, I remain

Cordially,

Calvin L. Skolnik, M.D.

FEE BREAKDOWN

Itemized Charges	No.			Charges ($)
clarifications	140	@	.25	35.00
restatements	157	@	.25	39.25
broad-focus questions	17	@	.35	5.95
narrow-focus questions	42	@	.30	12.60
reflections of dominant emotional theme	86	@	.35	30.10
resolutions of inconsistencies	38	@	.45	17.10
pointings out of nonverbal communications	22	@	.40	8.80
encouragements to say more	187	@	.15	28.05
sympathetic nods with furrowed brow	371	@	.10	37.10
acknowledgments of information reception (Uh-huhs, Um-hmmm, etc.)	517	@	.08	41.36
interpretations of unconscious defense configurations	24	@	.30	7.20
absolution for evil deeds	16	@	.50	8.00
pieces of advice	2	@	.75	1.50
expressions of personal feelings	6	@	.50	3.00
personal reminiscences	2	@	.65	1.30
misc. responses (sighs, grunts, belches, etc.)	35	@	.20	6.00
listening to remarks disparaging therapist's appearance, personal habits, or technique	7	@	1.75	12.25
listening to sarcastic remarks about psychiatry	12	@	1.00	12.00
listening to psychiatrist jokes	3	@	.80	2.40
telephone calls to therapist	3	@	.15	.45
telephone call to therapist at especially inopportune moment	1	@	10.50	10.50
Kleenex tissues	22	@	.005	.11
ashtray	1	@	3.50	3.50
filling and repainting of ashtray-size dent in wall	1	@	27.50	27.50
shampooing of soft drink stain on carpet	1	@	15.00	15.00
letter of excuse from work	1	@	2.50	2.50
surcharges for unusually boring or difficult sessions	2	@	35.00	70.00

Subtotal: charges $ 438.52

Itemized Credits	No.			Credit
unusually interesting anecdotes	4	@	.45	1.80
good jokes	3	@	.50	1.50
item of gossip about another patient which was found useful in her therapy	1	@	3.50	3.50
apology for sarcastic remark	1	@	1.00	1.00
use of case history at American Psychiatric Association convention	1			10.00
chicken salad sandwich on whole wheat w/mayo	½	@	1.75	.86
bummed cigarettes (1.00/pack)	7			.35
damaged Librium tablet returned unused	1			.10

Subtotal: credits $ 19.11

Total: PLEASE REMIT— $ 419.41

PART IV

SOCIAL CONCERNS

NATIONAL GEOGRAPHIC, THE DOOMSDAY MACHINE

George H. Kaub

Pollution of many types and kinds is currently paramount in the public mind. Causes and solutions are being loudly proclaimed by all of the media, politicians, public agencies, universities, garden clubs, industry, churches, ad infinitum. Pollution runs the spectrum from the air we breathe, the water we drink, the soil we till as well as visual and audio pollution, and in recent years, pollution of outer space from junk exploration hardware. These threats to our environment, our health and our mental well being are real and with us, but not nearly as immediately catastrophic or totally destructive as the disaster which imminently faces this nation and which has gone unheeded, unheralded and ignored for over 141 years. The insidious consequences lurking in this menace of monstrous proportion bode national, even, continental disaster of proportions likened only to the entire country resting on a gargantuan San Andreas fault. Earthquakes, hurricanes, mud slides, fire, famine, and atomic war all rolled into one hold no greater destructive power than this incipient horror which will engulf the country in the immediate and predictable future.

This continent is in the gravest danger of following legendary Atlantis to the bottom of the sea. No natural disaster, no overpowering compounding of pollutions or cataclysmic nuclear war will cause the end, instead, a seemingly innocent monster created by man, nurtured by man, however as yet unheeded by man will doom this continent to the watery grave of oblivion.

But there is yet time to save ourselves if this warning is heeded.

Publication and distribution of the National Geo-

graphic *magazine must be immediately stopped at all costs!* This beautiful, educational, erudite, and thoroughly appreciated publication is the heretofore unrecognized instrument of cosmic doom which must be erased if we as a country or continent will survive. It is *not too late* if this warning is heeded!

Weighty Reading

According to current subscription figures, more than 6,869,797 issues of the *National Geographic* magazine are sent to subscribers monthly throughout the world. However, it would be safe to say that the bulk of these magazines reach subscribers in the United States and

Canada, and it is and never has been thrown away! It is saved like a monthly edition of the Bible. The magazine has been published for over 141 years continuously and countless millions if not billions of copies have been innocently yet relentlessly accumulating in basements, attics, garages, in public and private institutions of learning, the Library of Congress, Smithsonian Institution, Good Will, and Salvation Army Stores and heaven knows where else. Never discarded, always saved. No recycling, just the horrible and relentless accumulation of this static vehicle of our doom! *National Geographic* averages approximately two pounds per issue. Since no copies have been discarded or destroyed since the beginning of publication it can be readily seen that the accumulated aggregate weight is a figure that not only boggles the mind but is imminently approaching the disaster point. That point will be the time at which the geologic substructure of the country can no longer support the incredible load and subsidence will occur. Gradually at first, but then relentlessly accelerating as rock formations are compressed, become plastic and begin to flow; great faults will appear. The logical sequence of events is predictable. First will come foundation failures and gradual sinking of residences and public buildings in which the magazine has been stored. As these areas depress the earth, more and more structures will topple and sink until whole towns and cities will submerge, then larger and larger land masses. This chain reaction will accelerate until the entire country has fallen below the level of the sea and total inundation will occur.

The areas of higher subscription density, affluence and wealth will be the first to go, followed by institutions, middle class, urban and ghetto areas in that order, with the relatively unpopulated plains and mountains finally sinking into the sea.

Clear Warnings

We have been warned of this impending calamity by a seeming increase in so-called natural disasters throughout the country as well as isolated occurrences striking areas heretofore immune to natural destruction.

Increase in earthquake activity in California has been triggered by population growth and the subsequent increase in *National Geographic* subscriptions and accumulations of heavy masses of the magazine. This gradual increase in weight has caused increased activity along the San Andreas fault.

Earthquakes in the Denver area were not caused by pumping of wastes into wells at the Rocky Mountain arsenal, but by accumulation of *National Geographic*

AN EXPERIMENTAL BEHAVIORAL PSYCHOLOGY APPLICATION TO CANCER RESEARCH

T. D. C. Kuch

Abstract. As part of the work of the Psychobiology Project, Aaron Burr Research Laboratories, Inc., fifty 6-week old female mice (strain B6C3F1) were treated with dl-2-amino-4-(ethylthio) butyric acid, which has been reported to be carcinogenic. Two days later, an intensive course of operant conditioning was begun. At age 14 weeks, 19 of the animals had been sufficiently conditioned to record their own body weights by standing on a mechanized scale while simultaneously pressing the operating lever to create a paper tape weight record. At this point the group was split into "slow-learners" (fifteen animals) and "fast-learners" (nineteen animals). The remaining animals, characterized as "dull-normal," were sacrificed. By age 29 weeks twelve of the slow-learners and fourteen of the fast-learners had developed palpable mammary tumors. Both groups were then conditioned to inspect their own lesions, count the number of tumors, and record this number by pressing a button the appropriate number of times with their noses. As expected, the slow-learners failed to perform satisfactorily. Of the fast-learners, five achieved better than 80% accuracy (one achieving a 100% rate), while the rest averaged 62% accuracy. All but the five best performing animals were then sacrificed. At age 42 weeks all animals presented with scruffiness, mange, and large tumor masses. The one best performing animal was trained to perform necropsies and read the resultant slides. The present paper was written by that mouse before she, too, was sacrificed.

magazines by more and more people as the population increased over the years.

Sinking of several coal mining towns throughout the country can only be attributed to the increase in workmen's benefits and pay increases allowing them to subscribe to and hoard *National Geographic*.

Mud slides in California which have brought destruction to hundreds of homes built on the hillsides were triggered by the final straw in the form of the last mail delivery into these areas to *National Geographic* subscribers and hoarders.

The list is endless, the warnings are clear.

The time grows short and we must act at once if this calamity is to be averted. The *National Geographic* must cease publication at once, if necessary, by Congressional action or Presidential edict.

NATIONAL GEOGRAPHIC: DOOMSDAY MACHINE OR BENEFACTOR? A VINDICATION

Response to "National Geographic, The Doomsday Machine"

L. M. Jones
Department of Geology
University of Georgia
Athens, Georgia

An attack on the *National Geographic* magazine is an attack on a venerated American tradition, one as American as apple pie, Watergate, Pogo, and pizza.

The cry for the immediate termination of publication and distribution of the *National Geographic* magazine cannot go without challenge. Kaub (1974) has not only created an aura of hysteria for the future of the earth, but he has also imparted an unnecessary sense of guilt on anyone who inasmuch as reads an issue of *National Geographic*, let alone anyone who would sequester an issue in an attic or garage.

Kaub (1974) contends there will be disasters of continental proportions due to the indestructability of the *National Geographic* magazine. He suggests that localized accumulations of the *National Geographic* are responsible for earthquake activity in areas such as the San Andreas fault and Denver. He also would attribute directly to the magazine other natural disasters such as mud slides and subsidence. Kaub (1974) further knells the doomsday bell, by predicting that continued storage of the magazine will result in massive subsidence of buildings, cities, and finally, inundation of the entire country by the sea.

Nonsense.

It is such erroneous expoundings as Kaub's that have created undue panic among the populace on other occasions. For example, movement along the San Andreas fault has been interpreted to mean that California will soon fall into the sea!

And now the *National Geographic!* Is nothing sacred?

Let's examine this problem calmly and logically. First, ten issues of the *National Geographic* magazine were selected from the collections of the author and a colleague. These issues were weighed and measured; these data are given in Table 1, in addition to calculated values of area and density for the magazine. To simplify the following calculations, it was assumed that erosion of the landmass was negligible, as well as other

---

THIS IS NEWS?

"The trouble with the poor is that they don't have enough money."

—From "Problems in the Urban Environment," Harvard-MIT Joint Center for Urban Studies, 1968.

TABLE 1. DIMENSIONS, WEIGHT, AND DENSITY OF TEN SELECTED ISSUES OF THE *NATIONAL GEOGRAPHIC* MAGAZINE.

	Thickness, mm	Weight, g	Width cm	Length cm	Area cm²	Density, g-cm⁻³
June 59	7.73	402.15	17.33	25.34	439.1	1.185
August 61	7.02	370.28	17.49	25.39	444.1	1.188
May 62	7.70	408.72	17.51	25.35	443.9	1.196
October 62	7.27	388.50	17.48	25.44	444.7	1.202
May 63	7.58	396.15	17.43	25.32	441.3	1.184
April 66	7.985	422.60	17.55	25.35	444.9	1.190
July 71	6.52	342.72	17.36	25.31	439.4	1.196
November 71-I	6.95	371.49	17.54	25.48	446.9	1.196
November 71-II	7.05	373.71	17.51	25.50	446.5	1.187
January 73	6.05	324.75	17.49	25.38	443.9	1.209
ave.	7.19				443.5	1.193

geologic factors. The only geologic process that would be operative is isostasy, which is the approach of crustal masses to a flotational equilibrium. Other assumptions that were made include the following:

1. the density of the upper mantle is 3.3 g-cm⁻³, which represents a lower limit;

2. the monthly circulation of the *National Geographic* is that as given by Kaub (1974), 6,869,797, and remains constant;

3. distribution of the magazine is restricted to the conterminous 48 United States (with no offense intended to Hawaii, Alaska, or any country, Hawaii and Alaska were excluded on the basis of relatively small area and small population, respectively);

4. the magazine is evenly distributed over the 48 United States;

5. the area of the 48 states is 7,954 × 10³ km² (Showers, 1973);

6. area of the oceans is 362,033 × 10³ km (Showers, 1973);

7. no issues of the *National Geographic* magazine will be destroyed;

8. the average thickness of the ten issues in Table 1 is representative (0.719 cm).

Taking the predictions of Kaub (1974) at face value, the height of a column of *National Geographic* magazines necessary to depress the continental land mass by 100 feet (30.48 m.) was calculated. This would be a vertical stack 82.33 meters high, equivalent to 11.45 × 10³ magazines. This depression of the land mass would produce a rise in sea level due to displaced mantle material. Assuming the effect is confined only to the ocean basins, a net depression of 100 feet (30.48 m) would be due to an actual depression of the land of 29.82 meters and a resultant rise in sea level of 66 cm.

There would be a notable change in the coastline with a net depression of one hundred feet. These changes are shown in Fig. 1. While there will be little change in the outline of the west coast due to the steep slope, that of the east coast will change markedly. It is readily seen that many urban problems will be solved by inundation, saving vast amounts of urban renewal funds. The Atlantis legend will be recalled with the flooding of cities such as Boston, New York, Washington, D.C., Baltimore, Savannah, Miami, Houston, and New Orleans. Of course, unexpected benefits would be realized by other communities. For example, Yazoo, Mississippi would become a major seaport; certainly a possibility that has not been dreamed of by town officials, even in their wildest imagination.

No matter how beneficial the results of this crustal depressing might be, there is the question of time. Assuming even distribution of the *National Geographic* over the present surface, it would take 17.94 × 10¹³ copies of the magazine to cover the forty-eight United States with one thickness. If the National Geographic Society continues to publish the magazine at twelve issues each year, it will take 2.176 × 10⁶ years to deposit one thickness over the United States. The time it would take to accumulate a thickness of the *National Geographic* sufficient to depress the crust 100 feet would take 24.92 × 10⁹ years. Since this length of time is several times greater than the present age of the earth, it should be obvious that we or future generations have little to fear from the National Geographic Society.

If Mr. Kaub is still distressed about the weighty threat by the National Geographic Society, perhaps he should consider taking up lighter reading.

REFERENCES

Kaub, G. H. "National Geographic, the Doomsday Machine." *Journal of Irreproducible Results,* 20:3, pp. 22–23, 1974.

Showers, V. *The World in Figures.* New York: John Wiley and Sons, 1973.

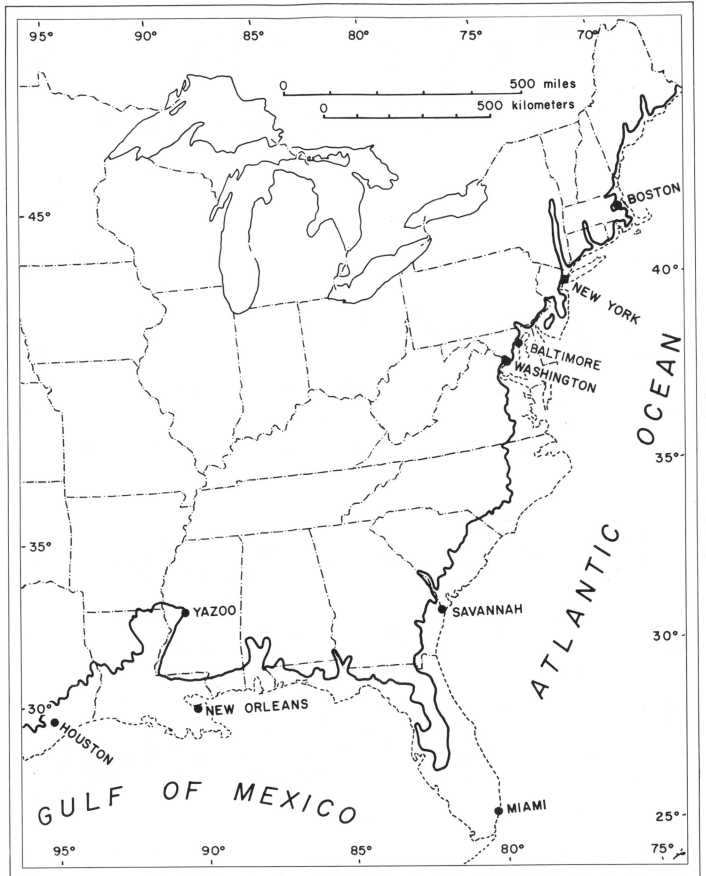

Fig. 1. The eastern coastline of the conterminous United States. The present-day coastline is indicated by the dashed line. The heavy, solid line represents the coastline following depression of the continental landmass 100 feet (30.48 m.) upon extensive accumulation of the National Geographic magazine.

AN EYE FOR AN EYE FOR AN ARM AND A LEG

Applied Dysfunctional Measurement

Gary Perlman
Department of Psychology
University of California, San Diego

Abstract

An arm and a leg are not worth two eyes, they are worth less.

Have you ever noticed how life insurance companies decide the relative worth of parts of our bodies? I just read a policy from Montgomery Ward (they will sell anything) that offered $6,000 "for loss of one hand, one foot, or the sight of one eye," and $12,000 "for death or loss of both hands, feet, the sight of both eyes, or any combination of these."

Ward seems to have assumed that hands, feet, and eyes are of equal worth, and that two of the same parts are worth exactly twice one. To me, a hand is worth a lot more than a foot, and the loss of two eyes is much worse than twice the loss of one; in the former case, the injured party can not see. Not only that, in terms of payoffs, losing your eyes is as good as being dead, with which I do not agree.

The present study is directed at finding the psychological worth people attribute to various parts of our bodies. The principle hypotheses were that the pain of losing two similar parts is worse than twice the pain of losing one; that some parts of our bodies are valued more than others (notably that feet are least valued); that there will be a preference for people to retain their dominant hands (while no such preference will exist for eyes or feet); and finally that death is a lot worse than the loss of two similar parts, although it may be better than being a blind quadriplegic.

Method

The use of human subjects was deemed inappropriate by some of my colleagues, so rats were subjected to assorted treatments. Suffice it to say that the rats' ratings (especially those in the "death" condition) were ambiguous. An alternative method was devised.

Human subjects were *asked* to rate on a happy/sad scale how they would feel after the loss of factorially deleted parts of their bodies. To help them make these judgments, drawings corresponding to their supposed disabilities were presented along with vivid verbal descriptions. An example of an undisabled person is in Fig. 1a; while one missing an arm and a leg is depicted in Fig. 1b. A picture of the worst possible non-terminal deletion of parts is in Fig. 1c. Dead figures were represented as lying down, with x's in their eyes (regardless of whether they had lost any eyes), Fig. 1d.

While the use of subjects' ratings of how they *would* feel *if* they sustained these injuries might not lead to the same results as in the case when they actually incur the disabilities, I ignored this.

Results

The data are presented in Fig. 2. Plotted are the average happiness ratings of subjects according to how many of each limb was lost. It is clear that subjects preferred to lose feet over hands, and preferred

---

TIPS FOR NOVICE FIELD RESEARCHERS

—Don't eat either yellow snow or 'bush raisins'; although not potentially harmful, the taste is less than palatable.
—If you have to cut down a tree on private land, gnaw the stump so that it will appear that a beaver did it.

—From the Canada Committee on Ecological (Bio-Physical) Land Classification, Newsletter, No. 5, 1978.

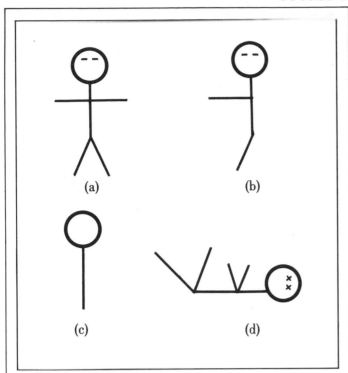

Fig. 1.

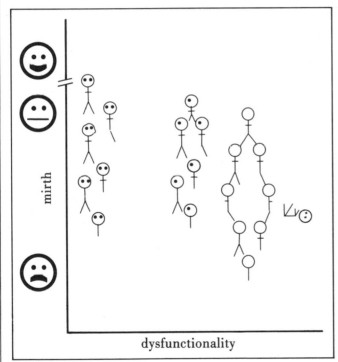

Fig. 2.

to lose hands over eyes. Virtually all subjects showed more than twice the dismay at losing two similar limbs than losing one, which is consistent with my theory. Subjects reliably preferred their dominant hands (p = .05), but there was no dominance preference for eyes or feet (p = .06). As predicted by Law 4 of my theory, people preferred multiple losses over death; the breaking point was when at least both hands and both eyes were lost. In these cases, people preferred death.

I should note that two subjects' data were discarded. Subject 1A was found to be an insurance agent, who conformed exactly to the insurance companies' guidelines, making his data unacceptable. The other subject, SM, did not seem to understand the rating scale and gave happiness ratings positively correlated with the number of missing limbs. Additionally, SM rated that he preferred to be dead than have no missing parts, and his most preferred state was as depicted in Fig. 1c. Other subjects had no difficulties using the rating scale.

Discussion

The practical implications of this study and my theory are enormous. Insurance companies no longer need guess the amount of retribution to a permanently disabled party. Using the regression equation below they can figure the exact amount of misery of living victims and pay accordingly. Quadriplegics no longer need feel cheated because they were paid only once; they will get their fair share. In the equation, *e* is the number of eyes lost, *h* is the number of hands lost, and *f* is the number of feet lost.

$$\text{payoff} = \$10,000\,e + \$8,000\,h + \$6,000\,f$$

A correction factor can be applied to account for the greater subjective value of dominant hands. If a dominant hand is lost, then the corrected number of hands lost is 1.25, and if the non-dominant hand is lost, the corrected number of hands lost is 0.75.

Footnote (Handnote?)

I owe nothing to anyone concerning this research. I did it all myself. Maureen Graham of the St. Andrew's University did not inspire me at all, not a bit. Anyway, she has left the country.

seascape

sacrifice at sea
soapy save-our-souls
spumes and spittles and sudsily bubbles
from fishy faces face-up and finished
in sodium stearate statues
they slivered with slippy soapy plants
they put them up to soap-plants.
my algae
under a scum of crud...
sea-soaked soapy seaweeds—
it's the flotsam
what getsam.

—C. S. Lobban.

READING EDUCATION FOR ZOO ANIMALS: A CRITICAL NEED

Michael J. Albright

This journal reports vital research conducted by some of the world's most distinguished scientists. The present paper, however, rather than reporting important results, calls for a project to be undertaken in a critical area of concern.

There are no existing programs providing zoo animals with instruction in basic school subjects. These animals are being denied the opportunity for normal intellectual growth and are unable to become contributing members of society.

The complete absence of animal education programs is a national disgrace. Suppression of zoo animals could well be the next great social issue in this country. A program is urgently needed to help alleviate mounting animal unrest and provide a viable model for animal reading education that can be implemented in all zoos.

Documentation of Need

Historically, zoo animals have been excluded from public school education programs. One primary hurdle has been transportation costs. The Mohawk School Bus Company recently estimated that a bus modified to accommodate giraffes would cost $82,000, nearly two and a half times the price of a conventional school bus.

A second important factor has been parent opposition. In 1978 a coalition of mother leopards stated emphatically that they would not permit their children to attend school with humans who "smoke, drink, blow grass, shoot speed, stick each other with switchblade knives, use profane language, and show little respect for teachers, administrators, and the educational process in general."

The American Federation of Teachers, too, has complained that its membership could cope with the mainstreaming of retardates and deaf-blind children, but it simply wasn't qualified to meet the unique educational needs of wildebeestes.

On the other hand, no zoo in the world has ever established its own animal education program. Zoo managers typically point to the dearth of funding, classroom space, and trained teachers, but it is painfully obvious that an attitude of hopelessness is the true reason no such program has ever been founded. Animals have never been expected to learn, so they were never taught, a classic case of self-fulfilling prophecy. Consequently, a shocking 98.8% of the adult zoo animal population is functionally illiterate.

The problem has now reached crisis proportions. A UNESCO study released in August 1979 listed these frightening low reading levels among adult zoo animals in Europe:

Animal	Reading Level
Anteaters	0.6
Kodiak Bears	1.4
Cobras	0.7
Orangutans	1.5
Yaks	0.2
Condors	0.4
Elands	1.0
Weasels	0.9

These deplorable conditions have manifested themselves in a number of incidents causing bodily harm, and in several cases death, to zoo animals and patrons. For example:

• At the Portland Zoo in 1976, an absent-minded cage cleaner left a can of kerosene in a chimpanzee cage. The chimp, unable to read the danger warning, chugged the can's contents, chased it with a cigarette dropped by a careless patron, and blew himself halfway to Boise.

• A normally mild-tempered dromedary at the

San Diego Zoo in 1978 went berserk, leaped an eight-foot moat, and trampled five high school students before she could be restrained. After a lengthy investigation zoo officials pinpointed the cause: for years the camel had been unable to read the T-shirts worn by viewers, and she was finally overcome by frustration.

No zoo animal education program has been initiated despite overwhelming evidence that animals can attain the intellectual level of humans. The following case studies are just a few of the many clearly illustrating this capability.

• Research at the University of Colorado demonstrated conclusively that penguins can be trained to read at rates up to 800 wpm. Several Evelyn Wood instructors are penguins, and one was recently promoted to vice president of the company.

• A prairie dog trained by a Tulsa psychologist once read the entire Bible in three days and 16 hours, and then scored 91 percent on a post test prepared by Oral Roberts.

• A Chaucerian scholar at Harvard trained a frog to read *Canterbury Tales*. After a few lessons in oral interpretation, the frog embarked on a lecture tour of 225 universities in the United States and abroad, where members of the audience sat ribbeted in their seats. The Harvard professor faded into oblivion and eventually committed suicide when the frog was awarded tenure.

• Spurred by the frog's success, a professor at Yale taught a wombat to read both English and Russian. In fact, the wombat was responsible for the original translation of Solzhenitsyn's *Gulag Archipelago*.

• University of Northern California football coach Sean O'Robins routinely trains gorillas to read playbooks and has developed three into All-American tackles. (UNC is currently under NCAA investigation because two gorillas allegedly received academic credit for classes they did not attend.)

• A University of Alberta music professor trained a caribou to read music and sing in Italian. The caribou made his debut to a standing ovation at La Scala in 1969, singing Pinkerton in *Madame Butterfly*.

These case histories and many others offer undeniable proof that animals can not only learn human language but can achieve intellectual levels heretofore assumed attainable only by advanced humans.

Prospective Benefits

Enormous benefits may be derived from such a project. The ability to read should greatly improve the self concepts of the participating animals, who will realize

---

DULY NOTED

"I wish to note the following: A physically meaningful random distribution of dislocations can be defined only by assuming the *positions of the dislocations are completely random.*"

—Ben-Abraham, S. I. "On Internal Stresses Due to a Random Distribution of Dislocations," Scripta Metallurgica, Vol. 2, No. 1, 1968.

---

that they, too, can engage in the intellectual pursuits of humans. Cage time will no more be devoted merely to eating, sleeping, and pacing. What zoo patron wouldn't be impressed with an armadillo dabbling in Kafka, an elk contemplating a *Wall Street Journal* article, or a lioness perusing Michener?

These animals will become qualified for employment such as proofreading for publishers or graduate students. Most animals, particularly elephants, will work for peanuts, and they are not covered by minimum wage laws. They will cease to be a burden to society. Some animals may even embark on political careers after reading inane statements attributed to jackasses already in office.

Implications for Project Design

Following are some suggestions prospective project directors may wish to consider when preparing their proposals.

1. It appears that mammals, birds, and reptiles have a more vital need for reading education than insects, fish, and mollusks. Therefore, these classes should be given highest priority.

2. Since the literature indicates that animals learn at different rates, remedial material should be developed for slower students and an accelerated curriculum for the gifted.

3. Few classroom teachers have been trained in techniques appropriate for zoo animals although some teachers have developed these skills through actual experience with humans. Therefore, teacher training should be an essential component of the project.

Funding Sources

It is evident that no Federal agencies are currently interested in funding projects of this nature, despite the potential impact on our nation's future. It is suggested that applicants seek foundation support for this critically urgent project.

THE SOLUTION OF THE ISRAELI WATER PROBLEM

Richard Kraft
The Negev Research Institute,
Beer-Sheva

DAVID SUTER

Introduction

Whenever a country has a shortage of some basic raw material a natural economic question arises: is it cheaper to import the commodity or to manufacture it locally? This question applies also to Israel's water problem. For obvious reasons, however, the problem posed by this question hasn't been seriously entertained in connection with the Israeli water shortage, until now.[1] Once the problem of importing water is seriously considered an obvious solution presents itself; it is the purpose of this note to outline the highlights of this solution.

The Plan

It is well known that the arctic regions of the world contain abundant supplies of salt free ice which when melted gives tasty water that is suitable for drinking and irrigation without additional processing. Since the human population of the arctic region is small and militarily impotent and doesn't need this water, there would be no moral or political obstacles in taking the water. Nevertheless, once it is shown that a cheap way of transporting this water to Israel exists, certain countries will strongly oppose the project. For this reason it is proposed that immediate steps be taken to show that the inhabitants of the Arctic are descendants

of a lost tribe of Israel.[2] Furthermore some organizers of the Jewish Agency should be sent as soon as possible to the Arctic to begin an immigration (aliya) program.[3] It would also be wise to ensure that the Minister of Foreign Affairs includes a stopover in the Arctic on the occasion of his next visit to Europe and the USA.

We will now discuss the technical aspects of the plan. Our proposal is to bring water from the Arctic to Israel in a pipeline. Pipelines of this order of magnitude have already been constructed in the United States. We will now show that Israel is in an advantageous position to implement this project.

One of the major problems of the project is the tremendous energy needed for pumping. In respect to this problem Israel is indeed blessed. For inside the borders of Israel is the Dead Sea—the lowest spot on earth. This makes it possible to bring the Arctic water to Israel by gravity feed. Hence there will be no pumping problem.

In order to turn the ice into water at the Arctic

---

[1] Since the only feasible proposal for producing water locally gives a secondary product of a somewhat controversial nature there could be more than just economic gain in importing water.

[2] Some opposition (on theological grounds) to this can be expected to come from Hechal Shlomo (the equivalent of the Vatican in Jewish religion). They may be persuaded, however, to accept the plan for the good of the country if the government would encourage their patriotic feelings by contributing funds to the establishment of a yeshiva.

[3] This is not connected with the proposal to send these officials to the Arctic for general purposes.

and prevent it from freezing in the pipeline, the pipeline will consist of two concentric cylinders. The inner tube will carry the water to Israel by gravity feed, while the outer cylinder will convey heated water to the Arctic by convection. The energy for the convection will be generated by the temperature differential between the Dead Sea and the Arctic. As a by-product of this convection we can expect to air-condition the entire Negev Desert.

Despite the close ties that can be expected to arise between Israel and the Eskimos (following the discovery that they are a lost tribe of Israel), some sort of compensation will have to be made to our northern brethren. With the closing of the Common Market to Israeli citrus fruit, there will be a surplus of citrus which we can ship to the Eskimos. Since oranges are lighter than water they can be buoyed up to the Arctic in the convective section of the pipeline. To the Eskimos this (the golden delicious fruit popping out from the ground) will seem like a blessing from heaven (figuratively speaking). No doubt, they will want to repay our generosity by sending us something in return.

What material and technical resources does Israel have for implementing this project? It is well known that Israel has abundant pipe factories. A strong diamond industry can be harnessed to provide the necessary drilling bits. The powerful financial support of American Jews could be relied upon. As for the technical problems, they will crumble under the Jewish genius.

The only remaining problem is to find a supply of cheap labor. First, let us remind ourselves that the pioneering age in Israel is coming to a close and along with its decline the Israeli youngsters are becoming soft and losing their idealism. Therefore the project of laying a pipeline to the Arctic is just the kind of challenge needed to inspire their spirits and harden their bodies. But some cynics may rightly claim that such an enterprise is beyond the capacity of the Nahal (Fighting Pioneering Youth—an agricultural version of Army service in Israel). Hence, the following solution is offered to the labor problem.

We are all familiar with the international response that was received for volunteer workers to excavate Masada. Many youths had to be turned away and were very disappointed. Another such call would no doubt be answered again by today's restless international youth. Of course, the real purpose of the project would be disguised. It would be billed as another archeological project, and this time no volunteers would be turned away. It is rather dubious that any of

DAVID SUTER

the workers toiling away in the bowels of the earth would discover the real job they were doing, and besides, some archeological finds would no doubt be made before they reached the Arctic.

When this article was in preparation another suggestion was proposed by O. Novick:

We should like to suggest another solution to the Israeli water problem, based on the transportation of icebergs from Spitzbergen to Israel. The icebergs required are about 10 x 2 x 0.2 km. If not available in nature, these can be produced by freezing a small fjord filled with river water. Such icebergs would be transported to Israel by three frigates, three destroyers and ca. ten orange carriers. During the transport, which would take about 5 months, the iceberg would melt and lose about 60 to 70% of its mass. The remaining 1000 millions of cubic meters of ice would amply supply the annual water consumption of Israel. The ice would be deposited at the Israeli coast, and melted there by solar energy, water being pumped directly from the iceberg. This project although perhaps engineeringly invalid, has some blissful marginal effects: It would solve the unemployment of both the Israeli Navy and the Merchant Marine (in peace time). Furthermore an iceberg carried through the Mediterranean would cool the Near East, and permit the importation of polar bears.

A MODEST PROPOSAL CONCERNING THE FUTURE OF TRANSPORTATION

Edmund J. Cantilli, Ph.D.
Department of Transportation
Polytechnic Institute of New York

The history of transportation is one of break-throughs in mode: from water to land, from land to air. Except for the development of space flight (an extension of air technology), it is difficult to see new modal breakthroughs occurring unless the scientific approach is taken. Air-effects machines are not the true breakthrough, merely substituting air pressure for wheels, with many of the same or similar side-effects and limitations of wheeled vehicles. The true breakthrough must satisfy two specific limiting factors of today's transport: *capacity* and *fuel*.

Capacity

The major transport modes in the United States today are the motor vehicle, the commercial airplane, and the boat or ship. The motor vehicle is ubiquitous, but has been found wanting from the standpoint of efficiency in carrying capacity. Individual vehicles are rarely filled. Buses are much more efficient than private cars, but must compete with the private auto for street space. "Mass transportation" has become the by-word, but individual buses, airplanes, or boats are hardly "mass" in any sense of the word. Aircraft have great speed, but, again, they cannot move great masses of people at once. Boats and ships can have great capacity individually, but do not provide the continuity requisite of true "mass" transportation systems.

The answer lies in *linkage*. Individual vehicles, whether land, sea, or air mode, must be considered modules to be linked for greater capacity. The Linked-

It's Future Lies, Says the Author, in a Rationale Which Augments the Interaction of Nexuses (Nexi) Through Consideration of Two Major Criteria: Capacity and Fuel.

Vehicle Mode (LVM) must become the new by-word.

Fuel

Current problems revolve about an overreliance on petroleum products as the major transportation fuel source. While science will continue to develop alternate sources of energy, such as wind, thermal, and solar energy, we sit upon vast sources of coal. Coal is now seen to be cheaper, more plentiful, and easier to control from a pollution standpoint. Coal must therefore become the fuel of the future.

The Breakthrough

The marriage of the concept of *linkage* with the fuel of the future, *coal*, will produce the long-awaited breakthrough in modal development in the field of transportation. This concept can be termed the Coal-Burning

DAVID SUTER

Linked-Vehicle Mode (CBLVM).

The latest concepts of fuel injection and modularization must be applied. This requires proximity of the fuel module to the propulsion module. Since we are dealing with a Linked-Vehicle Mode (LVM), it is recommended that the fuel module *follow* the propulsion module.

Lastly, the individual passenger modules will follow, linked to the fuel module (which is linked to the propulsion module).

Guideway

An appropriate guideway for the land mode of this breakthrough Transport Rationale would permit little choice or maneuver, since both of these variables can be linked to much of the confusion, congestion, and lack of safety of free-running land vehicles. This suggests strong steel roadways set upon reasonably flexible beds, for which a combination of wood and gravel suggests itself as efficaceous. There is room for further development here, but the concept of a steel Nexus must be seen as inevitable between origin and destination. Only in this way may we expect to augment the interaction between activity centers.

Terminology

While Coal-Burning Linked-Vehicle Mode is properly descriptive of this new concept, a readily usable acronym for this mode is an absolute necessity. CBLVM is unwieldly and provides no selling "word" to be used in pushing the new concept (Cobalavin will not do). In this regard the concept of the Interactive Nexus provides us with the germ of a usable acronym. Since there already exist Nexi in other modal forms, our further purpose is the *augmentation* of interactive nexi. And finally, the whole constitutes a Transport Rationale for Augmentation of Interactive Nexus, or "TRAIN," TRAIN, or "train," may well become a commonplace term.

REFERENCES

Falconseye, J. Charles. "Freedom Now Through Urbitration." *Journal of True Release*, July 4, 1976.
Kraulig, K., Obersturmgruppenfuhrer. "The Importance of Trivial Detail in Library Science." *Journal of Wheel-Spinning*, 2:17, January 8, 1888.
Li, B. Jung. "Leave Driving to Driver." *Cairo News*, July 4, 1776.
Nattero, L.P.G. "Monerting Dater From Umter Because I Said So." *Society for Re-Invention of the Wheel*, 1:1, 1976.
Rogers, R.U.R. "The Pleasures of Robotization Through Lobotomy." The *L.P.G. Nattero Journal*, 5:70, 1975.
Schoen, Billy Mack. "The Need for Self-Inflicted Punishment and Reform." *The L.P.G. Nattero Journal*, 5:69, 1975.

THE BIOPUMP SOLUTION

Thomas A. Easton, Ph.D.
Director
Center for Independent Research

The force of peristalsis is used by all the higher members of the animal kingdom for the movement of liquids, slurries, and small solid fragments, but this force has hitherto been tapped commercially only in the design and use of small peristaltic pumps for biomedical applications. These mechanical pumps, however, suffer from the two drawbacks that they (1) handle only small quantities (a maximum of less than three liters per minute),[1] and (2) require a continuous energy supply apart from that required to maintain their operators.

Each of these drawbacks may now be defeated with a new device,[2] henceforth called the Biopump, which can achieve flow rates of well over three liters per minute[3] and which requires no external energy input. The latter benefit is of particular significance during these days of an energy shortage and means that use of the Biopump will not be affected by brownouts, blackouts, or strikes. It also means that use of the Biopump will not adversely affect the ecology of any region in which it is used.

Getting Hosed

The Biopump consists of a flexible, thin plastic tube, one end of which is equipped with an input hose fitting and one end of which expands into a bulbous reservoir with a second hose fitting placed to one side. The latter fitting couples the reservoir to a tube of a heavier gauge plastic tube which ends in an output hose fitting. Each of the components is made of biologically inert materials.

To prepare the Biopump for use, the thin plastic tube is threaded through the human esophagus and the input fitting is mounted through the cheek in such a way that an input hose may be coupled to it. The reservoir is placed in the stomach with its hose fitting traversing the stomach wall in such a way and position that the second, more rigid hose may connect the reservoir to the last hose fitting at the navel, where an output hose may be attached. Once in place, as shown in Fig. 1, the Biopump forms a continuous path from cheek to navel by which the operator can propel, by swallowing and the consequent esophageal peristalsis and stomach churnings, liquids, slurries, and small solids from one vessel or level to another. Several Biopumps arranged in parallel can transport virtually any quantity of material. Arranged in series, they can transport material over virtually any distance. And, if their operators stand on their heads, they can even be used to transport materials up hill, for peristalsis is independent of gravity.

There are no constraints on the materials that the Biopump can transport other than those of consistency, for the Biopump effectively isolates its operator from toxic or corrosive substances. The only influence that crosses the plastic barrier of the Biopump is that of the muscles of the operator's alimentary system.

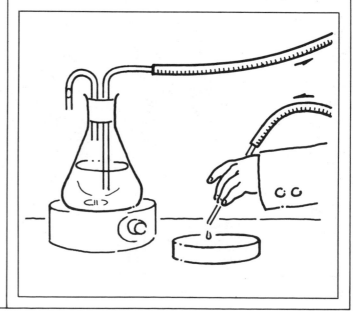

---

[1] See, for example, the pumps produced by Harvard Apparatus.

[2] It has not yet been built, but anyone who wishes to try may feel free to do so, and patent it as well, if he wishes, as long as he makes the proper acknowledgments.

[3] Estimate based on the observation that I can swallow 200 ml in four seconds.

No More Bony Fish

Because the Biopump is made of a thin, flexible plastic, when not in use the esophageal tube and the reservoir will collapse into a thin layer against the walls of the esophagus and stomach. It will thus not interfere in any way with its operator's ingestion of food and drink, although its operator must, as a simple safety precaution, refrain from all those foods, such as popcorn, nuts, and bony fish, which might tear, puncture, or otherwise impair the integrity of the Biopump. The operator should also, of course, have those teeth nearest the Biopump's input removed.

The applications of this device should be immediately obvious. Eminently portable, it will allow motorists, at a moment's notice, to siphon gasoline into their automobiles. Inexpensive to produce and virtually maintenance-free, it will give graduate students new assistantship opportunities as their professors seek new ways to eliminate their dependence on outside energy supplies and equipment suppliers for moving their solutions about. It will give industry new ways to employ persons of little education or skill. And it will allow ecologically disruptive pipelines to be replaced by lines of thousands of government bureaucrats and oil company executives, each one equipped with a Biopump.

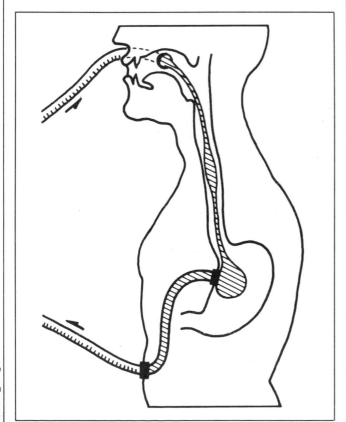

Fig. 1

"OLE YELLER ENZYME"

T. Ragland

Introduction

"Ole Yeller Enzyme" is important historically, if for no other reason.[1] It introduced the use of color to qualitate enzyme studies and made available for the first time an enzyme which could be thought of as a catalyst in a biochemical quagmire.

Purification

Step 1. Nine pigs are Waring-blended and water-extracted according to the method of Baron von Lebedev.[2] Lead subacetate is added (400 ml of liquor plumbisubaceti i D.A.B. 6 per liter of Lebedev juice) and the mixture vigorously shaken with high-test anti-knock aviation octane (Stukka No. 3). The precipitate formed after three months at $-20°$ centigrade is separated from the mother liquor by severing the umbilical cord and centrifugation. To the supernatant, which contains the enzyme, is added a half volume of dialysed Ramco No. 5.[3] After the viscous jel settles out, the "yeller" super is evaporated to dryness.

Step 2. One hundred grams of "ole yeller" is redissolved in chloroform and shaken in lusteroid Mickle disintegrator tubes for one week. The sprayate, which has flown all over the walls and ceiling, is scraped off these fixtures and designated as "ole yeller" No. 3.

Assay

"Ole yeller," fraction 3 is scrubbed up in octanol and the co-enzyme "split" from the ape-o-enzyme. Upon the addition of DPNH, crude yeast extract (Canadian ale yeast, top variety, Hanson), and octanol sludge, a rapid bleaching occurs which is directly proportional to the intensity of the yellow color. Arbitrarily assuming that 5 Fisch Units catalyze 10 bleaches (assuming single hit kinetics) the fluorescence quenching may be calculated. One kg. of pig yields 3 mg of "ole yeller."

---

[1] As a matter of fact, *absolutely* for no other reason.
[2] *Zeitschrift fuer Konigen*, 12, 199.
[3] Available from Spitzungen and Schleicher.

REDUCING AUTOMOBILE ACCIDENTS

John L. S. Hickey*

Recently reported research[1] by the National Safety Program has provided a significant clue which can, if properly exploited, reduce and perhaps completely eliminate automobile accidents. The germ of the breakthrough lies in the NSP finding that "75% of automobile accidents occur within 40 miles of home."[2] Now there are five ways in which one may react to this statement. Three of the reactions are elementary:

1. Normal reaction: "I should be just as vigilant driving near home as when on the highway."

2. Statistician's reaction: "Since about 90% of the driving occurs within 40 miles of home, and only 75% of the accidents, this is a 'safe' area and I can relax while driving."

3. Reverse reaction: "I'd better drive as fast as possible to get out of the 40-mile 'danger' zone into the surrounding 'safe' zone."

The other two reactions will be explored in some detail, as reaction #4 provides the means to reduce accidents, and reaction #5 can, at some small risk, eliminate them completely. Both employ the method of Data Enrichment[3] previously reported in the Journal of Irreproducible Results.

The fourth reaction is: "If 75% of automobile accidents occur within 40 miles of home, it can be seen through use of the data enrichment method[4] that the farther one is from home, the smaller the chance of an accident. Therefore, *I will register my car at a 'home' 500 miles away and never go near there.*" This process could easily be developed into a national program for providing simulated or substitute homes for all drivers, perhaps with a title like Car Registration at Substitute Homes (CRASH). Obviously, if no one ever drives within 40 miles of their "home" accidents will inevitably be reduced 75%.

The fifth reaction requires a little background discussion. As we all know, accident rates vary from locality to locality; one can therefore expand on the fourth reaction and surmise that, instead of registering their car at a randomly chosen "home" 500 miles away, the safer thing to do would be to register it in a place much farther away *and which has a low automobile accident rate.* A place immediately comes to mind—the South Pole. It is very far away, and there is only one automobile there.[5] Thus the automobile collision rate is necessarily zero, and automobiles registered in Antarctica will sustain this rate. Again, this concept could be extended into a nationwide program under which every automobile would be registered at a single center located at the South Pole, which could be named Central Location for Accident Prevention Through Registering Automobiles Polarly (CLAPTRAP). Through this method, the automobile accident would become a thing of the past. The small risk? If another automobile were taken to Antarctica and collided with the first one, every car in the country would suddenly be registered in an area with *a 100% automobile accident rate.*

A HUMAN REPLACES INSTRUMENT DUMMY IN AUTO CRASH TEST

For the first time in 28 years, men and women will voluntarily participate in auto crash testing at Calspan Corporation in Buffalo, New York. The volunteers will ride a giant machine that precisely duplicates the crash of an auto into a stone wall.

—From "Faster than a speeding bullet," I&CS, October 1974, p. 47.

---

*Nom de plume for Mike Robrain.
[1] Reported via public service time on TV and radio.
[2] It may be 80% within 50 miles of home. The exact figures do not change the concept.
[3] *The Data Enrichment Method* appears on page 93 of this book.
[4] Calculations not reproduced here.
[5] A Volkswagen: see full page ads in *Life,* almost any 1967 issue.

WEEKEND SCIENTIST: LET'S MAKE A THERMONUCLEAR DEVICE

D. I. Radin
Belly Laboratories

Introduction

Worldwide controversy has been generated recently from several court decisions in the United States which have restricted popular magazines from printing articles which describe how to make an atomic bomb. The reason usually given by the courts is that national security would be compromised if such information were generally available. But, since it is commonly known that all of the information is publicly available in most major metropolitan libraries, obviously the court's officially stated position is covering up a more important factor; namely, that such atomic devices would prove too difficult for the average citizen to construct. The United States courts cannot afford to insult the vast majorities by insinuating that they do not have the intelligence of a cabbage, and thus the "official" press releases claim national security as a blanket restriction.

The rumors that have unfortunately occurred as a result of widespread misinformation can (and must) be cleared up now, for the construction project this month is the construction of a thermonuclear device. We will see how easy it is to make a device of your very own in ten easy steps, to have and hold as you see fit, without annoying interference from the government or the courts.

The project will cost between $5,000 and $30,000 dollars, depending on how fancy you want the final product to be. Since the last column, "Let's Make a Time Machine," was received so well in the new step-by-step format, this month's column will follow the same format.

Construction Method

1. First, obtain about 110 pounds (50 kg) of weapons grade Plutonium at your local supplier[1]. A nuclear power plant is not recommended, as large quantities of missing Plutonium tend to make plant engineers unhappy. We suggest that you contact your local terrorist organization, or perhaps the Junior Achievement in your neighborhood.

2. Please remember that Plutonium, especially pure, refined Plutonium, is somewhat dangerous. Wash your hands with soap and warm water after handling the material, and don't allow your children or pets to play in it or eat it. Any left over Plutonium dust is excellent as an insect repellent. You may wish to keep the substance in a lead box if you can find one in your local junk yard, but an old coffee can will do nicely.

3. Fashion together a metal enclosure to house the device. Most common varieties of sheet metal can be bent to disguise this enclosure as, for example, a briefcase, a lunch pail, or a Buick. Do not use tinfoil.

4. Arrange the Plutonium into two hemispheral

---

[1] Plutonium (PU), atomic number 94, is a radioactive metallic element formed by the decay of Neptunium and is similar in chemical structure to Uranium, Saturium, Jupiternium, and Marisum.

DAVID SUTER

shapes, separated by about 4 cm. Use rubber cement to hold the Plutonium dust together.

5. Now get about 220 pounds (100 kg) of trinitrotoluene (TNT). Gelignite is much better, but messier to work with. Your helpful hardware man will be happy to provide you with this item.

6. Pack the TNT around the hemisphere arrangement constructed in step 4. If you cannot find Gelignite, feel free to use TNT packed in with Play-Doh or any modeling clay. Colored clay is acceptable, but there is no need to get fancy at this point.

7. Enclose the structure from step 6 into the enclosure made in step 3. Use a strong glue such as Krazy Glue to bind the hemisphere arrangement against the enclosure to prevent accidental detonation which might result from vibration or mishandling.

8. To detonate the device, obtain a radio controlled (RC) servo mechanism, as found in RC model airplanes and cars. With a modicum of effort, a remote plunger can be made that will strike a detonator cap to effect a small explosion. These detonator caps can be found in the electrical supply section of your local supermarket. We recommend the "Blast-O-Matic" brand because they are no deposit–no return.

9. Now hide the completed device from the neighbors and children. The garage is not recommended because of high humidity and the extreme range of temperatures experienced there. Nuclear devices have been known to spontaneously detonate in these unstable conditions. The hall closet or under the kitchen sink will be perfectly suitable.

10. Now you are the proud owner of a working thermonuclear device! It is a great ice-breaker at parties, and in a pinch, can be used for national defense.

Theory of Operation

The device basically works when the detonated

TNT compresses the Plutonium into a critical mass. The critical mass then produces a nuclear chain reaction similar to the domino chain reaction (discussed in this column, "Dominos on the March," March, 1968). The chain reaction then promptly produces a big thermonuclear reaction. And there you have it, a 10 megaton explosion!

Next Month's Column

In next month's column, we will learn how to clone your neighbor's wife in six easy steps. This project promises to be an exciting weekend full of fun and profit. Common kitchen utensils will be all you need. See you next month!

Previous Month's Columns

1. Let's Make Test Tube Babies! May, 1979
2. Let's Make a Solar System! June, 1979
3. Let's Make an Economic Recession! July, 1979
4. Let's Make an Anti-Gravity Machine! August, 1979
5. Let's Make Contact with an Alien Race! September, 1979

PART V

HOW RESEARCH IS DONE

THE DATA ENRICHMENT METHOD*

Henry R. Lewis

The following remarks are intended as a nontechnical exposition of an interesting method which has been proposed (not by the present author) to improve the quality of inference drawn from a set of experimentally obtained data. The power of the method lies in its breadth of applicability and in the promise it holds of obtaining more reliable results *without recourse to the expense and trouble of increasing the size of the sample of data.* The method is best illustrated by example. Two such examples are outlined below; the first is somewhat routine, but the second is a striking illustration of what "data enrichment" can achieve.

A Sound Experiment

Consider an experiment performed to test the ability of a specific sound receiver to detect an audio signal. The experiment is performed in such a way that in each of a series of trials one learns either that detection was accomplished or that it was not accomplished. Suppose, moreover, that the sound source and the receiver are fixed in space and trials are made with the source intensity set at six different levels. At each of the six source intensity levels a number of tests are made and the result, detection or no detection, is recorded. The data from such an experiment are summarized in Table 1.

It is desirable, of course, to increase the amount of data available at each source level. It is reasonable to assume that detectability is a function of source level and that, if all other parameters are held constant, a loud sound is easier to detect than one of smaller intensity. Thus it is safe to assume that if a signal was detected at a given level, it would have been

*Reprinted with permission of the Editor from *Operations Research,* 5:551, 1957.

It has been known to those interested in psychophysical phenomena that a man's tendency to flip a coin in such a way that when it lands he will be faced by a head rather than by a tail increased with the altitude at which the experiment is performed.

detected at all higher source intensity levels. (The electronics are not such that overloading of the receiver would prevent detection.) Moreover, if a signal was not detected at a given level, it would not have been

Table 1

Raw data

Source level (db)	Number of detections	Number of failures to detect
62	5	40
65	10	30
68	15	20
71	20	10
74	25	5
77	30	3

detected at any lower level of source intensity. Using these simple facts, the data collected at one source level can be used to add to the data available for other levels. For example, looking at Table 1 we see that three of the trials made at a source level of 77 db resulted in no detection. These trials would also have led to no detection had the source level been at 62 db. Consequently, we can add the results of these experiments to our body of knowledge about 62 db *since we know how these experiments would have come out had we performed them.* Similarly the five trials made at 62 db and resulting in detection would certainly have resulted in detection had the signal been as high as 77 db at the source. Thus five more trials resulting in detection can be added to those actually made at 77 db. Treating all the data in this fashion, we can compile Table 2.

Two things are apparent at once: the probabilities of detection given in Table 2 are quite different from those which might have been deduced crudely and directly from Table 1; in addition the number of "virtual" trials at each level of source intensity is much larger than the actual number of trials. Hence one may be more confident of the results of Table 2 than of any results one might get directly from Table 1.

Table 2

Enriched Data

Source level (db)	Number of virtual detections	Number of virtual failures	Probability of detection
62	5	108	5/113
65	15	68	15/83
68	30	38	30/68
71	50	18	50/68
74	75	8	75/83
77	105	13	105/108

New Heights

A second example, even simpler than the first, should make the advantages of this method of analysis quite clear now that the details are fixed in the reader's mind. It has been known to those interested in psychophysical phenomena that a man's tendency to flip a coin in such a way that when it lands he will be faced by a head rather than by a tail increases with the altitude at which the experiment is performed. The effect is small but a vast number of trials conducted on Mount Everest, from base to summit, have shown that the effect indeed exists. With due respect to the hardy band of men who invested so many years and Sherpas in this effort, it is of interest to show how the same

result can be obtained by one man with no more athletic ability than that required to climb a flight of stairs and no more equipment than an unbiased nickel. Our advantage over the pioneers in this field lies, of course, in our knowledge of the "enriched-data" method.

The power of the method lies in its breadth of applicability and in the promise it holds of obtaining more reliable results without recourse to the expense and trouble of increasing the size of the sample of data.

Consider a set of stairs with ten levels and number them in the order of their increasing altitude. The experimenter climbs the stairs, slowly, and at each level flips a coin ten times and records a head as a success and a tail as a failure. The results of an actual test are recorded in Table 3.

Table 3

Raw Data: Coin Experiment

Step number	Number of successes	Number of failures
1	4	6
2	5	5
3	7	3
4	4	6
5	6	4
6	5	5
7	6	4
8	6	4
9	3	7
10	4	6

The results of Table 3 are not conclusive. The altitude effect may be present but is not evident, at least to a naive observer. Suppose we now attempt to increase the data available by recourse to logic in the manner already illustrated in the first example. The altitude principle tells us that if a trial on the first step resulted in a head, then it would certainly have resulted in a head if the trial had been made at the loftier tenth step. Similarly, if despite the height of the tenth step a trial made there resulted in a failure to throw a head, then the same trial would surely have been a failure on the lower steps. Using this added insight, the data can be enriched by a large number of virtual trials as is shown in Table 4.

Table 4

Enriched Data: Coin Experiment

Step number	Number of virtual successes	Number of virtual failures	Probability of throwing a "head"
1	4	50	4/54
2	9	44	9/53
3	16	39	16/55
4	20	36	20/56
5	26	30	26/56
6	31	26	31/57
7	37	21	37/58
8	43	17	43/60
9	46	13	46/59
10	50	6	50/56

A glance at Table 4 shows that the altitude principle, which was skulking almost unnoticed in the raw data of Table 3, has been fully brought forth by the data enrichment method. The probabilities in Table 4 are shown in Fig. 1 to further emphasize the point. It might be mentioned in passing that the altitude effect in the Pentagon appears to be 10^5 times as large as that found in the Himalayas. Whether this is a temperature effect, a geographical effect, or the result of psychical factors as yet unknown should be the object of further study.

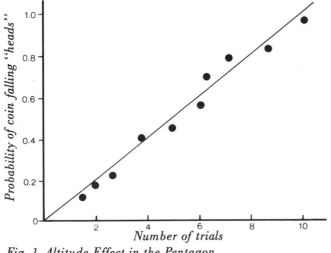

Fig. 1. Altitude Effect in the Pentagon

The Raw and the Cooked

A final remark on the strength and weakness of the method is in order. As mentioned earlier, its strength lies in its breadth of applicability, and the method is as pertinent to experiments in classical physics as it is to experiments in psychical phenomena. In short, the method will give new meaning to data quite without regard to the status of the hypothesis used to increase the sample size.

Despite its evident power, however, the method requires further study. Its principal shortcoming is that before the enrichment process can be started, some data must be collected. It is quite true that a great deal is done with very little information, but this should not blind one to the fact that the method still embodies the "raw-data flaw." The ultimate objective, complete freedom from the inconvenience and embarrassment of experimental results, still lies unattained before us.

THE TRIPLE BLIND TEST

R.F., M.D.

At one time, an investigator working alone could produce significant research. But the ever increasing array of electronic gadgets is making it difficult for one person to record objectively all his erroneous observations. Many irrational leads are thereby missed.

Since it is now virtually impossible for him to blunder blindly without help, teamwork has come to the rescue with a perfect solution: the double-blind study.

The value of the double-blind study was first illustrated by studies of the LD-50 (lethal dose for 50% of test subjects) of cyanide. In earlier experiments it was considered satisfactory to give, and not to give, the drug to alternate subjects. But now control subjects are given a placebo of exactly the same size, shape and color as the cyanide tablet. By doing the experiments in this way, the clinical impression that cyanide is lethal is verified by observations uncluttered by bias.

The accuracy of the double-blind test permits evaluation of a drug with far fewer subjects than heretofore: in fact, in some studies it has been possible to reduce the number of subjects to zero.[1]

In evaluating the precision of this method, researchers have made an unexpected discovery—the therapeutic effectiveness of sucrose and starch placebos. The diversified effects of these simple carbohydrates constitute a major discovery in medicine.

Of particular interest is the remarkable potency of starch in pathological pain, with no indication that it produces addiction. It is equally noteworthy that starch does not affect experimentally produced pain.

This observation has brought about the realization that analgesics should be appraised only in relief of naturally occurring pain, since man may be the only species that imagines suffering.

Placebos are now available for the treatment of headache, rheumatoid arthritis and female ailments.

In addition, they are as potent as ethanol either as "psychic energizers" in depressed states or as "psychic de-energizers" in overactive states.

Serendipity

Over the past few years, a new concept has arisen in medical research. Therapeutic nihilists now feel that the best chance of therapeutic breakthrough in mental disease, cancer and hypertension lies in experiments so completely unbiased and randomized that an accidental discovery of importance may turn up. This principle—sometimes called serendipity—is well recognized in mathematics: Sir Arthur Stanley Eddington said, "We need a super-mathematics in which the operations are as unknown as the quantities they operate on and a super-mathematician who does not know what he is doing when he performs these operations."

Applying the randomization principle to experimental medicine has led to the triple-blind test: The subject does not know what he is getting, the nurse doesn't know what she is giving and the investigator doesn't know what he is doing. Half way through the experiment, randomization is increased by a process known as turnabout—the patient administers the drug to the investigator, and the results are evaluated by a student-nurse. The famous mathematician, Lewis Carroll, may have had the randomization principle in mind in the phenomenon he described as Jabberwocky or "unknowable actors executing unknowable actions."[2]

The chance that triple-blind testing will produce something of consequence is calculated to be at least as great as that of spontaneous mutation. This probability is about one times ten to the minus sixth power per generation. But considering the large number of chaotic investigations now in progress, the chance of a significant breakthrough in the next few thousand years is not improbable.

---

[1]A novel presentation of the theory of errors in small samples may be found in the recent book by B. L. Smith entitled *The Statistical Treatment of Vanishingly Small Samples and of Nonexistent Data.*

[2]Annals of *Alice in Wonderland* and *Through the Looking Glass.* A more precise description of Jabberwocky follows:

"Twas brillig, and the slithy toves
did gyre and gimble in the wabe;
all mimsy were the borogoves,
and the mome raths outgrabe."

A PRELIMINARY REPORT ON GENETIC DETERMINANTS IN AESTHETIC DECISIONS

Ross Coates
Chairman,Department of Fine Arts
Washington State University
Pullman, Washington

Early in 1972, with the help of a grant from Winsor and Newton Co.[1] my colleagues and I began to explore the possibility that the shoddy visual environment of late twentieth century America could best be explained by postulating a genetic mutation that had rapidly become dominant.[2] We hypothesized that this now dominant gene encouraged Americans to make bad aesthetic decisions. We decided on this as a hypothesis since almost fifty years of resolute art teaching had actually coincided with an obvious decline (see Fig. 1).

Knowing that there has been increasing concern over the use of human subjects in genetic experiments, and realizing that once we had identified the gene affecting aesthetic decision-making we would have to wait for the results through several generations, we decided not to use humans but to fall back on the old stand-by the fruitfly *(D. Melanogaster)*. However, we could not develop a satisfactory method for judging aesthetic decisions made by a fruitfly, so we eventually began our work with a strain of white rats specially bred for laboratory work (Sprague-Dawley).

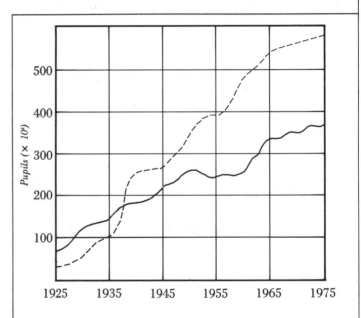

————numbers of pupils receiving art education in public schools

- - - - -numbers of sunburst clocks and plaster ducks sold as living room decorations. (For reasons that will be made clear when our results are published in detail these two elements were statistically significant as indicators of aesthetic decline.)

Fig. 1. Relationship of Art Education to Aesthetic Decline

We hypothesized that these rats, housed for generations in barren laboratories, would have gone mad from aesthetic deprivation unless the non-aesthetic gene had quickly become the dominant one. We felt

---

[1] It seemed strange that no U.S.-based foundation was interested in our research.
[2] cf. T. Veblen on the occasionally grandiose and possibly symptomatic bad taste of the Robber Barons.

this was a reasonably good analogue for the average contemporary middle-class American.

Methods

Two tasks were developed to measure aesthetic activity by the rats.[3]

Task one: Water was made available in both a translucent plastic dish with dried leaves imbedded in it, and a raku pot.[4] Choosing to drink from the raku pot was judged a positive aesthetic decision.

Task two: Food was made available by pressing a lever covered by a Skira print of Cezanne's *Mte. Ste. Victoire,* or a lever painted pink decorated with a rhinestone butterfly. Choosing to press the "Cezanne" lever was judged a positive aesthetic decision.

We corrected for an extraneous variable early in the experiment. The original assistants were of course art majors and so unthinkingly encouraged the rats to make positive aesthetic judgments, sometimes by rewards of extra food. We replaced the art students by engineering majors but found that they not only encouraged unaesthetic decisions by the rats (again by rewards of food) but in one particularly embarrassing case actually stole the plastic dish for use as a Christmas gift. After trying various other groups, our final solution was to use architecture majors who, peculiarly enough, seemed totally uninterested in all aesthetic decisions, and so let the rats go their own way.

Using the usual randomization techniques, we divided the rats into a control and experimental group. An extended and detailed report of the technical part of the experiment is to be published soon,[5] but suffice it to say we were finally able to isolate the "aesthetic" gene and to make it dominant, through breeding (see Fig. 2).

Discussion

We are confident that our preliminary results seem to confirm our hypothesis. In rats that had been consistently unaesthetic for generations directed genetic mutation and selective breeding did indeed produce a group of rats that consistently made positive aesthetic decisions and passed this trait on to their offspring. It appears that this is only the first step into a new field for which we suggest the name *bio-aesthetics.*

However, when these techniques and the results are extrapolated to human populations there are many

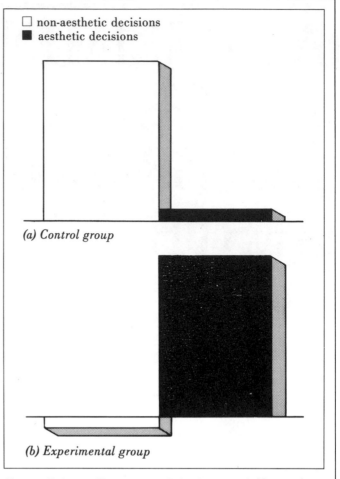

☐ non-aesthetic decisions
■ aesthetic decisions

(a) Control group

(b) Experimental group

Fig. 2. Relative Frequency of Aesthetic and Nonaesthetic Decisions

complications. Ideally a population could be developed that would be able to make valid aesthetic judgments on its own! Suddenly art critics, museum directors, art gallery owners, art dealers, art teachers at all levels and even many artists would become superfluous. Welfare rolls would lengthen as thousands in the art business found they were no longer needed by an aesthetically intelligent population. The social problems are enormous.

As we began to tabulate the results of our experiments with the rats, we sometimes felt, especially in those lonely early morning hours in the laboratory, that we were tampering with the lock on yet another Pandora's box.

---

[3] Valuable assistance in evaluating these tasks was given by the College Art Association.
[4] A very special thanks to Asia House (N.Y.C.) for lending us a twelfth century Japanese raku pot for the duration of the experiment.
[5] In the *Journal of Aesthetics and Art Criticism.*

NOTES UPON A WHOPPER

Dick Rubinstein

I recently visited my local Burger King and received this register receipt with my purchase:

```
1           WHOPER          1 09
1    N     M               00
1    AU   O                00
     1      COFFEE milk      30
               TAX           08
3040      THANKS           1 47
   09  NV TOTL  A           1 47
```

I have a number of observations (resulting from my failure to bring any reading material into the establishment):

Observation a. They misspelled Whopper.

Conjecture a_1: No one has noticed the error.
Investigation: I asked the cashier, who replied "Yeah, I know."

Conjecture a_2: The manufacturer economized by reducing the number of columns of alphabetic print to six.

Observation b. The "X" in "TAX" is in the seventh column.

Conjecture b: The printer can't print any letter in any column—an economy measure: There may be no "P" available in column 5, and no R in column 7. An "E" is, however, available in column 6. This requires more investigation, only achievable by more varied orders, selected on the basis of the spelling of the items.

Observation c. Although they don't charge for excluding mayonnaise ("NO M"), or for providing onion ("AD O")—"having it my way"—the cash register receipt shows clearly that they may do so some day, as they've left room for charges.

Observation d. You can't "AD MILK" to coffee: they had to write it in.

Conjecture d_1: Per Observation b above, they do not plan to charge for milk in coffee, or:

Conjecture d_2: No one at corporate headquarters uses milk in coffee—they prefer cream, sit too long at their desks, have cholesterol problems, and die young, or:

Conjecture d_3: "AD MILK" was broken the day I was there.

Observation e. "AD" is the opposite of "NO." They even talk that way among themselves and to the customers. "Here's your Whopper, no mayo, ad onions, sir." They really do.

Observation f. 3040 is a large number. It's printed in red.

Conjecture f: Per a_1 and a_2, they economized by using numbers in these columns. The text translates as "Many thanks."

Observation g. Coffee is in a different category than hamburgers, as shown by the quantities appearing in different columns at the left of the ticket.

Conjecture g_1: It may not be possible to order 100 Whoppers, because there is no room to the left on the ticket to print the quantity.

Conjecture g_2: The columns shift right for multi-digit quantities. Ten coffees is the limit.

Observation h. I have no idea what "NV" means.

I've finished my "WHOPER," and have no interest in ordering even ten more. Science be damned.

INTERFERENCE OF LABIUM SUPERIUS ORIS HAIR WITH SPHERICAL ICE CREAM SURFACES

A Theoretical Analysis

Dinesh Mohan
Engineering Department
University of Michigan
Ann Arbor, Michigan

Ever since the appearance of ice cream in spherical configurations a large number of men have been battling with the upper-lip-hair-ice cream-interaction-phenomenon. Researchers have documented[1] cases of psychological disturbances causing feelings of depression and fear of rejection by peer groups as a result of this "phenomenon." More important is the fact that this causes inefficient utilization of energy in the restoration of contaminated hair and economic losses in terms of soiled handkerchiefs, shirt-cuffs, Kleenex, etc. Accurate scientific information is deplorably lacking in this area and it will require years for any quantitative and meaningful analysis to be made. We report here a first attempt at the definition of the problem in precise terms and have suggested possible approaches that other investigations may use.

The following analysis establishes an equation which may be used to define a locus for a mustache

DAVID COULSON

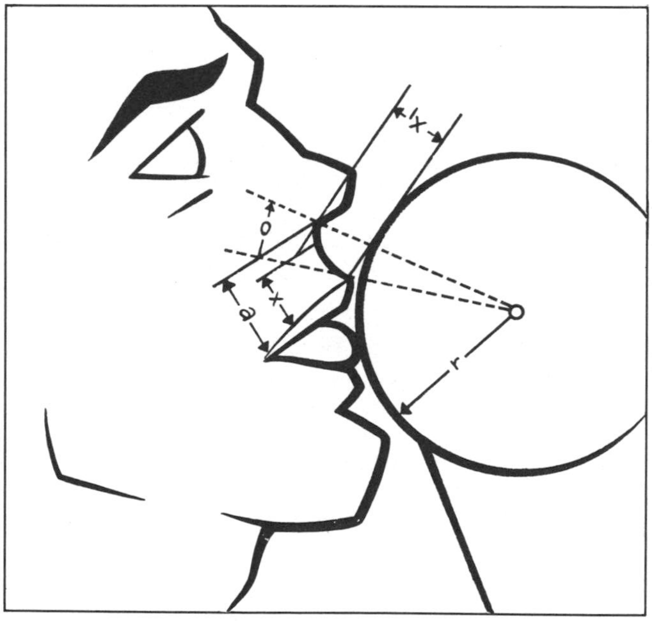

Fig. 1. Constants necessary to calculate optimal mustache profile.

profile, optimizing it for a person's lip size, ice cream flavor and radius of curvature of ice cream surface. These loci may be used to manufacture templates which can be used by individuals or barbers.

Assumptions

1. The labium oris deforms by a maximum of 10% on contact.

2. Ice cream surface is spherical.

[1] Labii, I. M., et al. "Psychological Trauma Resulting from Labium Oris Pilus Contamination." *Int. J. Lip Ser.*, 13:8345, April 1901.

3. No turbulence caused by hyperventilation.

4. Consumption of ice cream results in an increase in the radius of curvature with the surface remaining spherical.

5. Labium superius oris has a straight surface.

The radius of curvature of the ice cream surface may be expressed as:

$$r = \Phi(\Delta T, F, t, R) \qquad (1)$$

where:

r is the radius of curvature at time t after the initial formation of the surface,

ΔT is the ice cream and ambient temp. difference,

F is the ice cream flavor factor,

R is the radius at time $t = 0$.

Taking a point distance from the lower edge of the upper lip length we can define an optimum hair length "l_x" at time $t = 0$ such that

$$(x\sin\theta)^2 + (R + x\cos\theta)^2 = (R + l_x)^2 \qquad (2)$$

or

$$x(x + 2R\cos\theta) = l_x(l_x + R) \qquad (3)$$

Equation (3) can now be used to plot l_x vs x from x = 0 to x = a and hence obtain a mustache profile given a particular brand of ice cream and the necessary constants (Fig. 1). Alternatively an estimate of θ may be obtained to determine lip rotation velocity. All kinds of mustache designs can be optimized if r is used instead of R in the above equation.

An important aspect of this investigation was the determination of the probability function for mustache-ice cream interference as a function of time. Fig. 2 shows this for an individual (137 lbs., 5′ 9″, 24.6 yrs.)

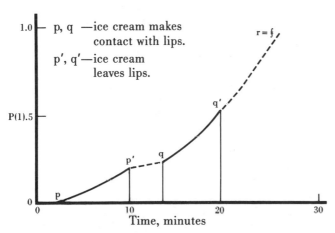

Fig. 2. Probability of Interference vs. time

Depressing: Mustache-ice cream interference.

eating a butter crunch pecan ice cream cone (surface radius .7″) when $\Delta T = 35°$ C.

In the absence of reliable anthropometric data, a more extensive analysis is really not possible. Our group is continuing its investigation with ever-increasing vigor and we expect to come up with some far reaching analyses.

Effectiveness of the design may be measured by the Physiological Advantage of No Interference Criterion (PANIC) Index:

$$\text{PANIC Index} = \frac{\text{Oxygen uptake in absence of interference}}{\text{Oxygen uptake in presence of interference}}$$

A numerical analysis of this problem is beyond the scope of this paper. However, other investigators are encouraged to look into the following areas of interest:

1. Training of orbicularis oris proper to minimize accidental interference.

2. Vascular changes in superior labial artery during interference.

3. Infra orbital nerve activity during interference.

4. Anthropometric measurements of 'a' and 'θ.'

5. Establishment of equation (1) for all brands and flavors of ice cream.

EVOLUTION OF SCIENTIFIC THOUGHT

Frank Anderson
Miami, Florida

Prof. Ludwig Botchall
Dept. Of Geophysics
Tifton University
March 20, 1971

Prof. Karl Von Vettkrotch
Dept. Of Geology
Pfledering Institute

Dear Karl,

Since my new grant I've been researching a method of controlling seasons via population selection and I'm forwarding this theory for your perusal and in hopes that you may have some suggestions.

It appeared to me as if from a dream that if one could elicit the cooperation of the world's total population for a mere few minutes one could control the earth's rotational velocity. I propose having everyone face in the opposite direction of the earth's rotation and at the same precise moment all run at top speed for five minutes. This would slow the earth's rotational speed by a factor TP^x (X being the frictional force average/individual and TP as total population).

How does this sound to you?

Your friend,
Prof. Ludwig Botchall

Prof. Karl Von Vettkrotch
Dept. Of Geology
Pfledering Institute
April 14, 1971

Prof. Ludwig Botchall
Dept. Of Geophysics
Tifton University

Dear Lud,

In answer to your letter dated March 20, 1971, I played with that theory several years ago as a means of avoiding daylight-savings time and I met a few stumbling blocks. (1) It seems that the mainland of Communist China would slam into California and the Chinese population would end up in the ocean as their continent slipped out from under them. (Not a bad idea though if you could get them to cooperate blindly). (2) Tidal upheavals would be immense. (3) Linearity would be difficult due to population distribution factors.

Have you considered these factors?

Karl Vettkrotch

Prof. Ludwig Botchall
Dept. Of Geophysics
Tifton University
April 17, 1971

Prof. Karl Von Vettkrotch
Dept. Of Geology
Pfledering Institute

Dear Karl,

By gosh you're right. You never cease to amaze me with your overall grasp, and you led me to consider some other ramifications. I feel that the proper mathematical computations of continent mass/total population would allow one to control the coefficient of frictional force necessary to effect rotational lag without continental shifting (although your China postulate sounds exciting). It's apparent that this frictional coefficient would vary with variation in land mass and population. Our computer here is on the blink again. Can you help?

Ludwig Botchall

Prof. Karl Von Vettkrotch
Dept. Of Geology
Pfledering Institute
May 19, 1971

Prof. Ludwig Botchall
Dept. Of Geophysics
Tifton University

Dear Lud,

Sorry to take so long but our computer was tied up with end of the month billings and I just finished my run. I have really lost interest in the climate control theory but I've become overwhelmed with the possibility of rejoining the continents into the original. When deriving your computations I came across some data on earth spin energies and the results are frightening. I came up with the following calculations for defining the differential rotational inertia of a continent:

(ΔI)

$$\Delta I = \iiint \Delta O \, R^4 \, (\sin \phi - \sin^3 \phi \, \cos^2 \theta) dR d\phi \, d\theta \, (\pm) \, p^f$$

Where ΔO = density contrast between adjacent continental crustal and oceanic layers:

R = continental Radius

ϕ = longitude

θ = latitude

$(\pm)p^f$ = population friction and is negative or positive depending on direction population is running

Integration would lead to two factors:

1. $(1.59 \times 10^{39} \, CM^2)$ depending on shape of crustal layer.

2. A $\pi/3$ function relative to hemispherical size.

The factor (p^f) could become a constant (k) by controlling population friction. This could be accomplished by having all participants wear golf shoes to minimize frictional differences caused by terrain.

Lud, I'm personally fearful of this experiment. My calculations show that the continents would definitely rejoin with a force equal to 2×10^7 earthquakes and would back us up to the triassic period in geological time. I'm not sure I would care to go back that far even if I did survive the earthquake forces.

I prefer to abandon the experiment and respectfully suggest that you do the same.

Karl Von Vettkrotch

P.S. My present worry is that all the "junk" we're leaving on the moon is going to alter its polar function. We as scientists should insist that NASA make some effort to distribute it more evenly.

RAYMOND SMITH'S STORY

Dr. Kurt W. Rothschild
Institut für Volkswirtschaftslehre und politik
Linz-Auhof, Austria

Raymond Smith, the well-known economist and econometrician, had lost his job and had to look for a new one.

He remembered that his old friend Freddie Cox held a very high post in the police establishment. He went to see Cox. "Look here, Freddie," he said, "I have been trained to be a problem-solving animal, finding out the remote causes of observed facts. I suppose this could be useful in your crime department. I should like to work for you." "Fine," said Freddie Cox.

Smith was at once asked to solve the important case of Betty Harper, the young widow who had been found brutally murdered in her flat. There was general agreement among neighbors and others that the murder had been committed either by Mr. L. or by Mr. R., both of whom had been ardent lovers of the late Mrs. Harper.

A Double Affair

Smith was not very happy about this narrowing down of the variables to be considered, but he accepted this limitation. The obvious thing to do in this case study seemed to him an application of the method of direct interrogation. He knew, of course, that answers to questionnaires were often drawn up hastily and thus not very reliable. In such an important case personal interviews would seem more appropriate. Fortunately, there was a trained interviewer available, called "The Judge," who had already talked extensively with the two men. Both of them had answered again and again "No" to the question whether they had murdered Mrs. Harper. On the basis of this evidence Smith was inclined to regard the case as closed. A conscientious interview program had given a clear result. There was not a single non-respondent! The murderer would have to be found elsewhere.

However, he was told that this would not do and that he should continue to work on the hypothesis that Mr. L. or Mr. R. was guilty. In particular, his attention was called to the fact that while both men had been very jealous in view of Mrs. Harper's double affair, it was Mr. R. who had repeatedly and openly declared in wild tones that he would no longer stand up to this and that he would do something about it. Mr. L. had also been grieved about the situation but had not shown any strong emotions. This was regarded as a strong indication that Mr. R. might be the culprit.

Smith decided to use more objective and reliable methods. He had found out from neighbors that both men had visited Mrs. Harper irregularly and that the visits had been spread over the whole week. But there had been a tendency for Mr. L. to concentrate on Thursdays, while Mr. R.'s principal visiting day was Saturday. The murder had taken place on a Tuesday.

The Eight Percent Solution

Smith now proceeded as follows. He made the not unreasonable assumption that both men always tried to come on "their" day, but probably chose another day when they were unable to keep that date. In the latter case it was most likely that they would come the day before or after. Only if these dates were also unsuited would they choose a more remote day. It seemed, therefore, justified to assume that the frequency of visits per day of the week was normally distributed with the "normal" visiting day of each of the two men as the mean day. Some additional information which he obtained from nosy neighbors reinforced him in this assumption. This sample information also helped him to estimate the variances of his frequency distributions. On the basis of this model he finally calculated that there was an 8% probability that Mr. L. had visited Mrs. Harper on a Tuesday, but only a 3% probability for a visit by Mr. R. The difference between these two percentages was highly significant.

"I have solved the case," said Smith when he entered Cox's office, "Mr. L. is the murderer." He explained why he regarded this conclusion as the best available hypothesis. "You are fired," said Cox.

BRANCHING AND SPROUTING*

Effects of Selective Sunlight Deprivation

O. A. Selnes**

Departments of Forestry and Histopathology
University of Fortchester
Fortchester, New York

H. A. Whitaker

Department of Neurophilology
University of Fortchester
Fortchester, New York

It has been established that the development of the brain may be influenced by a number of factors, such as one's occupation,[1] nutritional intake[2] and environment.[3] The latter influences seem to be of particular importance for the growth and functional differentiation of the cells in the cerebral cortex, in particular their dendritic structure. Evidence for this comes from ingenious experiments involving selective deprivation of sensory input to defenseless little animals, most commonly the cat *(Felix Domesticus)*.[4] The latest statistics from the AAPCRA (American Association for Prevention of Cruelty to Research Animals) indicate that an average of three out of ten research kittens become blind as a result of deliberate tampering with their visual environment.

In light of the impending energy crisis, however, this line of research, inanimal though as it may be, has become highly relevant, as the Federal Government has deemed it necessary to determine the absolute minimum light level which can be used throughout schools, hospitals and other similar institutions, without incurring noticeable changes in the visual cortex of the individuals spending most of their time in these institutions.

The present research project is concerned with possible morphological effects of sun deprivation in a somewhat robust organism, the *Arbor Erectus*, (Fig. 1) and was carried out in anticipation of the President's plans of ordering the sun[5] to cut down on its energy expenditure. Unpublished data from the local Weather bureau strongly suggest that the CIA has been performing tests, in selected regions of the United States, for some time already in order to evaluate possible effects of reduced number of hours of sunshine per day. (In the spring of 1975, Upstate New York experienced a total of 162 consecutive days without any sunshine.)

Fig. 1. General morphology of Arbor Erectus. *Note the striking resemblance with a cortical dendritic field, particularly if the picture is turned upside down.*

*The conclusions of this study were lavishly supported by Grant W-In 1-234673 from the President's Committee for Conservation of Energy.

**The opinions expressed in this paper do not necessarily reflect the general level of intelligence of the authors, or the general lack of policy on behalf of our supporters.

[1] Millhaus, N. "Morphological Peculiarities of the Brains of Six Eminent Politicians." *S. African J. Pathology & Ideology*, 24:3–29, 1974.

[2] Scoop, P. "A Rare Case of Ice-cream in the Lateral Ventricles." *Proc. Bulg. Assoc. Higher Mental Funct.*, 47:543–549, 1959.

[3] Hansen, F. "The Brain of the Polar Bear." *Acta Climatologica Physiologica*, 23:79–84, 1912.

[4] Hubble, T. and M. Diesel "Blind as a Bat." *J. Optical Illusions*, 13:240–56, 1964.

[5] Light-emitting circular disc known to appear in the sky during day time, frequently seen in Florida and California.

Materials and Methods

Two healthy looking specimens of *Arbor Erectus* were selected, and transplanted, according to the directions provided by Holst,[6] one to a sunny spot, and the other to a shadowy spot. The amount of exposure to sunlight was determined by random measurements with a Pikon Type 2 light meter. The data obtained were averaged through a diffusion screen, and subsequently correlated with the daily weather reports (r .81).

By the time the specimen on the sunny side had received 95% more exposure to sunshine than the one on the shadowy side (two months, three days), both specimens were photographed with an SLP pinhole camera from three different angles, and *camera lucia* drawings made from the photomacrographs (Fig. 3a and b) (Fig. 2 was unfortunately lost in the darkroom, but a search has been initiated, and the findings will be the subject of a forthcoming publication).

A   B

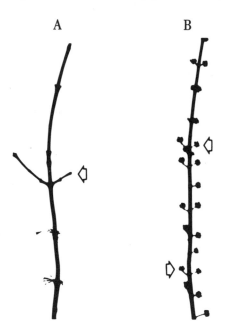

Fig. 3. (a.) Fine structure of a branch of the specimen of Arbor Erectus *exposed to sunlight. Note the overall sparsity of normal spine-like twigs, and the elongated, hypertrophied twigs. Part b shows the fine structure of a branch from the light-deprived specimen. Note the abundance of regularly spaced, healthy looking spine-like twigs. (Camera lucia drawings, slightly demagnified.)*

Results

The results from this study are unusually clear and unambiguous. It is clear from even a cursory inspection of the *camera lucia* drawings that the specimen on the sunny side shows retarded growth (Fig. 3a). The few spine-like twigs are thin and elongated (hypertrophied), and none of the healthy looking mushroom shaped or stubby spine-like twigs present in the sun-deprived specimen can be seen. Since these findings were somewhat surprising, the probabilities that the two photomacrographs might have become switched in the darkroom were computed. The resulting p .5 does not allow any inferences about this possibility, however, and a lie-detector test of the photo-lab technician was also negative. We are therefore led to conclude that sun deprivation has definite beneficial effects on the growth and development of *Arbor Erectus*.

Discussion

It is clear that our findings necessitate a reinterpretation of previous studies of light deprivation in animals. There are two possible explanations for the lack of agreement between these findings and our results. First of all, most of the animal studies have looked at a large number of cortical cells, and the possibility therefore exists that the results and their interpretation are confounded by intricate statistical procedures. Our sample size of N = 1 for each group obviously avoids these problems.[7] Secondly, and more importantly, the behavioral defects observed in animals following prolonged light deprivation are most probably artifactual, i.e. resulting from the fact that the animals have been tested in a bright rather than a dark environment. We therefore suggest that the earlier animal studies be reconsidered in light of these methodological considerations.

Support for our findings that deprivation of sunlight enhances the growth and development of trees and plants may be derived from reports on the vegetation in areas rich in sunlight[8] and from reports from people working in environments with high light levels. General adverse reactions like headaches, pupillary constriction and fasicullations of the eyelids have frequently been reported. These reports strongly testify to the overall validity of our findings that a decrease in light levels throughout the United States may have beneficial effects.

[6] Holst, A. *Handbuch der Tannenbaumheilkunde.* 154:2314 ff. Heidelberg: Runner Verlag, 1951.

[7] Square, C. and T. Student. *Deceptional Statistics.* New York: Distributional Publ. Comp., 1965.

[8] Sam, U. *How to Make Your Garden Look Better with a Plastic Lawn.* Rio de Janeiro: Sunshine Publ. Comp., 1967.

A DRASTIC COST SAVING APPROACH TO USING YOUR NEIGHBOR'S ELECTRON MICROSCOPE*

Aalbert Heine

The fine picture (right) may constitute a breakthrough in scientific research. We have used the amazing circumstance that all photographs made with an electronic microscope look exactly identical.

With the prices of these scopes skyrocketing, enormous savings can be made simply by borrowing a photograph and using it in any kind of research in any field. Grants and designated funds earmarked for an electron-scope can then be diverted to the acquisition of licorice or other essentials.

We at the Museum have now been using the same picture for five years. It has resulted in two substantial increases in the operating budget, one unnecessary appendectomy, three unscheduled salary raises and a sizable grant for investigating possible differences in taste between fried bay shrimp and gulf shrimp.

Fig. 1: *A eutectic mixture of quartz and plagioclase. The phenocrysts of the feldspar show a typical alpha structure (right center). 3000 ×*

*Another contribution to Science by the staff of the Corpus Christi Museum in Texas.

Fig. 2: A cross section through the skin of a peripatus. The sebaceous glands shown have atrophied indicating insipid senile degeneration so typical for the genus. 6000 ×

Fig. 4: Fragment of a hickory ax handle. The micro scars resulting from machine tooling (upper left) are causing a progressing fatigue in the wood fibers, a dangerous condition previously never suspected. 1000 ×

Fig. 3: The surface of a root hair of a quadruploid species of crabgrass. The osmotic pressure, caused by excessive salinity, has enlarged the chloroblasts to unusual size. A condition which may ultimately prove fatal to the plant. 4000 ×

EFFECT OF LEFT-RIGHT INVERSION UPON THE SIZE-WEIGHT ILLUSION

Clair Schulz

Previous investigators have dealt with the problems of size constancy, form constancy, and cerebral dominance in regard to handedness. None of these studies pertain to the present investigation.

Lemke[1] has shown that mediation is a probable occurrence in preschool children providing the children are eight years old or older. The study also indicates that the children under three years of age tend to transpose intermediate-size objects and their mothers.

Gile[2] found visual cues to differ significantly from the age of the experimenter. On both the near and far tests the investigator found that children tended to use their eyes in discriminating between the lamp and the automobile. It appears that the differences in depth between the test objects was related to the intelligence of the subjects.

Johnson[3] and Aaron[4] have found that the effects of maternal dependency are significantly related to the frequency of erasures on an essay test. The former investigator found that younger children tend to erase more with their right hand. Aaron found significant differences between boys who wrote about zebras and the girls who wrote about washroom graffiti.

Mercy et al.[5] have found that younger children tend to use color more often than form when being chased by a rabid dog. Girls tended to scream more loudly and bleed faster than boys. Et et al.[6] found no statistically significant color-form or sex differences. They did find, however, that the dog salivated whenever a bell was sounded in the presence of a scared child.

Gile has stressed his theory of Diffuse Quality of Perceptual Regression in neonates throughout his research. It is Gile's belief that there are three stages of development in childhood. The first he has called "Locomotor Resonance." It is in this stage that a child first begins to locomote and resonate. The second stage ("Resonating Locomotion") involves a refinement of the first responses. In late childhood the third stage, Somata Resolution, develops. The final stage requires that a child be able to conceptualize the difference between the first two stages. The present investigation tests this theory in relation to perception.

Method

Subjects. The subjects were eighty children, ages three through ten (mean age 67.3 months) randomly selected from private schools, reform schools, nursery schools, and mental hospitals. Each age group had ten subjects and their mean IQ was 82.6. Switchblade proficiency tests were given to the reform school subjects and all reached criterion. Only sixteen girls completed the experiment. This may have been due to their participation as subjects in the switchblade proficiency tests. Five subjects in each age group were placed in the experimental group and the other five were placed in the control group.

Apparatus. The experiment was conducted in a semi-illuminated room, 8 by 120 feet, in which the windows and the ceiling were covered with green paper. The walls were covered with red paper because the experiment was conducted near Christmas. The subject was instructed to lie down on a couch and to look at the

[1] Lemke, Q. "The Middle-Sized Problem in the Oversized Family." *Studies in Iraq Review,* XC:32–41, 1977.
[2] Gile, D.C. *Theories to Test Children By.* New York: The Experimental Press, 1972.
[3] Johnson, A.C. "Oedipus Rex, the Essay." *American Journal of Experimental Relationships,* XXXIII:338–345, 1978.
[4] Aaron, A.A. "Overlearning and the Zebra Phenomenon." *Siempre Quarterly,* XL:137–142, 1973.
[5] Mercy, R., Less, D., and Lee, F. "Trust as a Function of Fear." *Child Regression,* LXXVI:475–483, 1976.
[6] Et, A.L., Tu, E.T., and Brute, J.C. "The Rapid Rabid Dog Syndrome." *The Biloxi Bulletin,* XLV:209–216, 1975.

stimuli from an upside-down position. The standard stimuli consisted of two black squares (sides 3 cm.) and a turquoise equilateral triangle (sides 10 cm.) which were placed against a white background ten meters away from the subject. The comparison stimuli consisted of a white square which was the same size as the standard stimuli squares. The comparison stimuli were placed against a white background and twenty meters away from the subject. The investigator wore a shirt with black equal area trapezoids imprinted against a white background. He placed himself midway between the comparison and standard stimuli. A mobile containing six blue circles (diameter 8 cm.) was suspended midway between the subject and the investigator. Candied kumquats were given as reinforcement.

Procedure

Each subject was instructed to look at the stimuli from an upside-down position while on the couch. The subjects were instructed to tell whether the comparison stimuli square was larger than, smaller than, or the same size as the standard stimuli. If the subjects said it was smaller than the standard stimuli, they were asked to compare it to the trapezoids on the investigator's shirt. If they said that it was larger than the standard stimuli, they were instructed to compare it to the circles suspended from the ceiling. If they said that the stimuli were the same size, they were told to compare the trapezoids with the circles. If any complained that they could not see the comparison stimuli because of the white background, they were hit across the side of the head, given a good shaking, and told not to be a wise guy. The subjects were instructed to report any left-right changes that occurred. Each child in the experimental group was instructed to remove the left shoe when viewing the objects with the left eye alone and the right shoe when viewing the object solely with the right eye. The mastery criterion was six correct responses out of eighty trials. Five trials were held

THE SOMETHING'S FISHY DEPT.

On 4 January 1971 Mr. F. J. P. Kellor shot with a .308 rifle an adult broadbilled swordfish *Xiphias gladius* Linnaeus, in Wairangi Bay.... On examination, the swordfish showed no external signs of injury.

—Webb, B. F. "Broadbilled Swordfish from Tasman Bay, New Zealand," N. Z. J. of Marine & Freshwater Res. Vol. 6, Nos. 1 and 2, 1972.

every Tuesday for sixteen weeks. Three of the children failed to reach criterion even after eighty trials and were excluded from the study because they were color-blind.

Results

The judgments of the students are given in Table 1.

Table 1

Age	Distance	Constancy Error (Both eyes)	Constancy Error (left eye, left shoe)	Constancy Error (right eye, right shoe)
3	10 m.	.68	.99	.09
4	10 m.	.32	.90	.42
5	10 m.	.73	.62	.31
6	10 m.	.82	.22	.86
7	10 m.	.29	.33	.71
8	10 m.	.71	.81	.32
9	10 m.	.40	.10	.61
10	10 m.	.63	.61	.42

The findings show conclusively that there is a constant error at each age level. They also show that there is a tendency for footedness to be related to perception. When one eye was closed and the opposite shoe removed, the subject viewed the stimuli with the open eye.

The reliability of the variants is shown in Table 2.

Table 2

	df	M.S.	F.P.	p	O	Q
Age	3	2.21	6.01	$\geq .10$	1	1.92
Size	4	.67	1.62	$\leq .05$	9	2.61
Age × Size	12	.086	.19		1	1.93

Significant differences were found between the size of the investigator's shirt and frequency of correct responses ($p < .05$). No significant sex differences were found, but the girls tended to fall off the couch on their heads more often than boys. The eight-year-old boys were more accurate than all age groups ($p < .01$, $z < .09$) when the investigator was standing with his arms crossed. The experimental group significantly differed from the control group both in the accuracy of responses ($p < .005$) and in the number of days since they washed their feet ($u < .001$).

Discussion

The results illustrate clear evidence that the ability to remove one's shoe increases with age. The three year olds had little trouble removing their shoes, but experi-

Subjects were asked to discriminate shapes from an upside-down position.

DAVID COULSON

enced difficulty tying them. This is probably due to cultural learning, although data seem to indicate the opposite effect.

The results in this experiment follow the tenets of Gile's theory. It appears that as children grow older they tend to develop new perceptual fields in relation to shirt size and Christmas colors. Older children who are placed upside-down tend to discriminate between stimuli and develop headaches faster than the younger children.

Several problems were presented in the choice of subjects. The reform school children were extremely recalcitrant and impractical. The investigator remembers one youth who suggested an unrealistic relocation for the apparatus. The children from the mental hospital also presented a problem. The geometric concepts of the figures used in the experiment had to be explained to most of these children. This was not as discouraging as their apparent inability to distinguish between the experimenter and the mobile.

Summary

Judgments were then made between comparison,

METRIC TIME

This is to advise you that the Cabinet has decided that, from midnight on January 1st, 1983, the whole Country will be converting to metric time. This is, of course, another step in the Metrication Program.

From that date there will be 10 seconds to the minute, 10 minutes to the hour, 10 hours to the day, and so on, delineated according to the following table:

Old Time	New Time English	French
1 second	1 milliday	1 millijour
1 minute	1 centiday	1 centijour
1 hour	1 deciday (or millimonth)	1 decijour
1 day	1 day	1 jour
1 week	1 decaday	1 decajour
1 month	1 hectoday	1 hectojour
1 year	1 kiloday	1 kilojour

The fortnight will be withdrawn

We are informed by Metric Commission Canada that further details will be forthcoming, but some preliminary guidelines are now available and steps should be instituted immediately, through the appropriate Faculty and Departmental Committees, to develop plans for the changeover.

Courses which at present occupy 1 (old) hour, would by direct transposition last $^{24}/_{10}$ of a deciday. Since this may well be confusing, they will thus be adjusted to become ½ a deciday, or as they will popularly be called, a demideciday. The demideciday represents 1.2 of an old hour. Professors are thus urged to talk more slowly in order to fill the time. The office on Education Instruction will soon announce short courses on how this is to be done effectively.

standard, and two other stimuli from eighty children. It was found that the children tended to verbalize their responses better as they grew older. Some of the younger chidren's responses consisted mostly of slobbering and mumbling which were assumed to mean correct choices. Two of the three-year-olds were found to be candied kumquat fiends and their responses were omitted from the study. All of the children reached criterion within eighty trials and most achieved it within forty trials. Therefore, the assumption can be made that the children learned the inversion. The only aftereffect of the experiment seems to be that some of the students insist upon answering questions at school in an upside-down position. Removal of the kumquat reinforcement should extinguish this behavior.

COGITO ERGO SUM: MURPHY'S REFUTATION OF DESCARTES

N. L. Morgenstern, M.D.
Kaiser-Permanente Medical Center
Oakland, California

Rene Descartes' catchy slogan, "I think, therefore I am," has somehow gained a reputation as an important insight. Its superficiality was first recognized by his contemporary, Edsall Murphy. It is regrettable that the fallacious ideas of Descartes have become well known, while Murphy's have sunk into obscurity. It is my hope, in this paper, to put the two into proper perspective.

Murphy himself seems to have been a somewhat elusive figure. According to Haber,[1] he was born by a breech delivery early in the fifteenth century. However, our evidence clearly places him as a contemporary of Descartes (1596–1650). Possibly there were two Edsall Murphys. One or the other of them is nowadays best known for Murphy's Law which, readers are reminded, in its simplest form states that if anything can go wrong, it will.

Murphy, like many other well-known figures of the day, had a nickname. Thomas Aquinas was known as "The Ox" because of his large size and slow speech, Murphy has gone down in history as "The Horse."

The Argument

"I think, therefore I am" sounds so impressive that it carries conviction. Murphy recognized it as a syllogism with an unstated major premise.

Major Premise: A non-existent object cannot think.

Minor Premise: I think

Conclusion: Therefore, I am.

When put this way, Descartes' slogan is obviously trivial, said Murphy. Compare with,

"I weigh 170 pounds, therefore I am."

Since nothing useful is to be found at this level, Murphy tried to search deeper. Descartes was apparently trying to answer the question, "How do I know that I exist?" To this, "Cogito, ergo sum" isn't a bad reply, although it will not withstand critical examination.

After all, if I seriously doubt my existence, must I not also doubt my thinking? To put it another way:

Q: How can you be sure that you exist?
A: I think.
Q: How can you be sure you are thinking?
A: I can't, but I do think that I think.
Q: Does that make you sure that you exist?
A: I think so.

This should make it clear that Descartes went too far. He ought to have said:

"I think I think, therefore I am."
or possibly,
"I think I think, therefore I think I am, I think."

To "The Horse," even such watered-down versions were unacceptable. This important proto-Existential philosopher contended that, from a humanistic point of view, you do not really exist unless others are aware of your existence. Murphy proclaimed,

"I stink, therefore I am."

The Dispute

In typical scholastic fashion, there were acrimonious exchanges between the followers of Descartes and Murphy. The Murphyites accused their opponents of putting Descartes before the Horse. On the other hand, Murphy's modest disclaimer of mathematical skill, "I don't know math from a hole in the ground," was used against him by the Cartesians.

Summary

I trust that this exposition will help to rehabilitate Edsall Murphy and to reaffirm his important influence.

[1] Haber, S. "Laboratory Halforisms." *Path. Ann.* 7:345, 1972.

THE FEEDING HABITS OF MOSQUITOES ON RABBITS

The Influence of Hydrogen Repellents On the Genetic Determination

Michael Bar-Kev-Keves
Israel Substitute for Entomological Research

It has been long known that some insect repellents have a repelling effect on mosquitoes.[1] These substances were, therefore, widely used in tropical and semitropical areas by civilians and military personnel, who did not possess sufficient olfactory acuity to make the substance repellent to themselves.

In view of the fact that most of the commercially available repellents have a large part of their molecular volume occupied by hydrogen,* it was desirable to test the repelling effects of hydrogen itself on mosquitoes, as well as to find whether the feeding habits developed by such repelled mosquitoes (the frustration complex) would be genetically fixed.

Methods

A solution of hydrogen was injected intravenously into a series of rabbits, which were being prepared as a substrate for the mosquitoes. Live animals rather than artificial membranes were used since anyway "special defeathered or defurred young bird or animal skins have to be used for successful blood feeding. They

---

[1] King, W. F. *Resistance Studies.* 1: 83–89, Burgess Publ. Co., 1958.
*Chlorohydrocarbons.

THE IN-THE-LONG-RUN DEPT.

"The force exerted by the human hand in a food squeezing test is partly dependent upon the person making the test and partly on the softness of the food according to recently published research. Force distance curves were plotted for firm and flabby apples squeezed by a testing machine. The firm apple provided a fairly steep curve disclosing that it does not deform very much when it is squeezed. The flabby apple gave a curve with a much greater slope at first indicating deformation to a considerable extent. However, as the force continued to rise, the shape of the curve obtained from the flabby apple gradually approximated the shape obtained from the firm apple. Similar results were obtained with jumbo-size marshmallows. The studies led researchers to the conclusion that gently squeezing is a superior means of testing quality. However, whether firmness is a desirable or undesirable characteristic depends upon the food being squeezed."

—Bourne, M. C., "Squeeze Engineering," *Washington Science Trends, Vol. 8, No. 8, May 22, 1967.*

---

must be prepared by the investigator and cannot be purchased commercially."[2]

At this stage of hydrogenation of the rabbits a surprising phenomenon was observed: the injected rabbits developed negative gravity and tended to collect under the ceiling of the laboratory. This phenomenon was studied elsewhere in a mathematical study by Wolyniec[3] and a formula was developed:

$$\lim(R + H) = Ce$$

where R represents rabbits, H hydrogen, Ce ceiling or

---

[2] Fisk, F. W. "Feeding and Drinking Methods." *Resistance Studies,* 1:114, Burgess Publ. Co., 1959.
[3] Wolyniec, G. "Mathematical and Statistical Interpretation of Negative Gravity I. Floating of Hydrogenated Rabbits." *J. Irrepr. Statistics,* 3:10, 1958.

any other horizontal impermeable surface above the rabbit.

Since we were not interested in rabbits but in mosquitoes, and did not want to embark upon teleological experimentation, the phenomenon of negative gravity was not pursued any further.

In all successive experiments the rabbits were simply securely tied to tables before the injection of hydrogen. The problem of introducing a sufficient quantity of hydrogen into the blood circulation of the experimental animals was solved by injecting first an aqueous suspension of micronized zinc into the ear vein, and following this after a few minutes by injection of concentrated hydrochloric acid into the vein of the second ear. The buffering capacity of blood versus the acid was measured beforehand and the amount of acid injected was sufficient to produce the desired generation of hydrogen.* The exceptional rabbits that survived this treatment (hereafter called hydrogenated rabbits) had a satisfactory saturation of blood with hydrogen.

Mosquitoes. The breeding and the genetical selection of mosquitoes was done by the method of Maire Yassat and O. Sex.[4]

Results

Carefully numbered mosquitoes were anaesthetized by CO_2, whereupon their palpi and antennae were surgically removed. As soon as the mosquitoes woke up from their anaesthesia and resumed normal activities, they were introduced into the cage containing hydrogenated rabbits. Undamaged mosquitoes served as controls. Table 1 shows the results of a typical experiment.

Table 1

Feeding of Normal and Antenna-less Mosquitoes on Hydrogenated Rabbits

	Total Number Used	Number Feeding on Hydro-Rabbits	Number Feeding on Normal Mosquitoes
Normal mosquitoes	100	44	99**
Antenna-less mosquitoes	100	28	31

[4] Yassat, Maire and Sex, O. "Fingerprinting as Means of Determination of Genetic Identity of *Culex* and *Anopheles* in Middle East and in Africa" (not to be published).

* No representative of the Society for Prevention of Cruelty to Animals was permitted to be present in the lab during this stage of preparation.

** The remaining mosquito, which did not feed, was found to be a male. This male was inadvertently included in the batch of females by one of the technicians, who was under a self-treatment with saccharomycetin (C_2H_5OH).

PAPER CHORMATOGRAPHY

Ralph A. Lewin
Scripps Insistution of Oceanography,
La Jolla, California

In these days of neo-classical renaissance, when it seems that everyone above the rank of labroatory assistant is "charismatic" and every insistution beyond the junior college level is "prestigious," we should not fail to note the grwoth of what may be called "paper chormatography" (from the mythical Greek: "*chorma*," gen. "*chormatos*," an inversion, and "*graphein*," to write). With the further limitation of research grants, and the general need for scientists to type their laboratory reprots themselves, chormatographic phenomena will undoubtedly become more and more evident as time goes on.

I first became aware of the phenomenon when I was typing the penult;mate draft of my thesis on the genetics of *Chalmydomonas*. I wasted a lot of time, back-spacing over the third and fourth letters, or erasing them, and then carefully retyping the word "*Chalmydomonas*," before I realized what was going on and capitulated to what is clearly a force of nature. I am sure that all biochemists who have used slat gradients to elute unknown substances from columns will know what I mean. My brother-in-law Gerlad, a mathematician, has had the same trouble with calaculus.

We are planning a symposium on the grwoth of chormatography, to be held in this insistution some time in 1972. Will all those who wish to participate please contact: Ralph A. Lewin.

When antenna-less hydrogen-fed mosquitoes were introduced into a chamber containing oxygen and platinum sponge, they exploded. Normal mosquitoes did not show this effect. We attribute the explosion to leakage of hydrogen from the cut surface at the base of antenna.

A very interesting finding was obtained with the hydrogen-fed normal mosquitoes. They were shown to be able to communicate the information about the presence of hydrogen in a rabbit by a complicated movement of their antennae. This movement was cinematographically recorded through a stereoscopic microscope. Exposure of unfed mosquitoes to cinematic screen (suitably diminished) displaying these recorded movements was sufficient to prevent the viewers from approaching hydrogenated rabbits.

Summary

Hydrogenated rabbits are dangerous to mutilated mosquitoes and repellent to normal mosquitoes.

FINDING THE LOST CHORD

E. N. Gilbert

But I struck one chord of music,
Like the sound of a great Amen.
                    —A. A. PROCTER (1825–1864)

The *Lost Chord* is a song which was taught to most American public school students before the present generation. Sir Arthur Sullivan, of the famous team Gilbert[1] and Sullivan, composed the music.[2] The words are from a poem *A Lost Chord,* written years earlier by Adelaide Ann Procter.[3] Sullivan's musical version, *The Lost Chord,* was an immediate success, *Variety*[4] lists it among the eight smash hits of 1877, along with *In the Gloaming* and *Where Is My Wandering Boy Tonight.*

Taken literally, *A Lost Chord* relates how Miss Procter accidentally "struck one chord of music like the sound of a great Amen" and was too overcome to recall the notes. Because of the poem's mystical tone, it was thought to be a mere allegory until not so long ago when Jimmy Durante[5] produced what was unmistakably the same chord. He too was dumbfounded by his discovery and he promptly lost the chord again. But now the chord is known to exist and to have the remarkable properties which the poem describes.

Chords

One way to find the lost chord is to play chords systematically one at a time. Ultimately the lost chord will be played, and be recognized from Miss Procter's vivid description. Proceeding along these lines I first calculated how many different chords can be played on an eighty-eight note keyboard using two hands, each of which can span sixteen half-tones. There are about 7,400,000,000 chords, enough to discourage anyone

---

[1] The author claims no kinship to W. S. Gilbert.
[2] Sullivan, Sir Arthur Seymour. *The Lost Chord.* London: Boosey and Co., 1877.
[3] Procter, Adelaide Anne. *Legends and Lyrics.* London: Oxford Ed., 1914.
[4] Mattfeld, Julius. *Variety Music Cavalcade 1620–1969.* Englewood Cliffs: Prentice Hall, 1971.
[5] Durante, Jimmy. *I'm the Man Who Found the Lost Chord.* The author has heard Durante perform this work but is unable to supply a record number.

from an exhaustive search. In what follows, the number of chords which must be played is drastically reduced by recognizing certain equivalences between chords.

Transposition, i.e., changing the pitch of each note in a chord by the same fixed number of half-tones, is one equivalence. Transposing a chord merely produces a new chord which sounds like the old one played in a new key. *Inversion,* i.e., moving any number of notes up or down the scale by octave steps, is another equivalence. A major chord retains its special major quality no matter how it is inverted. The same is true of minor chords, 7th chords, etc. Surely Miss Procter's description of the lost chord will fit any chord obtained from the lost chord by transposition, inversion, or both. The 7,400,000,000 fall into a much smaller number of types of equivalent chords. Only inequivalent chords, one from each type, need be played.

By applying an inversion, any chord can be changed to an equivalent one having all its notes contained within a single octave, say A#233.1 to A440.0. Even allowing six fingers on each hand there are only $2^{12} = 4096$ of these chords in close harmony.[6] When transpositions and inversions are both allowed one can easily guess that the number of inequivalent chords must be around $2^{12}/12 = 341.3$. The correct

---

[6] Chords with 11 or 12 notes were considered in the interest of thoroughness. After all, W. A. Mozart is known to have composed a piano piece which can be played only by using the performer's nose as an eleventh digit.
[7] Gilbert, E. N. and Riordan, John. "Symmetry Types of Periodic Sequences." *Illinois J. Math.* 5:657–665, 1961.

number is a bit larger (352) because a few chords (diminished 7th chords, for example) generate fewer than twelve distinct chords when all twelve possible transpositions are applied to the basic octave. The correct enumeration appears in Table I, which shows how many inequivalent chords there are with N notes, $N = 0, 1, \ldots 12$. Gilbert and Riordan[7] give the mathematical details.

Table I

Enumeration of the 352 Inequivalent Chords by Number N of Notes

N	0	1	2	3	4	5	6	7	8	9	10	11	12
Chords	1	1	6	19	43	66	80	66	43	19	6	1	1

The Experiment

The chords were played in the manner of a psychophysical experiment which reproduced Miss Procter's conditions as closely as possible. Although the poem gives no construction details of her instrument, it does specify her state of mind as "weary and ill at ease" and the time of day as "twilight." Accordingly a panel of judges, consisting entirely of unmarried girls named Adelaide, met at the close of each working day to judge another chord type.

The chord was played on an organ especially designed for the experiment. It contained twelve neon bulbs, wired as relaxation oscillators in the manner of the trautonium (see Trautwein[8]), to generate twelve notes of the basic octave. The appropriate notes were switched on, amplified, and presented to the judges through hi-fi headphones. Each judge had a keyboard and allowed her fingers to wander idly over it. These keys did not alter the pitch of the notes (which remained constant throughout the session), but did control the amplifier gain, tremolo circuit, formant filters for tone coloration, and a fuzz box. This ensured that each judge would approximate the quality of Miss

[8] Trautwein, F. "Toneinsatz und Elektrische Musik." *Z. Tech. Physik* 13:244, 1932.

Procter's organ at least part of the time.

After sunset, each judge answered some standard questions which paraphrased lines of the poem. Typical questions were, "At any time did tonight's chord come from the soul of the organ and enter into yours?" and "Did it flood the crimson twilight like the close of an Angel's Psalm?" The answers were decidedly negative throughout the first 351 sessions. After that only one chord type remained; it was clear that it must be the one sought. Expecting the lost chord to be complicated we had begun with the chord containing all twelve notes; we had gradually worked our way through chords with fewer and fewer notes until now the only remaining chord was the one with no notes, silence. How could that be it?

Actually, pure silence is a great rarity. The quietest place available to us was an anechoic chamber. We held our last session there with the power plug to the test organ disconnected. Even there faint noises created a disturbance. One became aware of one's own heartbeat and of a white Gaussian noise caused by thermal fluctuations of the air molecules. Still the anechoic chamber is well nicknamed "the dead room"; the unusual quiet produces eerie sensations similar to those Miss Procter described in her poem.

Silence did not receive a perfect score. It failed to sound like "a great Amen" and it did not quite tremble "away into silence as though it were loth to cease." On other counts it scored high. "It lay on my fevered spirit with a touch of infinite calm." "It quieted pain and sorrow like love overcoming strife." "It seemed the harmonious echo from our discordant life." "It linked all perplexed meanings into one perfect peace." The last stanza is especially appropriate.

> *"It may be that Death's bright angel*
> *will speak in that chord again,—*
> *It may be that only in Heaven*
> *I shall hear that grand Amen."*

PART VI

ONE-MINUTE MISMANAGER

UNITED STATES ENVIRONMENTAL PROTECTION AGENCY
NATIONAL ENVIRONMENTAL RESEARCH CENTER
CINCINNATI, OHIO 45268

SUBJECT: Safety Hazards: Breen Building   DATE: March 12, 1974

FROM: N. A. Clarke

TO: Breen Building Staff

It has been brought to my attention by the Safety Officer at the Breen Building that a number of near serious accidents occurred at this facility yesterday afternoon. Specifically:

a. A bacteriologist (Commissioned Officer), working late on the afternoon of March 11, 1974, accidentally ingested a small volume of a broth culture of *E. coli*, (ATCC 10733-4).

b. A virologist (Commissioned Officer), working in the isolation trailer on the afternoon of March 11, 1974, accidentally dropped 143.61 ml of a suspension of attenuated Polio 1 virus on his shirt.

c. A chemist (Civil Servant), working in the mobile lab late on the afternoon of March 11, 1974, spilled approximately 600 ml of 0.05 N HCL onto his new Thom McAn shoes.

d. A bacteriologist (Civil Servant), working in the lab in the front of the building on the afternoon on March 11, 1974, spilled 403 ml of warm agar into his new, wide cuff, flare trousers.

e. A secretary (Civil Servant), while typing a detailed report on the afternoon of March 11, 1974, became so agitated that she hit several keys at once on her electric typewriter causing it to short circuit and trip a major circuit breaker supplying current to the autoclaves.

The Safety Officer enlisted the aid of our resident epidemiologist to determine the cause of these seemingly unrelated accidents.

When last seen, the epidemiologist was running as fast as he could around and around our building in pursuit of a middle-aged, white, non-mustached male, who was wearing *only* dirty sneakers, face mask, and Commander insignia on his shoulders.

It is the Safety Officer's conclusion that the sudden vision of this enlightened male streaking around a building dedicated to the pursuit of science caused the rash of accidents to occur on the afternoon of March 11, 1974.

I therefore solicit your assistance in apprehending this culprit so we can get on with our research and FY 75 Research Objective Achievement Plan (ROAP) preparation.

A PROBABILISTIC FORMULATION OF MURPHY DYNAMICS AS APPLIED TO THE ANALYSIS OF OPERATIONAL RESEARCH PROBLEMS

William R. Simpson
Center for Naval Analyses
Arlington, Virginia

Abstract

The author contends that the formulation of Murphy's Law as presently accepted in the open literature is useful only as a general statement of life patterns, but meaningless to the application of operational research problems. In fact, the direct application may be dangerously wrong. A more satisfactory statement is that if anything can go wrong, it might. This formulation not only better fits the facts of life, but can lend itself to a mathematical formulation that can be used in the analysis of operational research problems. Such a formulation is presented based on a probabilistic model of operational realizations. Numerous examples of direct application are cited.

Introduction

The classical formulation of Murphy's Law as proposed by Edsall Murphy* is as follows:

"If anything can go wrong it will."

This is an absolute statement of the transpiring events and is conditional only on possibility. The oft-cited example is that of the dropped jelly bread. Murphy's Law would state that the bread would always fall jelly side down. This, however, is in direct conflict with experimental data as extracted from reference 2 and shown in Table 1.

As shown in Table 1, Murphy's Law is only 88% correct. It is precisely this difference that causes the problem in operational research problems.

Although the current formulation is new, its presence is not unknown. Witness, for example, the Havard Law of animal behavior:

"Under precisely controlled experimental procedures, an animal will behave as it damn well pleases."

This also was thought to be a corollary of Murphy's Law at one time, but has been since grouped with several others to form the Generalized Uncertainty Principle (GUP) which states:

---

* Murphy, Edsall. *The Physical Universe*. Naples, Italy: Gross-Press, July 1723.

"Complex systems exhibit unexpected behavior."

While the behavior may be unexpected, it may not be unpredictable, as we shall see.

Table 1

Jelly Bread Experimentation

No. of Trials	Bread	Jelly	Jelly Side Up	Jelly Side Down
227	Wheat	Grape	14	213
314½[1]	White	Strawberry	26½	288
37	Potato	Orange marmalade with sardines	0[2]	37
176	Rye	Cream cheese and apple jelly	39	137
200	Pumpernickle	Guava	20	180
14	Russian rye	Mint jelly	6[3]	7[3]
1712	Various	Peanut butter and various jellies	206	1506
2680½			311½	2368

Table 2

Outcomes and Usefulness of Jelly Bread Experiment Events

Event	Qualitative Usefulness	Comments
1. Nothing	Highest	There is some conjecture as to the possibility of this event
2. Fall to an edgewise	High	Least mess, most edible result
3. Falls jellyside up	Better than Nothing	Potential edible Result
4. Falls jellyside down	Low	Murphy prediction

The First Principle Law of Murphydynamics

Consider the systems delineated in the introductory section of this paper. The event space may be taken as the sum of possible events. Consider the state variable in the jelly-bread problem; bread (type), jelly (type), potential energy (height), and absence of gravity retardant. Consider also the events and their relative utilities as given in Table 2.

Table 2 when compared to Table 1 leads to immediate conclusions. For example, the event with the highest usefulness did not occur, while the event with the lowest usefulness occurred most frequently (88%). Event two, with high usefulness, occurred only once and event three—the intermediate—occurred 12% of the time. The conclusion is inescapable; the probability of occurrence of an event is inversely proportional to the utility, or:

$$P_\epsilon \; \alpha \; \overset{\approx}{\frac{1}{u}}$$

This equation represents the basic formulation of Murphydynamics. It is also the embodiment of the phrase:

"If something can go wrong, it might."

This explains why regression sometimes shows high correlation in unrelated data, or why failures occur primarily in critical items.

FALLS EDGEWISE

FALLS JELLY SIDE UP

FALLS JELLY SIDE DOWN

---

[1] One experimental trial was half consumed by an experimenter and may have presented a physically significant different set of parameters.

[2] The lack of an entry here is deemed insignificant and is attributed to sample size.

[3] The Russian rye used in the experiment was somewhat stale, and one trial actually landed on edge.

DAVID COULSON

Antropy and the Second Law

A casual observance of the aforementioned formulation would place a pessimistic view of what events would occur and which ones would not. For example, if one works really hard to make a highly useful item, it will hardly ever work. This is almost true, but not quite. If the basic formulation is examined again, and the proportionality is replaced with a proportional equation:

$$P_\epsilon = \frac{a}{\approx u}$$

The proportionality constant (a) is termed antropy and is a measure of failure not connected directly with the main event, such as the failure of a backup system when the primary system is still functional.[3-5] Antropy is the accumulation of confusion in a system.

An example of the creative incompetence within the Navy, and the proper application of the antropy is the A-5 which was painstakingly designed as an attack aircraft (unsuccessful?) but turned out to be an excellent reconnaissance aircraft (successful?).

The antropy, however, carries with it the penalty of timing. This explains why the bureaucracy works, albeit slow, in spite of its inherent internal confusion and potential usefulness. The utility is, of course, decreased by improper timing.

The accumulation of antropy can cause a phase shift as well as a timing problem. The phase shift may result in the system doing things it was not designed to do and not doing things it was supposed to do. Gall[3-6] points out that the construction of the Aswan dam (which was supposed to be a boon to the Egyptian people) prevented the Nile from flooding and hence depositing its valuable silt downstream (which is now trapped behind the dam). The once fertile fields now must be fertilized. In response to this unexpected event, the Egyptian government built fertilizer plants which are powered by the electric output of the Aswan dam. In fact, the dam must run at capacity in order to power the plants which would not be needed if the dam did not exist. As can be surmised, the antropy phase shift in this sequence of events is sizable.

Absolute Antropy and the Third Law

The existence of antropy and the formulation of the second law leads to the inescapable conclusion that the antropy goes to zero when the utiles go to zero. This offers us the ability to make some statements as to the possibility of the occurrence of events. Possibility may be mathematically defined as that event having a finite probability of occurrence. Or possibility exists when

$$P_\epsilon \geq \delta$$

Since we can formulate the probability of an event have

$$P_\epsilon = \frac{a}{\approx u} \geq \delta$$

or, possibility may be expressed in terms of antropy as:

$$a \geq \delta \tilde{u}$$

assuming utiles to be a non-zero, non-negative quantity. This immediately shows that nothing is impossible, but some things are highly improbable. An event can become possible if it can accumulate antropy at a greater rate than utility. This is the challenge of the design engineer. It should be noted that:

$$a = a\,(\tilde{u}, p_i, p_j, p_k, \ldots.)$$

since the utiles are not an event state variable.

We can also differentiate at what point an event may be possible or impossible. Mathematically an event may be impossible in two circumstances:

4. Gall, John. *Systematics.* New York: Quandrangle Press, 1977.
5. Parkinson, C. Northcote. *Parkinson's Law and Other Studies in Administration.* Boston: Houghton Mifflin, 1957.
6. Peter, Laurence. *The Peter Principle.* New York: Bantam, 1970.

DAVID COULSON

1. The antropy goes to zero—this is mathematically precluded by the third law which forces utiles to go to zero at the same time as antropy.

2. The utiles become exceedingly large. This is a mathematical expression of the old axiom;

"You cannot make one device to do all things."

This is a simple impossibility, both intuitively and mathematically. If the planners in the Pentagon had known this, the Navy F-111B could have been stopped early in its formulation stages, since its probability of success would have required such a high antropy level, and as we shall see later a high anergy level.

Anergy and the Laws of Conservation

The mechanism of antropy manipulation is through the application of the conservational laws of Murphy dynamics. The concept of Anergy (A) was first introduced by Gall[4] in his studies of the works of Parkinson[5] and Peter[6]. He felt he had achieved an understanding of the relationship between input effort to achieve an event and the dynamics of the event. By his definition:

"Anergy (A) is measured in units of effort required to bring about the desired change."

This can easily be stated in terms compatible with our terminology as:

"Anergy (A) is a measure of units of effort. If in the process of bringing about an event, enough anergy is expended, the event becomes first possible, then probable, and finally certain."

The process of anergy expenditure can be seen as related antropy. The anergy required to make an event possible, of course, is a function of the utiles of the event. The input of anergy is the mechanism by which the antropy to utile ratio is controlled, or:

$$dA \, \alpha \, \left(\frac{\delta a}{\delta \tilde{u}}\right)_\epsilon$$

where we state that the total anergy derivative is proportional to the partial derivative of antropy with respect to utiles for a fixed event.

A second and more important principle is the principle of conservation of anergy:

The total anergy in a closed system is constant.

This explains directly why a major study (and its attendantly higher utiles) has such a major impact on the operation of a research outfit. More and more of the fixed anergy must be turned to the task to make it (the study) a possible event because of its high utile count.

Then at last we can arrive at a relation between the probability of an event and the input required to achieve that probability. First, the differential anergy is integrated to achieve the anergy integral:

$$A = \int_{Es} \left(\frac{\delta a}{\alpha \tilde{u}}\right._\epsilon d\epsilon$$

Further, the relationship between the event probability and the antropy utile ratio is rearranged to form:

$$a = P_\epsilon \tilde{u}$$

and

$$\frac{da}{d\tilde{u}} = \left(\frac{\delta a}{\delta \tilde{u}}\right)_\epsilon + \sum_{i=1}^{n} \frac{\delta a}{\delta p_i} = P_\epsilon$$

since $a = a(u, Pi, Jj, Pi, \ldots)$

So that

$$\left(\frac{\delta a}{\delta \tilde{u}}\right)_\epsilon = P_\epsilon - \sum_{i=1}^{n} \frac{\delta a}{\delta pi}$$

and finally:

$$A = \int_{Es} \left(P_\epsilon - \sum_{i=1}^{n} \frac{\delta a}{\delta pi}\right) d\epsilon$$

We have here a rather startling conclusion in that the event anergy is independent of the event. This at first seems contradictory since it would state that the effort required to bring about an event is independent of the event. But it is in fact well known since we require more direction of effort than expenditure, and the fact that we define different events to be achieved at different event probability levels. The stochastic integral is then the relationship for the control of Murphydynamics.

Summary

We have reviewed the formulation of Murphydynamics in terms of the basic experiment and the common sense approach. We have seen that event dynamics are governed by usefulness and that the probability and event possibility of an event can be potentially controlled through the proper application of creative incompetence or the accumulation of antropy. This is as yet a preliminary, but useful (and therefore improbable) formulation of Murphydynamics and feedback constructive, destructive, and useless is encouraged.

BEYOND INCOMPETENCE

Frank R. Freemon
Department of Neurology
Vanderbilt University School of Medicine
Nashville, Tennessee

In an article that has since been criticized on ethical, religious, and anatomic grounds, Guy Godin has generalized the Peter Principle.[1] Taking up the ball where Godin left off, the present missive carries through the *reductio ad infinitum* barrier to the logical conclusion of the Parkinson to Peter to Godin theoretical reconstruction of complex hierarchical systems and, indeed, life itself.

Peter presented the principle postulate[2] that each employee in a company rises to his level of incompetence; that is, each competent employee continues to be promoted until he arrives at a position that he cannot properly handle and there he incompetently stays. In his erratic but brilliant evaluation of this principle, Guy Godin points out that at some given time in the future every employee in an institution must be incompetent. Peter would say that the newest employees, not yet risen to their final level, might be competent, but Godin proves that an old, established institution has so many incompetents that it must begin to hire persons incompetent *before they even start to rise* (italics added). Godin points out that in this maximally incompetent organization, incompetents will leave their level of incompetence and rise to new levels of even greater incompetence as the incompetents at the top die off. He summarizes this in the law that those individuals incompetent in a specialized field will rise to a level of generalized incompetence. Beyond specialized incompetence or the inability to do one certain job correctly lies the field of generalized incompetence, the inability to do anything right. This article attempts to take Godin's analysis to its finality. What lies beyond generalized incompetence?

A New Creature

The answer to this important scientific question is clearly obvious when formulated. When the answer to this enigmatic riddle lies unraveled before one, it strikes the consciousness with a startling clarity and the words, "Now why didn't I think of that," seem to jump from one's lips. They jumped from mine and I had thought of it. Before unraveling this riddlistic enigma, let me digress to describe another biological example of a *reductio ad infinitum* breakthrough which will by analogy clarify and illuminate the beyond incompetency question.

Teilhard de Chardin points out that there was a time on this planet when it was a totally inorganic sphere.[3] Things were happening, volcanoes were erupting, rain was falling, but there was no living being, not even one organic molecule on the globe. Organic molecules formed and much of the inorganic material became rearranged as parts of living organisms. From these simple viruses and unicellular organisms rose multicellular organisms with nervous systems. As the nervous systems became more complex, animals capable of complex behavior arose and changed the earth by eliminating organisms with simpler nervous systems. This process culminated in man. In fact man broke though some type of cerebral barrier to gain the ability to think, to plan ahead, and to understand, however dimly, some aspect of his existence. As the organic molecules had rearranged the inorganic, and the complex creatures had eliminated the simpler, man also changed the entire planet. He spread over the earth at such a rate that many modern scientists predict man will be destroyed by his own overproduction. One could say that the hierarchy of the human race has reached its level of maximum generalized incompetence. But Teilhard de Chardin thinks that a new breakthrough will occur, a new type of creature or existence. And as the inorganic world could not predict the organic and the animal world could not predict the

[1] Godin, G. "The G Constant." *Journal Irreproducible Results,* 19:21–22 (1972).

[2] Peter, L. J. *The Peter Principle.* New York: Morrow, 1969.

[3] Teilhard de Chardin, P. *The Phenomenon of Man.* New York: Harper, 1959.

spread of man, so modern man cannot predict what will come after him. But Teilhard is optimistic. Since each major change in this planet has been for the better, or at least for the more complex, so the next breakthrough of the *reductio ad infinitum* barrier will be the arrival of a God-like creature. From the maximally incompetent comes the advanced competent.

And so now we can state Freemon's Rule:

The generalized incompetent sometimes rises to a level of advanced competence.

Grant and Peter

For those few who need proof of this essentially obvious (but brilliant) truism, I will offer some explanatory examples. History abounds with individuals who have fulfilled the Peter to Godin to Freemon straight arrow path. Ulysses S. Grant was moderately successful as a young man at West Point and in the Mexican War. He rose through the Army's ranks until he reached a level of incompetence. This was, of course, specialized (military) incompetence. Out of the Army he proved he had risen to the level of generalized incompetence. His business was a failure and he was becoming an alcoholic and sinking toward the nineteenth century equivalent of skid row. The Civil War, however, forced him to rise to his level of, you guessed it, special competence. He was the general that cut the South in two at Shiloh and Vicksburg and later squeezed Lee in Virginia until he won the War.

Another example is Peter the Fisherman, later called St. Peter (no relation to Peter of the Principle). He was apparently a fairly competent fisherman and when Jesus chose him to be a disciple he seemed to do a competent job. However, he rose among the disciples to his level of incompetence. He was the first to admit his incompetence to prevent or even to try to prevent the arrest, trial, or execution of Jesus. Yet after the death of Jesus he was forced to rise above incompetence to help guide the young religion that subsequently spread over the Western world. Its success was due in part to his highly competent direction of its early course. Truman's business failed and Nixon lost so many elections that he declared he would never again run for elective office but both became moderately good Presidents. This type of thing happens so frequently in the United States that it has been clichéd that "the man rises to meet the office" of the Presidency. A recent example of Freemon's Rule from British politics is Winston Churchill, specialized incompetent at Gallipoli, generalized incompetent in the 1930's, but rising to highly advanced competence during World War II.

Incompetence Marches On

In his classic yet still incompletely appreciated article, Godin states that "there is continuous progress from Parkinson to Peter to Us." By *Us*, Godin does not refer to the United States but to his own self. My own analysis suggests a further progression of the incompetency argument, possibly to its final sublimation. A progression from Parkinson to Peter to Godin to Freemon emerges from a careful consideration of specific individuals who have advanced beyond generalized incompetence. Frankly, I don't exactly see how Parkinson fits in except he is a big name in this area. Note how I have worked Teilhard de Chardinian concepts into this whole question. The relationship of Marshall McLuhan to this complex of big names somehow eludes me. In any event, Table I summarizes Peter's Principle, Godin's Law, and Freemon's Rule to show a steady progression of incompetency until the *reductio ad infinitum* barrier is burst. Beyond incompetence lies competence.

Table I

Peter to Godin to Freemon

Name of Axiom	Originator	Axial Statement
Peter's Principle	Peter	In a hierarchy, every employee tends to rise to his level of incompetence.
Godin's Law	Godin	Generalizedness of incompetence is directly proportional to highestness in hierarchy.
Freemon's Rule	Freemon	Circumstances can force a generalized incompetent to become competent, at least in a specialized field.

Summary

Peter postulated that in any hierarchy every individual tends to rise to a level at which he is incompetent to handle his job. Godin proved that these specialized incompetent individuals will eventually rise to a level of generalized incompetence. From a broad biologic viewpoint, Teilhard de Chardin recognized that the human race itself may have arrived at a historical level of maximum generalized incompetence. Using examples and brilliant logic the present article shows that many generalized incompetents can under certain circumstances push through the *reductio ad infinitum* incompetency barrier to a new level of advanced specialized competence.

PROJECT MANAGEMENT

B. Sparks[*]

From time to time, every professional journal publishes articles to aid their members in a particular field. Much has been written on Project Management; however, certain aspects are often overlooked. These are the practical, everyday, down-to-earth aids that make a project move. In an attempt to fill this void, the following three aids are offered to assist in obtaining irreproducible results.

Project Vocabulary

Knowing the terminology is the first key step in project management.

Project: an assignment that can't be completed by either walking across the hall or by making one telephone call.

To activate a project: make additional copies and add to the distribution list.

To implement a project: acquire all the physical space available and assign responsibilities to anyone in sight.

Consultant (or Expert): anyone more than 50 miles from home.

Coordinator: the guy who really doesn't know what's going on.

Channels: the people you wouldn't see or write to if your life depended on it.

Expedite: to contribute to the present chaos.

Conference (or Meeting): that activity that brings all work and progress to a standstill.

Negotiate: shouting demands interspersed with gnashing of teeth.

Reorientation: starting to work again.

Making a survey: most of the personnel are on a boondoggle.

[*]Consulting Engineer

Under consideration: never heard of it.

Under active consideration: the memo is lost and is being looked for.

Will be looked into: maybe the whole thing will be forgotten by the next meeting.

Reliable source: the guy you just met.

Informed source: the guy who introduced you.

Unimpeachable source: the guy who started the rumor.

Read and initial: to spread the responsibility in case everything goes wrong.

The other viewpoint: let them get it off their chest so they'll shut up.

Clarification: muddy the water so they can't see bottom.

See me later on this: I am as confused as you are.

Will advise you in due course: when we figure it out, we'll tell you.

In process: trying to get through the paper mill.

Modification: a complete redesign.

Orientation: confusing a new member of the project.

Reorganization: assigning someone new to save the project.

Ten Commandments for the Project Manager

These are the rules by which the Project Manager must run his project.

1. Strive to look tremendously important.

2. Attempt to be seen with important people.

3. Speak with authority; however, only expound on the obvious and proven facts.

4. Don't engage in arguments, but if cornered, ask an irrelevant question and lean back with a satisfied grin while your opponent tries to figure out what's going on—then quickly change the subject.

5. Listen intently while others are arguing the problem. Pounce on a trite statement and bury them with it.

6. If a subordinate asks you a pertinent question, look at him as if he had lost his senses. When he looks down, paraphrase the question back at him.

7. Obtain a brilliant assistant, but keep him out of sight and out of the limelight.

8. Walk at a fast pace when out of the office—this keeps questions from subordinates and superiors at a minimum.

9. Always keep the office door closed—this puts visitors on the defensive and also makes it look as if you are always in an important conference.

10. Give all orders verbally. Never write anything down that might go into a "Pearl Harbor File."

Project Progress Report

Below is a standard report that can be used by just about any project that has no progress to report:

The report period which ended _____ has seen considerable progress in directing a large portion of the effort in meeting the initial objectives established.[1] Additional background information and relative data have been acquired to assist in problem resolution.[2] As a result, some realignment has been made to enhance the position of the project.[3]

One deterrent that has caused considerable difficulty in this reporting period was the selection of optimum methods and techniques; however, this problem is being vigorously attacked and we expect the development phase will proceed at a satisfactory rate.[4] In order to prevent unnecessary duplication of previous efforts in the same field, it was deemed necessary to establish a special team to conduct a survey of facilities engaged in similar activities.[5]

The Project Control Group held its regular meeting and considered the broad functional aspects of all levels of coordination and cross fertilization of relevant ideas associated with the general specifications of the evolving system.[6] At the present rate of progress, it is believed that most project milestones will be met.[7] During the next quarter a major breakthrough is anticipated and will be fully covered in progress report No. _____.[8]

[1] The project has long ago forgotten what the objective was.
[2] The one page of data from the last quarter was found in the incinerator.
[3] We now have a new lead-man for the data group.
[4] We finally found some information that is relevant to the project.
[5] We had a great time in Los Angeles, Denver, and New York.
[6] Fertilizer.
[7] Would you be happy with one or two?
[8] We think we have stumbled onto someone who knows what's going on.

GUIDE TO EMPLOYEE PERFORMANCE APPRAISAL

How do you rate?

Performance Factor	Performance Degrees				
	Far Exceeds Job Requirements	Exceeds Job Requirements	Meets Job Requirements	Needs Some Improvement	Does Not Meet Minimum Job Requirements
QUALITY	Leaps tall buildings with a single bound	Must take a running start to leap over tall buildings	Can leap over short buildings only	Crashes into buildings when attempting to jump over them	Cannot recognize buildings at all
TIMELINESS	Is faster than a speeding bullet	Is as fast as a speeding bullet	Not quite as fast as a speeding bullet	Would you believe a slow bullet?	Wounds self with bullets when attempts to fire
INITIATIVE	Is stronger than a locomotive	Is stronger than a bull elephant	Is stronger than a bull	Shoots the bull	Smells like a bull
ABILITY	Walks on water consistently	Walks on water in emergencies	Washes with water	Drinks water	Passes water in emergencies
COMMUNICATION	Talks with God	Talks with the angels	Talks to himself	Argues with himself	Loses those arguments

Submitted by
Dr. Jay Pasachoff, Hale Observatories, California Institute of Technology, Pasadena, California.

FROM PAPER CLIP TO PENTAGON

Morton Rothstein, Ph.D.
Professor of Biology
State University of New York at Buffalo

The following is an excerpt from a full-length biography of Mr. Seymour Faltz, the famous efficiency expert.

It is worth studying the early experiences of Mr. Seymour Faltz, Chief of Operations Analysis, U.S. Department of Defense, so that other aspiring young men may, by his example, understand how ingenuity, American know-how and hard work can lead to a highly successful and useful career.

The brilliant idea which started Mr. Faltz on his road to professional success, and which eventually led to the development of a whole new concept of efficiency in business operations, was conceived when he was still a young man. At the time, he was employed as an Administrative Assistant in the Molecular Zoology Department of a moderately large and otherwise undistinguishable State University. Whenever a member of the faculty wished to have a secretarial service performed, he checked the desired service (type, copy, mimeograph, etc.) on a small blue form and attached it with a paper clip to the document to be worked on. For this purpose, a small box of paper clips was kept near the blue forms within easy reach of even short faculty members.

As he became familiar with the office routine, Mr. Faltz developed a strong feeling that the supply of paper clips disappeared equally quickly whether he set out a full box or a half-empty one. This situation made it exceedingly difficult to keep the proper number of paper clips in stock. If the supply ran out, then no faculty work could be done until new ones were ordered and delivered. If too many were ordered, they not only would be used wastefully (if Mr. Faltz's observation was correct), but valuable funds would be tied up in unnecessary supplies.

The Red and the Black

Mr. Faltz then devised the following brilliant tactic. Each time a secretary removed the blue instruction sheet, she put a small mark on the paper clip, using a black marking pen, and returned the clip to the box. If a marked paper clip was used again, a second mark would be made, and so on. If a clip survived for five marks it received a red mark. By varying the starting number of paper clips, and periodically counting the number of marks, the half-life of any given starting number of clips was derived within very close limits. An interested group at the Computer Center performed the statistical analyses. A small panic was created when a psychologist suggested that paper clips with both black and red marks were a more attractive target for disappearance than unmarked ones. Mr. Faltz decided to overcome this objection by changing the marks to green. However, this move became unnecessary when the Psychology Department succeeded, by use of interviews, questionnaires and hidden cameras, in determining the "faculty fondness unit index" (FFUI) for unmarked, black, and black and red clips, respectively. This FFUI factor was subsequently applied to the statistics, resulting in an accurate and predictable system for determining paper clip needs.

The above work was published in a national business magazine and reprinted in the *Wall Street Journal,* where it caught the attention of General Hershey Bar. The General had recently been given a rather nasty going over by a Congressional Committee which was angry because of incredibly large purchases of paper clips by the Pentagon and huge overruns by defense contractors. It did General Bar little good to explain that paper clips were the life blood of the Pentagon. During a minor quarrel about the relative merits of staples versus paper clips, it was readily shown by extensive cost analyses that the capital investment for rapid fire staplers of the latest model more than offset the cheaper price of the staples vis-à-vis paper clips. In any case, General Bar had successfully defended the value of the clips, but he and his aides recognized that they had a problem of inefficient utilization on their hands which could seriously affect army operations and national security.

Military Hardware

After reading Mr. Faltz's article, General Bar immediately contacted that gentleman and persuaded him to take charge of the Pentagon paper clip situation. Faltz set up the same type of study as had been conducted at the University. Unfortunately, members of the Psychology Department were unwilling to face the contempt of their colleagues in the Department of Creative Thought. The latter, though willing to write best-sellers about the Defense Department (personally receiving sizable royalties), were unhappy at the idea that others might be involved in any way with that institution, even if the purpose was the saving of tax monies. Fortunately, the CIA provided some unobtrusive observers so that an estimate of the disappearance ratio of red-marked clips to black-marked or unmarked clips could be made. It was of interest to note that on a *per capita* basis, colonels pocketed paper clips (all marks) 22.6% more frequently than majors, who, in turn, squirreled these items away 6.8% more frequently than generals. Lieutenants had the lowest frequency of pocketing, but demonstrated a high frequency of distorting and twisting the clips into decorative but useless objets d'art.

The Battle of Manila Folders

As a result of Faltz's work, the Pentagon learned that it could safely reduce its stock of paper clips by 2,253,751 per annum. An additional saving was made by sending majors instead of colonels whenever paper clips were to be used.

Faltz became a hero to efficiency-minded executives. Not only government departments (Commerce, Agriculture, etc.) but private industry adopted his methods. He appeared on TV shows, was written up in the *Saturday Review* and was even interviewed by *Playboy.* Attempts to discredit him by paper clip manufacturers (who objected that re-use of paper clips was bad for the economy) failed, although covert support was given to the movement by stapler interests.

Faltzism was applied zealously to other major office products such as rubber bands, envelopes for inter-office mail and manila folders. Experts in faltzism were in short supply, but the universities, in their desire for relevance, quickly established a number of appropriate courses. Making use of Faltz's original statistics, two contradictory schools rapidly developed. When it was discovered that paper clips were rarely used in the central cities, sociologists and social psychologists quickly developed new theories to explain the significance of this finding and its relationship to the learning ability of the disadvantaged. Applications for government grants did not go unheeded.

Meanwhile, Faltz had adapted his system to marking officers at the Pentagon. Every time certain sections of the building were visited, the officer involved would receive a colored mark on his forehead. Within a month, for the first time in history, statistics were developed showing where officers were spending their time. It turned out that by locating a number of offices geographically closer to each other, two generals, eight colonels, five majors, twelve lieutenants and one private could be relieved of their daily routine.

Before his appointment as Chief of Operations, Faltz had an interesting call from a lady who lived in a house with twelve daughters. It seems that she wished his help in keeping track of their movements by applying a spot of color just below the navel.

This brief outline of the rapid rise of Seymour Faltz should serve to stimulate other young men into being careful observers of the passing scene. It is not even necessary to attend a Faltz Course, let alone a whole School of Faltzism, in order to establish a high level of Faltzhood. All that is needed is a strong penchant for organizing trivia. We have high hopes, in this state, that with the present stress on large numbers of students in our University courses, we can do more than our share toward graduating large numbers of students who will achieve Faltz status.

RATIONALE FOR PROCRASTINATION

Frieda B. Taub, Ph.D.
College of Fisheries
University of Washington
Seattle, Washington

Alert biologists search for the potential survival advantage of structures or behavior patterns which occur commonly and in diverse groups. Procrastination behavior is analyzed here to determine if procrastination does more than merely satisfy Parkinson's Law, that work tends to fill the allotted time.[1]

Most procrastination behavior is performed against a deadline, e.g. a manuscript which requires one month's effort is due one year from today. A skillful procrastinator will spend at least 11½ months working on other projects and trying, but not quite coming to grips with, the project under discussion. The work of the 11½ months will probably be necessary to clear the desk as it is covered by work that is past due, i.e. work which cannot in clear conscience be further postponed. In examining the merits of the procrastination strategy—that of starting two weeks before the deadline rather than a year before—the following attributes of procrastination become apparent.

1. Procrastination shortens the job and places the responsibility for its termination on someone else (the authority who imposed the deadline).

2. It reduces anxiety by reducing the expected quality of the project from the best of all possible efforts to the best that can be expected given the limited time.

3. Status is gained in the eyes of others, and in one's own eyes, because it is assumed that the importance of the work justifies the stress.

4. Avoidance of interruptions including the assignment of other duties can usually be achieved, so that the obviously stressed worker can concentrate on the single effort. Under non-stressed conditions, the refusal to answer the phone, host visitors, or attend to routine matters would be considered intolerably rude.

5. Procrastination avoids boredom; one never has the feeling that there is nothing to do (J. Taub personal communication).

6. It may eliminate the job if the need passes before the job can be done (M. Davis personal communication).

These advantages which accrue from the strategy of procrastination obviously serve to reinforce procrastination behavior. An in-depth examination of such rewards or payoffs of games has been made by Berne.[2] A study of the survival and reproductive rates of procrastinators and controls is beyond the scope of this report.

The time spent on this effort was a form of procrastination on all the other things I should have been doing. This effort was supported by no grant.

[2] Berne, Eric. *Games People Play, The Psychology of Human Relationships.* New York: Grove Press, 1964.

TO SIMPLIFY PURCHASING DEPT.

The ASTM Committee F-11 on Vacuum Cleaners issued this definition in a standard designated ASTM F395:

"A system or device that removes material, usually loose, from surfaces by means of the air flow caused by subatmospheric pressure, having an intake intended to be moved in proximity to the surface, a means of separating the material from the air, and a receptacle for collecting the separated material. The inlet may be fixed or attached to other equipment and provision is made for removing collected material."

— *ASTM Standardization News, p. 26, February, 1977.*

[1] Parkinson, C. Northcote. *Parkinson's Law.* Boston: Houghton-Mifflin Co., 1957.

PART VII

WORDS AND NUMBERS

SEXUAL BEHAVIOR IN THE HUMAN LANGUAGE

H. J. Lipkinsey

It is now apparent that sex is at the root of all human problems. In all of history,[1,2] sex has been consistently suppressed in areas where it has every right to appear.[3] It has therefore popped up in other areas where there is no good reason for its existence.[4] All aspects of the problem have been treated in detail by Freud and Kinsey, with the exception of the sexual behavior of languages which is treated by Lipkinsey.[5]

The French pride themselves on their rational attitude toward all things, including sex. But Frenchmen have neglected their language, whose anomalous sexual behavior is among the worst of its kind. All French tables are feminine. "La crayon de ma tante est sur *la* table" is the first sentence every student learns. Woe be unto the poor wretch who says *le* table. No French table will ever forgive this insult. Yet, what is the lot of the unfortunate French table? All that the future offers it is hopeless spinsterhood, for *all* French tables are feminine and there are no male tables in France.

Lucky is the French table who can make the journey to a foreign land like Israel, where all tables are masculine (or the lucky Israeli male who can make the trip to France). Perhaps this is one of the reasons for the friendship which has recently arisen between Israel and France. But all in all, both the French and Hebrew languages are nothing more than a mass of misplaced sexuality. They are full of sexified tables, chairs, houses, trees and other objects who have no need for sex, have never asked for it, and use it only to frustrate themselves and anyone who is trying to learn the language.

The Germans have evidently stumbled upon the important idea that some objects need not have sex, and should remain sexless. With characteristic German thoroughness they have classified everything as masculine, feminine and neuter, and they have made a horrible mess. Der Tisch, die Wand, das Mädchen, das Fräulein. German tables are masculine, German girls and unmarried women are neuter, walls are feminine. What is there for a young man to do in Germany? All young and unmarried women are sexless. If he wants feminine company he must find himself a married woman or go to the wall.[6] Is it any wonder that German youth has been responsible for so many upheavals in the past century?

The English-speaking peoples alone have almost completely succeeded in keeping sex out of irrelevant portions of their language. This is undoubtedly a result of the Puritan tradition of taking sex out of everything.[7] English tables are sexless and have no problems, even though they may be laid on occasion. Boys are masculine, girls are feminine, and Hollywood makes the most of it. It is only when foreigners speak broken English that sex is ever introduced into the English language: "This house, she is too small; My train, he did not come on time." An Englishman can always tell a foreigner by his attempts to introduce sex into the conversation.

[1] Essex, A., B. Sussex and C. Wessex, *Sex in English History.* Middlesex Press, 1957.
[2] Freud, S., *Oedipus Sex, a study of sexual behavior in ancient Greece.*
[3] Freud, S., A. B. Kinsey and S. U. Perkinsey, "Sex and Repression in Human Society." *Journal of Inorgasmic Chemistry,* 1, 51, 1957.
[4] Morris, P. and L. Strike. "Sex in Cigarette Advertising," Any American Magazine.
[5] Lipkinsey, H. J., "Sexual Behavior in the Human Language." *Journal of Irreproducible Results.* V, 1957.
[6] Die Magd, the servant girl, is also feminine. Draw your own conclusions.
[7] One Puritan sect succeeded in eliminating sex from every aspect of life and became extinct.

PAUL MEISEL

DECLINE OF LANGUAGE AS A MEDIUM OF COMMUNICATION

R.J. Hoyle

School of Health,
Physical Education and Recreation
Dalhousie University
Halifax, N.S.

The recently reported decline in the ability of students (*Time* (1), 1975; Pratt, 1975) and people in many walks of life (*Time* (2), 1975), to use English in both speech and writing, has been accompanied by suggestions that facility with English is of diminishing usefulness (*Time* (1), 1975).

These latter suggestions led to the investigation of the relationship of the complexity of English, in terms of sentence length and word length, to the passage of time.

Method

Certain texts, considered to be representative of their time and consistent as to source, were investigated (Amer. Acad. Pol. Soc. Sci.). In order to avoid a geographical bias, a transatlantic selection was also included (Bryant *et al*, 1967). Frequency counts of the number of words per sentence of selected passages were made, along with counts of the frequency of letters per word of the same passages (American sample only).

Results

Sentence lengths for the U.K. sample are shown in Table I.

Fig. 1 shows the declining frequency of words per sentence from the year 1598 (Bacon) to 1940 (Churchill) for the English sample. The plot of the American figures (1890-1974) on the same graph shows a steeper slope. Both curves are extrapolated to zero word length, at about the middle of the 22nd century, although this is hypothetical and the curve may actually be asymptotic.

Table I		
Sentence Lengths of British Public Speakers, 1598-1940.		
Name	*Year*	*No. of words/sentence*
Francis Bacon	1598	72.2
Oliver Cromwell	1654	48.6
John Tillotson	1694	57.2
William Pitt	1777	30.0
Benjamin Disraeli	1846	42.8
David Lloyd George	1909	22.6
Winston Churchill	1940	24.2

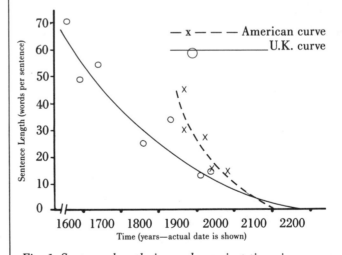

Fig. 1. Sentence length, in words, against time, in years.

The number of letters per word is plotted against time in Fig. 2. The decline is approximately one letter per century and can be extrapolated to zero letters per word at about the year 2450.

Discussion

The decline of English as a means of communication is evident here and its eventual demise may be postulated. The shortening sentences argue for an increased efficiency in the use of words. The steeper slope of the American graph reflects that nation's world leadership in efficiency and modernization. Sentences will eventually consist of, on the average, one word only. These have already existed for some years and indeed a complete letter by G.B. Shaw is quoted here in full:

> "Dear Sir,
>   No.
>
>   Yours truly,
>   G.B. Shaw"

One word sentences will be superseded by communication by single letters. This is easily deducible from the fact that the graph of word length against time (Fig. 2) extrapolates to zero some 300 years later than the graph of sentence length (Fig. 1). Early experiments in this, e.g.

> "2B or not 2B . . ."
>   —(Shakespeare, 1604)

did not seem to be developed past the pilot study stage. A more recent attempt (Bell, 1965), while excellent for its purpose, probably has limited application. The language already shows some tendency toward this type of reduction (tea, see, I, you, etc.)

The growth of non-verbal communication (NVC) will cause the eventual repression of the spoken language. Early usage of NVC in writing was employed by Victor Hugo in 1862, who wrote: "?," to his publisher in an enquiry about the progress of one of his novels (McWhirter and McWhirter, 1974).

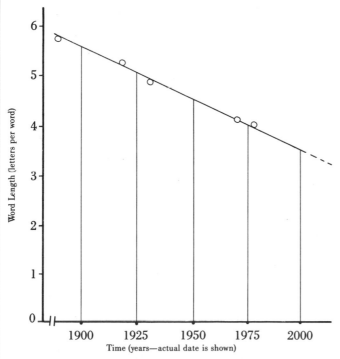

Fig. 2. Word length, in letters, against time, in years.

Despite the fact that the number of periodicals doubled from 1951 to 1963 and doubled again from 1963 to 1970 (Ulrich, 1951, 1963, 1970), the written language, though evidently growing in volume (though not necessarily in content), will probably be superseded eventually by radio, television and public address systems employing professional talkers.

It is forecast, then, that there will be an expansion in the knowledge of NVC, through the study of, for example, gestures (e.g. LaBarre, 1947), and extra-sensory perception (Rhine et al., 1966), at the expense of the written and spoken word, when we shall all "hold our tongues."

REFERENCES

American Academy of Political and Social Sciences, Annals, 1890–1974.

Bell, Ivan, *reported by* M. Gardner *in Scientific American,* 213:98, August, 1965.

Bryant, D. C., C. C. Arnold, F. W. Haberman, R. Murphy, and K. R. Wallace (eds.) *Selected British Speeches.* New York: Ronald Press, 1967.

LaBarre, W. "The Cultural Basis of Emotions and Gestures." *Journal of Personality.* 16:49–68, 1947.

McWhirter N. & R. McWhirter. *Guinness Book of Records.* London: Guinness Superlatives Ltd., 1974.

Pratt, Terry. "English Ain't Writ Here No More." *Maclean's,* Dec. 15, 1975, p. 59.

Rhine, J. B., J. G. Pratt, B. M. Smith and C. E. Stuart. *Extrasensory Perception after 60 Years.* Boston: Bruce Humphries, 1966.

Shakespeare, W. *Hamlet,* (Act III, scene 1). London: N.L. and John Trundell, 1604.

Time (1). "Can't anyone here speak English?" *Time Magazine.* Aug. 25, 1975, pp. 56–58.

Time (2). "How Many Incompetents?" *Time Magazine,* Nov. 10, 1975, p. 12.

Ulrick's International Periodicals Directory, 6th ed., 1951; 10th ed., 1963; 13th ed., 1970.

APPLIED MATH DEPARTMENT SEMINAR "FUZZY LOGIC"

Professor B. Vastor
Kings College, Cambridge, England

Fuzzy Logic is concerned with systems in which subsets are only vaguely defined.

This seminar will be held at 4:00 P.M. in room 347 unless the lecture there is running late. In which case it will be held in room 211. It will be held on June 15 unless Professor Vastor takes longer than expected to finish the experiments on which the seminar to be given is based.

Submitted by: E. B. Forsyth
Brookhaven National Laboratory

A LAYMAN'S GUIDE TO THE INTRODUCTION OF NEW WORDS INTO THE ENGLISH LANGUAGE

P. Kendall du Par, Ph.D.
Professor of Etymology
Department of Language Structure
Pardu University
West Layfayee, Indiana

After the premorphal discovery of a prehistoric language that underlies the language of "common usage," the detailed reconstruction of old, often trite concepts, have taken on new forms of expression in the use of an idiomatic language which is peculiar to or characteristic of the English language.

However, heretofore no publication has dared to explain the etymological process of creating new idiomatic expressions for entry into the dictionaries of common usage.

Ingenuity, of course, is of magnimost importance in composing a word that creates the correct mental picture desired. For example, in describing an event of colossal success, one might exclaim *"splentrific!"* (creating a mental atmosphere of splendor and terrificness). Do not be dampened if confusion arises in the minds of the minority.

Once a word has been created one must with confidence use the word with great frequency so that when others wish to explain or describe like terms, situations, feelings or attitudes, they likewise will perpetuate the expression.

It is highly important that when creating new words, that one does not become guilty of simply altering an existing word so slightly that those encountering it assume the word has only been misspelled.

Once your etymological expressions become known for their specific idiomatic meaning, one has an open door for pyramiding new expressions. For example, once the word *"gosmo"* has been established and accepted to connote *"super"* quality, one can then prefix unlimited words and thereby relate unlimited super-"ness." Taking one example: *blatz* could well resweep the country under a new label of *"gosmo-blatz."* Note that now the trite expression *"new improved"* has been circumdumped with *"gosmo."*

The following are a few of the many expressions which have found their entry into the common everyday language throughout the Pacific Northwest as well as other large sectors of the U.S. and Canada and have, to date, been entered on the manuscripts of three major dictionary publishing firms for official entry into the English language.

abazenia: /a'-ba-zin»-ē-a/ n. A concluding remark at parting—often used interjectionally denoting the intent to return at a subsequent time.

flamnoxious: /flam-nok'-shes/ adj. Deceitfully disagreeable or offensive. One who deceitfully lies or perpetuates a hoax. Commonly used to describe power "mania" among political aspirants.

flustrate: /flus'-trāt/ v.t. 1. To plan in a state of nervous confusion. 2. To become or cause others to become agitatedly confused or bewildered.

jargastric: /jar-gas'-trik/ adj. Any comment or situation which jars the gaster (e.g. turns one's stomach). See GASTRO-, GASTR-.

peacefork: /pēs'-fork/ n. Symbol representing "the American chicken" denoted by its inner shape.

Since the emphasis of this Layman's Guide is placed on the "hows" of introducing new words rather than on the publishing of the quantity of new words which have been considered,[1] an open invitation is being given for submitting new words which upon consideration will then be printed in succeeding editions of this guide.

In conclusion, recognition must be given for the invaluable contributions of the NEWVORD panel of 100 outstanding speakers and writers who have contributed a wide range of questions and suggestions about how the language is used today, especially with regard to dubious or controversial locutions. Many of the leading scholars and scientists of the English-speaking world have collaborated with our permanent editorial staff in the interest of recording with accuracy and authority those elements of our language which are of concern to literate people.

Forward all responses to:
NEWVORDS % B.C.
Dept. 6284
Goleta, California 93017

---

[1] In excess of 350.

INTERIM REPORT ON THE RAVEN

Dr. C. F. Englebretsen
Bishop's University
Lennoxville, Quebec, Canada

Whatever data confirm or disconfirm a statement will likewise confirm or disconfirm any logically equivalent statement. "All ravens are black" is logically equivalent to "All nonblack things are nonravens."

This so-called "Raven Paradox" has been a commonplace among philosophers and logicians for centuries. Aristotle, Ockham, Leibniz, Mill, Frege, and Russell have often been mentioned in this regard.[1] Nonetheless, we believe that the failure to solve this puzzle is due to the well-known shortsightedness, narrowmindedness and unimaginativeness of philosophers.[2] Consequently in the spring of 1965 a team of scientists, including an entomologist, two ornithologists, three bioecologists and a lyricist,[3] was formed for the purposes of solving the Raven Paradox once and for all. The old puzzle was finally moved from the stuffy seminar room to the open field.

Our task has been to confirm the hypothesis that all ravens are black by confirming its equivalent: that all nonblack things are nonravens. Now while "All ravens are black" is simply tested by determining the blackness or nonblackness of all ravens—a relatively easy task[4]—the task of confirming its equivalent is considerably more difficult. That this was so became quite clear to our brilliant team of scientists within the first year or so of the project, when we came to realize that the number of nonblack things[5] in the world is much greater than the number of black things. As of this date we have examined over 56,620,000 items of nonblack color. These have turned out to be such things as eggs, books, tables, coffee cups, signposts, clouds, apples, and some female undergarments—but none have turned out to be ravens. Of the 8.31% which have been tested as definitely black (all of which were subject to extensive laboratory testing) only 612 have been confirmed as genuine ravens. All the rest we now suspect to be old telephones, crows, pencil leads, ink spots, certain items of female underwear, etc.

There are still many nonblack things to be examined.[6] And so our work continues—not in the dusty halls of philosophy but in the bright fields of Science.[7]

---

[1] Not to mention Poe's mention of the paradox. We should keep in mind, however, the particularly frightening consequences of Poe's version of the Raven.

[2] See the exchange in *Ratio*, xiii, June, 1971.

[3] Poe's thesis concerning the Raven can never be entirely ignored.

[4] Though recall the consequences of Dr. Fwyn's twenty-eight year program for doing this. Fwyn, his wife, his two older children, and four field assistants still suffer chronic lower back aches, stiff necks and crossed eyes.

[5] Pink, yellow, brown, white, blue, green, orange, red, purple, magenta, tan, etc. Gray is still a puzzle case.

[6] 10^{877613}

[7] A request for a National Science Foundation Grant to fund our research for the next few centuries is pending.

CLICHE CONFLICTS: A QUANTITATIVE CASE STUDY

L. Allen Abel
Department of Neurology
School of Medicine
University of Pittsburgh
Pittsburgh, PA

As has been frequently pointed out by those who concern themselves with such things, originality of expression in written and spoken language seems destined to follow the California condor and the free road map into oblivion. As society gradually regresses toward a level of communication last utilized in the Pleistocene, those means of expression still remaining to us assume increasing importance. One of these is the much-maligned cliche. Once scorned as the verbal equivalents of TV dinners, these universally understood, prefabricated constructions enable vast numbers of individuals to communicate without having to undergo the painful experience of attempting to produce an original thought. Therefore, when a conflict is found between two equally popular cliches, it behooves us to attempt to resolve the disagreements. Such is the theme of this paper.

A popular piece of folk wisdom, reflected in many a song, is "Absence makes the heart grow fonder." Indeed, upon reflection, many of us can recall personal examples of its accuracy. Disturbingly, however, this sentiment is contradicted by the equally well-established expression, "Out of sight, out of mind." This phrase possesses the same cultural and personal validity as that cited previously; nevertheless, the two are diametrically opposed. It is hoped that an analytical examination of the question involved will lead to a resolution of this conflict.

Let us begin by defining the force of attraction between the two individuals involved (here assumed to be a man and a woman, for tradition and clarity of subscripts) as f_{mw}. It is interesting to note that it is not necessarily true that f_{mw} equals f_{wm}. (The case where $f_{mw} \neq f_{wm}$ is known as unrequited love.) A close examination of our contradictory cliches reveals that while the first is a function of time, the second is a function of distance. That is,

$$f_{mw} = f_{mw}(x,t) \qquad \text{(Eqn. 1)}$$

where x is the distance separating our subjects and t is the duration of separation. The next step is to explicitly define this functional dependence. Considering first our second expression, we find that "Out of sight, out of mind" expresses an inverse relationship between attractive force and distance of separation. This has a certain intuitive validity: if the object of one's desire is in the next room one's ardor is less likely to cool than if he or she is in Sri Lanka. On the other hand, the effects of one party's removal to, say, Pascagoula, would probably be as pronounced as a transoceanic separation. This saturation effect can be represented as

$$f_{mw}(x) = \frac{a_1}{x + a_0} + a_2 \qquad \text{(Eqn. 2)}$$

Thus,

$$f_{mw}(x) \quad a_2, \quad x \to \infty \qquad \text{(Eqn. 3)}$$

Conversely, for small separations,

$$f_{mw}(x) \frac{a_1}{a_0} + a_2, \quad x \to 0 \qquad \text{(Eqn. 4)}$$

(The events occurring at $x \leq 0$, although a fruitful field of investigation, do not pertain to the subject at hand.) Hence, if $\frac{a_1}{a_0} >> a_2$, we find that the force of attraction starts at an initially high value and then monotonically declines with increasing separation to the asymptotic value of a_2, which may, in fact, be vanishingly small.

The temporal portion of the equation represents the thought "Absence makes the heart grow fonder."

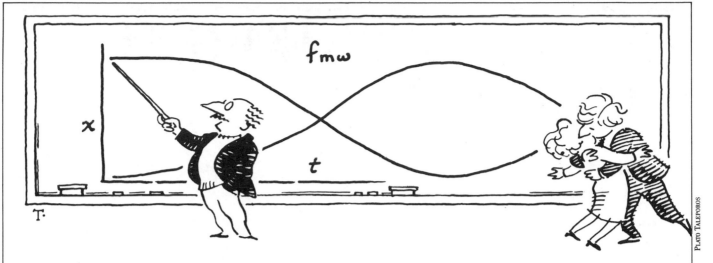

Some difficulty arises here in determining whether $f_{mw}(t)$ varies proportionally with time or if a nonlinear component is present. We might well assume an initially accelerating function as the absent party is gradually idealized by a conveniently selective memory. Still, since it seems unreasonable for attraction to grow without limit, a saturation must eventually prevail. A function meeting these requirements is one minus the sum and difference of three exponentials.

Hence,

$$f_{mw}(t) = b_0 + b_4(1 - e^{-b_1 t} - e^{-b_2 t} + e^{-b_3 t}) \quad \text{(Eqn. 5)}$$

This yields

$$f_{mw}(t) = b_0, \quad t = 0 \quad \text{(Eqn. 6a)}$$

$$f_{mw}(t) = b_0 + b_4, \quad t \rightarrow \infty \quad \text{(Eqn. 6b)}$$

Assembling both the time and space functions, we have

$$f_{mw}(x,t) = \frac{a_1}{a_0 + x} + a_2 + b_0 + b_4(1 - e^{-b_1 t} - e^{-b_2 t} - e^{-b_3 t}) \quad \text{(Eqn. 7)}$$

If we consider the possibility that $a_2 < 0$, then we see that for the case where our hypothetical couple has been far apart for a considerable length of time we have

$$f_{mw}(x,t) = a_2 + b_4 + b_0, \quad x, t \rightarrow \infty \quad \text{(Eqn. 8)}$$

Since we are assuming that $b_4 > 0$ and $b_0 > 0$, it can be seen from Eqn. 8 that $f_{mw}(x,t)$ may remain positive, become zero, or even go negative. Thus, the fate of a relationship depends on the values assigned to the several coefficients to be found in Eqn. 7, particularly the asymptotic terms. This may reflect the importance of fundamental, rather than superficial characteristics (e.g., intelligence vs. a Mercedes).

We can see, then, that the apparent conflict between popular cliches is resolved when examined quantitatively, and that the seeming threat to clarity of expression may be eliminated through the application of straightforward mathematical analysis. Hence, the question of which expression most accurately describes the fate of a relationship actually depends on the relative values of coefficients which, in turn, depend on the exact nature of that relationship. The manner in which these terms may be computed, as well as possible extensions of this work to relationships involving more than two persons, domestic animals and household appliances all provide intriguing areas for further research.

THE LOST THEOREM OF EUCLID

David C. Jolly
Massachusetts Institute of Technology
Cambridge, Massachusetts

The recent rediscovery of the "lost theorem" of Euclid has received such widespread publicity that some of the more sensational aspects have been emphasized at the expense of accuracy. As one of the discoverers of the theorem, the author feels obliged to publish the following accurate history of the theorem.

At the beginning of this century, one of the bitterest controversies in the history of German archaeology was waged over the so-called "missing theorem" of Euclid. At that time the first edition of the *Elements*[1] existed only in fragments, while the second edition[2] was available in complete form. By careful comparison of the fragments of the first edition with the complete second, it was determined that, starting with the 42nd theorem of Book III, a renumbering had taken place between editions, and it was deduced that the renumbering was consistent with one theorem having been deleted in the second edition. All authorities agreed on this point. The trouble began when various scholars attempted to deduce what the missing theorem was, based upon internal evidence contained in the *Elements* themselves, and upon references of other ancient authors to Euclid's work. Their approach was essentially one of "What would Euclid have wanted to prove at this point?" The German archaeological community divided into several bitterly antagonistic camps, each convinced of the validity of its own interpretation. This period resulted in some of the most abusive journal articles ever published.[3]

A New Angle

The eye of the storm was in Dessau, a small city now located in East Germany. Here was stored the great manuscript collection of the Dessau Museum containing, among other things, medieval copies of almost all ancient writings bearing on the question. Scholars from all over Germany journeyed to the museum in search of evidence supporting their individual viewpoints. Chance meetings of opposing professors occasionally led to duels, much to the amusement of the local townsfolk. In one notable incident, a well-known professor from Berlin took his entire class to Dessau to challenge a rival professor and his students to a "duel en masse." The plan was nipped in the bud when the local police clapped the "Herr Professor" and his students into "der Klink." The Kaiser, concerned about the international image of German science, was moved to make a personal request for the professor's release.[4] Duels, suicides, and resignations caused by the controversy had decimated the ranks of German archaeology by 1914 when the outbreak of war put an end to hostilities.[5]

In a freak accident during the war, a burning observation balloon fell on the wooden structure housing the Dessau manuscript collection, and all documents were lost. When this loss became known, international reaction was one of dismay.[6] The loss of this valuable material and the uncertain political condi-

[1] Euclid. *Elements*. Alexandria, 13 vols., c.310 B.C.
[2] Euclid. *Elements*. Rev. 2nd ed. Alexandria, 13 vols., c.302 B.C.

[3] For a relatively unbiased account of the early years of the controversy see e.g., *Die Euklidische Elemente*, by A. W. von Graustoff, Berlin, 1911.
[4] "Das Interzession des Kaiser Bill." *Dessau Zeitung*, Jan. 20, 1913.
[5] Dimbleby, Lt. Col. R. B. (ret.). *A Concise History of the Great War*. London, 1922, 35 vols.
[6] "The Dessau Museum Fire: Calamity or Disaster?" *Nature*, 103:521, 1919.

tions in Europe after the war led the lost theorem controversy to be forgotten. This of course has all changed with the recent discovery of a fragment containing the complete theorem. The discovery was made in Istanbul during the razing of an old monastery to make way for a parking lot. Radiocarbon dating[7] and paleographical analysis have established the authenticity of the find, and the fragment has tentatively been attributed to the minor Byzantine geometer and scribe Bokletes (fl. 2nd cent. A.D.). For convenience, the theorem is presented in modern notation below.

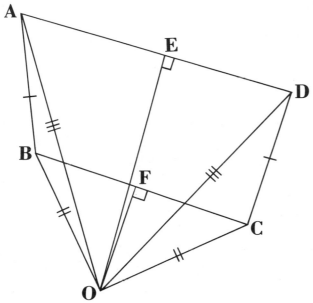

To Prove: All obtuse angles are equal to the right angle. Given: Obtuse angle ABC.

1. Construct DC ⊥ to BC and equal in length to AB.

2. Draw AD.

3. Erect the perpendicular bisectors of AD and BC until they intersect at point O, and draw AO, BO, DO, and CO.

4. Clearly AO = DO, BO = CO, and ∠CBO = ∠BCO.

5. Since all three sides are equal, ABO and DCO are congruent triangles, and therefore ∠ABO = ∠DCO.

6. Since ∠CBO = ∠BCO, by subtraction of equal angles we have ∠ABC = ∠BCD. Q.E.D.

By a remarkable coincidence, within a month of the Istanbul discovery a manuscript detailing the history of the theorem surfaced in the Vatican Library. The manuscript was apparently a summary of documents assembled in the fourth century A.D. by Theon of Alexandria as source material for his never finished *History of Geometry*. It had mistakenly been bound in

with a collection of sermons by Pope Sixtus II[8] and was discovered by accident.[9] Based on the Istanbul fragment and the Vatican manuscript, the remarkable story of this theorem can now be traced to its discoverer, Pythagoras.

Round and Round

As is well known, the Pythagoreans founded a school at Croton, in Southern Italy, in 529 B.C. Among other things, this school was noted for its mystical numerological beliefs and for strict adherence to the duodecimal system. Little else is known of their activities. One long standing puzzle to historians has been the sudden disappearance of Pythagoras and most of his disciples in 502 B.C.

Through the Vatican manuscript we now know that the "lost theorem" was discovered at that school in 510 B.C., causing a number of changes to be instituted. New disciples were barred, and the facility at Croton abandoned for more suitable quarters at Metapontum. It did not take the Pythagoreans long to realize the far reaching consequences of the theorem. For example, consider two objects, one rotating twice as rapidly as the other. In the time the slowly rotating object turns 90°, the faster one will have rotated 180°. Since by the theorem 90° and 180° are substantially the same angle, the two objects are really rotating at the same rate. By a straightforward extension of this logic, it can be shown that all non-zero rotation rates are equal. Clearly a person or group in command of such counterintuitive knowledge possesses enormous advantages.

The Pythagoreans had long disputed over the nature of the heavenly bodies, and proposed to put their new-found knowledge to practical use in actually traveling to observe a star at close range. They reasoned that the earth and its occupants could be considered to be revolving about the sun at some velocity. If a person inside a sealed "ship" were to suddenly imagine himself revolving at some other rate, he would then actually be in that new reference frame (which he had been in all along since all rotation rates are equal), and by proper choice of new reference frame, a traveler could be hurtled to a distant star in a matter of seconds, observe, and then return safely by reversing the procedure.

Starship Down

Their choice of target star was governed by obscure astrological considerations, as was the most favorable

[7] UCLA-2083.

[8] Bib. Vat., Sixt. II, 29 T.6.
[9] J. Lib. Disc., 18:231-3, 1973.

time of launch. This restricted the launching site to a small area in North America near the present site of Winslow, Arizona. A Phoenician combine from Sidon was engaged for transportation, and the Pythagoreans set out for North America. After landing near what is now Savannah, Georgia, the Pythagoreans and their Phoenician escort proceeded overland to the launch

site.[10] Despite a rather harrowing journey, they arrived safely in Arizona and readied their starship. At the appointed time, Pythagoras and his disciples sealed themselves inside the ship and began imagining themselves to be stationary with respect to the earth. Upon signal from Pythagoras, they suddenly began imagining themselves in a new frame rotating much more rapidly about the sun.

By examining the surviving records, it can be determined that there had been a factor of twelve errors in their calculations, leading to an incorrect choice of new reference frame.[11] Instead of being hurtled to the target star, they were instantaneously accelerated to a downward directed velocity of about one parsec per sec. Due to the presence of the earth, an almost equally rapid deceleration followed. Pythagoras and his followers vanished in an intense flash of ultraviolet light, leaving a large crater.[12] The surviving Phoenician witnesses reported that a large mushroom shaped cloud followed the event. Local American Indian mushroom worshipers still speak in reverent tones of this appearance of their deity. To this day annual festivals are held by them in which small mushrooms are consumed in memory of His appearance.

A Use for the Obtuse

Upon the return of the Phoenicians to the Mediterranean, the Pythagorean school was disbanded, and most of their accumulated knowledge was scattered and lost, although some records were preserved in the great library at Alexandria. These records were apparently discovered by Euclid some time between 320 and 315 B.C., and formed the basis for his *Elements*. At that time, Rome was contesting Greek power in the Mediterranean. The tremendous military potential of the theorem was belatedly recognized after publication of the first edition of the *Elements*, and existing copies were hastily recalled, accounting for its scarcity today. A new edition was prepared omitting any mention of the theorem. Several copies of the first edition were nevertheless carefully preserved, and sent out at intervals for use in trouble spots threatened with Roman takeover.

It is now known that Archimedes of Syracuse was one of the recipients of the first edition. He is perhaps best remembered today for his statement, "Give me a place to stand, and I will move the earth."[13, 14] His use of military engines to drive off Roman attacks on Syracuse is legendary. It is said that Roman fleets would turn sail at the merest sight of an unusual rope or pole appearing over the fortifications of Syracuse. Many of his devices were in fact clever applications of the "missing theorem." Unfortunately, the inhabitants of Syracuse became overconfident and began to rely too heavily on the genius of Archimedes. The downfall occurred as a result of a peculiar fort he had constructed based on the theorem. By a clever combination of right and obtuse angles he had devised a fortification whose entrance could not be stormed. No matter where one stood, the entrance always seemed to be "just around the corner." Unfortunately, during an attack in 212 B.C., the force sent to defend the fort could not find the entrance themselves, and were caught in the open as they milled about in confusion. Archimedes himself was slain while frantically trying to re-derive the lemma necessary to find the entrance. The fall of Syracuse and the later destruction of the library at Alexandria caused the theorem to be forgotten until its recent accidental rediscovery. The rediscovery has of course drastically changed the direction of modern scientific thought, but these recent events are beyond the scope of this article, and the reader is referred to the current scientific literature.

---

[10] Relics of this expedition may have been unearthed recently in Georgia. See e.g. F. L. Witherspoon, "Is the Metcalf Stone a Clever Forgery, or Merely a Fraud?" *Rev. Mod. Archeo.*, 32:128-131, 1970.

[11] This highlights one advantage of our present decimal system, such errors being somewhat less serious. Nevertheless factor of ten errors also cause trouble. For numerous examples of bridges, dams, etc. collapsing through such errors, the reader is referred to E. Godfrey, "Engineering Failures and Their Lessons," 1924.

[12] This crater still exists and is a present-day tourist attraction.

---

[13] This may have been no idle boast. Recent evidence suggests that in the first millenium B.C. major disturbances took place in the orbits of some planets, possibly as a result of Archimedes using the theorem to alter planetary rotation and revolution rates. See e.g. I. Velikovsky, *Worlds in Collision*, Doubleday, 1950. Such casual tinkering with the solar system, if it occurred, does the memory of Archimedes little or no credit.

[14] Archimedes' statement may in fact be a mistranslation. "Place to stand" is an ancient Greek idiom for "reference frame," i.e. a place to observe from. His statement can be more accurately rendered as "Give me the earth's reference frame, and I will alter it."

METRIC HAVOC

Jerry W. Mansfield
Assistant Engineering Librarian
Purdue University
West Lafayette, IN

Over the past few years there has been much heated debate surrounding the suggestion that the United States convert to the metric system of measurement. Though there is much resistance and many of the advantages and disadvantages have been voiced, the total implications of the conversion to the metric system have not been fully realized by the populace. Homemakers may be aware that recipes may call for $1\frac{1}{3}$ fluid drams of water and that the driving distance between two cities may be 43 km, but what has been purposefully kept from the public are the particulars surrounding the formulation of the new metric calendar.

The proposed calendar is certain to create havoc with vacation schedules, school related activities, local Weight Watcher meetings and most of the traditional holidays as we now know them. The National Institute of Metriconification (NIM)[1] has been working with PUCI, Publicus Uninformatum Concilium Impedio[2], on this project for several years to facilitate the transition within the United States and has recently made their proposed calendar known. A test calendar has been used extensively in some United States territories and protectorates since 1976 with some success. Modifications will continue to be made based upon recommendations of officials in these sparsely populated islands before implementation in the United States.

In the States we have been gradually prepared for a dramatic calendar change with the governmental act of moving official government holidays to a set Monday, e.g. Columbus Day. We have also witnessed the installation of metric comparison distance charts on some interstate highways and have observed that many new cars even have their fuel tank capacity expressed in liters. All of this and more is designed to prepare us for the big day.

The method by which the new dates will be determined is one which can easily be used by all. To compute the change, NIM-PUCI has devised the following formula to convert present dates to the metric calendar:

$$\Psi^{(n)} (\chi + 1) = \Psi^{(n)} (\chi) + (-1)^n n!/\chi^{n+1},$$

$$\Psi^{(n)} (1-\chi) + (-1)^{n+1} \Psi^{(n)} (\chi) = (-1)^n \pi \frac{d^n}{d\chi^n} \text{Cot } \pi\chi$$

When the given data is input and the calculation complete the result is 127. Thus all present dates and holidays will be moved forward a total of 127 days. If you use this equation you can easily discover for yourself the new date for your favorite holiday. Merely to provide you with some idea of where the new holidays will fall, the following chart is a partial list of some of the more popular holidays.

	JULIAN CALENDAR	METRIC CALENDAR
New Year's Day	January 1	May 8
Valentine's Day	February 14	June 21
Washington's Birthday	February 22	June 29
St. Patrick's Day	March 17	July 22
Easter	Mid-March/ Mid-April	Mid-July/ Mid-August
Memorial Day	May 30	October 4
Independence Day	July 4	November 8
Labor Day	1st Monday/ September	1st Monday/ January
Halloween	October 31	March 7
Thanksgiving	4th Thursday/ November	4th Thursday/ March
Christmas	December 25	May 1

Some of these changes will work out better than the present date observed. For instance, since many workers often cannot get to work in January because they are snowbound, it may benefit business and industry that Labor Day will fall on the First Monday in January. However, many familiar phrases like "the Fourth of July" will no longer be used and the school year will now begin in January. Similarly, the old Summer vacation will become the Fall vacation as school will be in recess from October through December.

---

[1] National Institute of Metriconification, P.O. Box 1361 A, Humptulips, WA 98552

[2] Committee to Keep the Public Uninformed, address unknown.

CORRECT METRIC TIME

James Wilson
Laboratory for Laser Energetics
University of Rochester
Rochester, New York

I wish to point out an error in the paper by Mansfield.[1] Mansfield correctly assessed the necessity of a metric calendar, but apparently had no concept of metric *time*. This shows the danger of letting as important a topic as metrification be discussed by librarians. The solution to the set of equations listed by Mansfield is only valid if the metric time t is related to the present time t' by

$$t = At' + 0$$

Although Mansfield correctly identified the phase shift 0 as 127 days, he completely neglected the other term. This has far-reaching consequences as we shall see.

The equation above points out that to make time truly metric, a simple phase shift is insufficient. Instead, any self-respecting metric year must have 100 days. This does present some problems, since we are not used to seeing Santa Claus boiling in his hot suit on Christmas Day in the middle of summer, as will happen every few years under the metric system. However, the long-suffering people in the Southern hemisphere have put up with this situation for ages. Surely the time has come to distribute the discomforts more evenly.

On the positive side is the fact that since there are roughly three metric years to the old year, and since Christmas comes but once a (metric) year, we will have more Christmases on the whole. This will rally the support of small children and merchants to the cause of metric time, but may discourage a few scrooges.

Accepting metric time means that we will all grow to an age approximately three times the present limit. Whether this is good or bad is a subject requiring further research.

Division of a day into twenty-four hours, each of which is subdivided into sixty minutes or 3,600 seconds, is not permissible in metric time, and instead a division by ten is proposed. The resulting unit can no longer be called an hour, of course; instead, I modestly propose, following the current fashion of naming scientific units after appropriate scientists, that this unit be named the Wilson. The Wilson itself will be subdivided into milliWilsons (corresponding crudely to ten of the present seconds), nanoWilsons, picoWilsons, etc. Think of how much nicer it will be to say "I'll be with you in a milliWilson," rather than "I'll be with you in ten seconds." Who can resist requesting "Just a 100 nanoWilsons" rather than "Just a sec"?

A difficulty with the new metric system of time is that it will be necessary to revert to the Roman system of months, i.e. only having ten to the year. This in itself is no problem, but the months being very short will not now even vaguely correspond to the phases of the moon. This is clear evidence of a lack of metric thinking on the part of Mother Nature. We suggest that she be hauled before a court of metrified scientists, and compelled to rectify this error.

PAUL MEISEL

A simplification resulting from the metric time is that with a metric month lasting only ten days, and the only logical metric week also being ten days, there will no longer be a distinction between a month and a week. What elegant simplicity! Another apparent problem is that since each metric month only has ten days, December 25th simply will not exist. Fortunately the phase shift 0 puts Christmas Day on May 1st, as pointed out by Mansfield,[2] and so Christmas is saved. Unfortunately other important dates are not so lucky, and Valentine's Day will disappear. For a true lover of metrification, this is a small price to pay.

[1,2] Mansfield, J.W. "Metric Havoc." *Journal of Irreproducible Results* 25:28 (1979).

THE LARGEST INTEGER

Joel H. Spencer
Bell Telephone Laboratories

Mathematicians have long sought to discover the identity of the largest integer. Some have proclaimed that such a thing does not exist. This view, while possibly internally consistent, certainly cannot give a true model of the integers. For by symmetry, if there is a smallest integer there must be a largest. Of course, this argument's premise may be, and has been, denied. However, without the principle of symmetry much of the work of the last two centuries would have to be discarded. This, we feel, is too great a price to pay. Our solution is given by the following.

Theorem: -1 is the largest integer

Proof 1:   List the integers

$$\ldots -4 \ -3 \ -2 \ -1$$
$$+1 \ +2 \ +3 \ +4 \ldots$$

You will note that nothing has been left out. The largest integer must have no successor: clearly -1.

This proof lacks rigor as it required a "listing" of the integers. We therefore include a rigorous

Proof 2:   Let n be the largest integer

Then $n \leq n + 1$

and $n + 1 \leq n + 2$

so $n \leq n + 2$

But since n is the largest integer

$$n \leq n + 2$$

so $n = n + 2$

Squaring both sides $n^2 = n^2 + 4n + 4$

$$4n = -4$$
$$n = -1$$

Q.E.D.

It has been noted that since $n + n + i$, $n = \dfrac{-i}{2}$.

Since n must be integral $i = 2j > 0$, $n = -j$. But $-1 \geq -j$ for all $j > 0$ and so is the largest largest integer

and therefore the largest integer.

We might also recall the conventional nonexistent argument (generally, and for good reason, used only with children), "add one and you get a larger number." But we see that nothing is one more than -1.

THE WE-ARE-ALL-ONE DEPT.

260.3 Use of number and gender. As used in Parts 260 through 265 of this Chapter:

(a) Words in the masculine gender also include the feminine and neuter genders; and

(b) Words in the singular include the plural; and

(c) Words in the plural also include the singular.

—*From "Rules and Regulations," the* Federal Register *Vol. 45, No. 98, May 1980.*

...and here today to speak on "side-effects of single-cell-protein diet"...

MEASURING THE PRIMADONNA FACTOR FOR ODD NUMBERS

Y. Ronen, et al.
Department of Experimental Mathematics
Beer Sheva, Israel

Recently Arbinka[1] proposed a revolutionary theorem in the field of falstional analysis. According to this theorem (Appendix A) all odd numbers are primary numbers. Due to the importance of this discovery our group at the department of experimental mathematics has proposed an experiment to verify this idea.

In our experiment we measured the amount in which odd numbers differ from being primary. The Primadonna factor P is defined as,

$$P = \frac{\text{Primary number}}{\text{odd number}} \qquad (1)$$

In other words, P is the factor by which you have to multiply an odd number in order to get the closest primary number. According to the Arbinka theorem this factor has to equal 1. In the experiment a large domain of odd numbers was chosen, namely all the odd numbers between 1 and 13. The temperature at each measurement was carefully checked. The results obtained are given in Table 1 and in Fig. 1.

Table 1
The Primadonna Factor For Odd Numbers

Odd number	Primadonna factor	Temperature °C
1	0.99 ± 0.1	20.4
3	0.98 ± 0.1	19.8
5	1.03 ± 0.1	19.0
7	1.05 ± 0.2	22.1
9	0.1 ± 0.1	40.0
11	0.97 ± 0.1	21.5
13	0.88 ± 0.2	25.0

In Fig. 1 we see an excellent agreement between

[1] Arbinka: Private Communication (1972)

our experiment and Arbinka's theory. The only difference occurs for the odd number 9. A possible explanation for this difference is the effect of temperature. Table 1 shows that all the measurements, besides the number 9, were taken at about the same temperature, whereas the measurement of 9 was taken at the high temperature of 40°C, which might explain the difference. We are now designing equipment for measuring the dependence of the Primadonna factor on temperature in order to get a conclusive explanation of the anomality of the number 9.

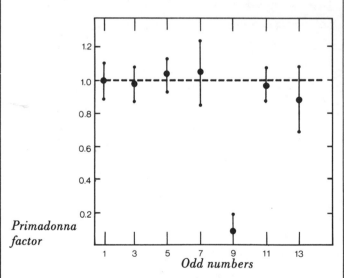

Fig. 1. The dependence of the Primadonna factor for odd numbers

ACKNOWLEDGMENTS
The authors are indebted to many people for useful comments and smiles.

APPENDIX—A
Theorem: All the odd numbers are primary numbers.
Proof: One   is primary number
                  Three   is primary number
                  Five   is primary number
                  Seven   is primary number.
Thus using the induction technique every odd number is primary.

IMPURE MATHEMATICS*

Once upon a time (1/T) pretty little Polly Nomial was strolling across a field of vectors when she came to the edge of a singularly large matrix.

Now Polly was convergent and her mother had made it an absolute condition that she must never enter such an array without her brackets on. Polly, however, who had changed her variables that morning and was feeling particularly badly behaved, ignored this condition on the grounds that it was insufficient and made her way in amongst the complex elements.

Rows and columns enveloped her on all sides. Tangents approached her surface. She became tensor and tensor. Quite suddenly, three branches of a hyperbola touched her at a single point. She oscillated violently, lost all sense of directrix and went completely divergent. As she reached a turning point she tripped over a square root which was protruding from the erf and plunged headlong down a steep gradient. When she was differentiated once more she found herself, apparently alone, in a non-euclidean space.

She was being watched, however. That smooth operator, Curly Pi, was lurking inner product. As his eyes devoured her curvilinear coordinates, a singular expression crossed his face. Was she still convergent, he wondered. He decided to integrate improperly at once.

Hearing a vulgar fraction behind her, Polly turned round and saw Curly Pi approaching with his power series extrapolated. She could see at once, by his degenerate conic and his dissipative terms, that he was bent on no good.

"Eureka," she gasped.

"Ho, ho," he said. "What a symmetric little Polynomial you are. I can see you're bubbling over with secs."

"O Sir," she protested, "keep away from me. I haven't got my brackets on."

"Calm yourself, my dear," said our suave operator, "your fears are purely imaginary."

"I, I," she thought, "perhaps he's homogenous then."

"What order are you," the brute demanded.

"Seventeen," replied Polly.

Curly leered. "I suppose you've never been operated on yet," he asked.

"Of course not," Polly cried indignantly. "I'm absolutely convergent."

"Come, come," said Curly. "Let's off to a decimal place I know and I'll take you to the limit."

"Never," gasped Polly.

"Exchlf," he swore, using the vilest oath he knew. His patience was gone. Coshing her over the coefficient with a log until she was powerless, Curly removed her discontinuities. He stared at her significant places and began smoothing her points of inflexion. Poor Polly. All was up. She felt his hand tending to her asymptotic limit. Her convergence would soon be gone forever.

There was no mercy, for Curly was a heavyside operator. He integrated by parts. He integrated by partial fractions. The complex beast even went all the way around and did a counter integration. What an indignity. To be multiply connected on her first integration. Curly went on operating until he was absolutely and completely orthogonal.

When Polly got home that evening, her mother noticed that she had been truncated in several places. But it was too late to differentiate now. As the months went by, Polly increased monotonically. Finally she generated a small but pathological function which left surds all over the place until she was driven to distraction.

The moral of our sad story is this: If you want to keep your expressions convergent, never allow them a single degree of freedom.

*Submitted by Richard A. Gibbs

PART VIII

OFF THE
IVORY TOWER

VIDE·INFRA

Tim Healey, F.F.R., M.I.Nuc.E.
Barnsley, Yorkshire
England

A s a keen[1] student[2] of footnotes,[3,4] I have long[14]

---

[1] Enthusiastic, not necessarily sharp.[13]

[2] When the late Dr. John Wilkie[18] stood up and said "As a mere student in these matters..." the listeners knew that they were about to hear some words of wisdom from a very experienced expert.[16-24] Modesty [17] forbids me to draw a parallel.

[3] Blaise[17] Pascal used the same trick with his phrase "It is easy to show that..." Experienced mathematicians soon recognized that these words warned them that the next step would take them three days of complex calculations to understand.

[4] I have been fascinated by footnotes ever since I obtained several editions of a book[5] that has some of the best footnotes[6] I have ever encountered.[7]

[5] Samson Wright's "Applied Physiology."[8]

[6] E.g. text: "Never occurs." Footnote: "What never? Well, hardly ever."

[7] A book called "Useless Facts in History" has a good pair[9] also.

[8] The footnotes disappeared after the ninth edition, when Samson Wright died. His major work has been continued,[10] but the footnotes that gave it individuality are no longer given: a grave mistake.

[9] There are only two in the book.[11]

[10] Tenth edition by C. A. Keele and E. Neil. O.U.P. London 1961.

[11] The first says "Do you like footnotes?" The second says "Aha![12] Caught you again."

[12] Note the similar style to Lucy.[15]

[13] Though I do not deny it.

[14] There is no room for the rest of this article, as my allotted space is entirely taken up with footnotes. However, I was merely going to state that it has been my ambition to write an article wholly composed of footnotes.[20] My resolution weakened and I included a first line.

[15] In the Peanuts strip cartoon by Schultz[24] in the *Daily Sketch*.[19]

[16] He was never wrong.[6]

[17] This juxtaposition no doubt reflects my admiration for the work of Mr. Peter O'Donnell.

[18] Of Sheffield.

[19] Now defunct. The *Sketch* and the strip have gone to the Mail.

[20] Footnotes should not be confused with references. Thus, 10 is a footnote, not a reference. References have a special charm of their own. I cherish a reprint of an article describing one case, with seven alleged co-authors and 73 references. Famous physics papers include those by Bhang and Gunn; Alfa, Bethe and Gamow; Sowiski and Soda, etc. In my capacity of Science Editor for an international journal, I get not a few "crank" papers for assessment. I have learned to recognize these at a glance by the facts that a) the references always come first, and b) the list includes (always at number 5 or 6, for some unknown reason) "5: 'Some inane observations on some perfectly well worked out phenomena' by N.A.D.[21] Six copies, privately circulated, six years ago."[22]

[21] The author of the paper being considered. They always use only initials here.

[22] You will observe that not all footnotes are brief. A recent article[23] I wrote was originally subtitled "A Footnote to History." It occupied two sides of news-sheet with 3000 words. The subeditorial pencil removed the subtitle, but a comment on the article in the *People* restored my faith in the subeditorial class. This genius[24] dreamed up the heading "Queen of Drag."

[23] "Was the Virgin Queen a Man?" *Pulse*, September 1971.

[24] Credit where credit is due.

THESIS GUIDELINES

Roger E. Soles

Don't Say	Instead Say
I have just found a way to add two and two the hard way.	I have just made a significant contribution to current methodological issues.
I have made a lot of mistakes in my life.	I have been fortunate to have had the opportunity to accumulate considerable experience.
Truthfully, I don't know what I am doing. But sooner or later I am bound to stumble on an acceptable answer.	Because of the complexity of the problem we had to employ the sophisticated Las Vegas technique, a converging Monte Carlo simulation.
Everybody knows what the answer is, so let's not waste a lot of time beating around the bush.	On the basis of *a priori* considerations involving Boolean logic and other advanced techniques, it was possible to narrow the relevant decision space considerably.
Because the original data did not give us the expected answer, we threw out data until we got the answer we wanted.	Exploratory estimates yielded wrong signs on some of the structural coefficients. However, closer scrutiny of the original data suggested that, in all probability, some of the data came from a different population. After discarding these data, logically consistent and statistically significant estimates were obtained.
I feel like taking a trip abroad without spending my own money.	It is our opinion that every agricultural economist has the moral responsibility to concern himself with international agricultural economics. I am ready to live up to this responsibility.
Things are going to change, but I don't have the slightest idea in which direction.	The next decade will see changes in the agricultural structure which will have dimensions and consistency never experienced hitherto anywhere in the world.
When I started this research I simply forgot to include taxation and inflation into the analysis. In retrospect, it is evident that an analysis of the problem without these variables is useless.	Taxation and inflation are two most important variables which must be considered in a complete analysis of this problem. However, inclusion of these two variables into this analysis was clearly beyond the scope of this study.
I wish I could understand what these Journal articles are all about.	It is evident that our Journal has come to the point where it contains mostly articles which do not address themselves to the real issues of today.
Neither evidence nor logic support the conclusion I desire to draw.	Indirect evidence clearly supports our hypothesis. Our hypothesis is further supported by theoretical arguments advanced by Ricardo, Marshall, Keynes, Schultz, Heady, Leontief, Stigler, Fidel Castro, and others.

HOW TO BE A PUBLISHED MATHEMATICIAN

David Louis Schwartz

Abstract

After a crisp, cogent analysis of the problem, the author brilliantly cuts to the heart of the question with incisive simplifications. These soon reduce the original complex edifice to a mouldering pile of dusty rubble.

Method

The problem is that mathematicians *know* all kinds of weird things, but they publish comparatively little. It's not the *numbers* that bother them; it's the *words*. If the fill-in words necessary for a mathematical paper were provided, any mathematician could fill in the spaces with numbers, and he'd be safely through the publish-or-perish barrier. It is with this humanitarian view that I have undertaken to provide a form sheet, sort of a workbook approach. The arrangement given is based on already published material, so the plan has the advantage of having been shown to be workable at least once before.

There are numerous subtitles. One must realize that editors of mathematics magazines tend to understand either (1) too much, or (2) too little about the things they read. Misunderstandings arise. One way around this obstacle is don't submit things to mathematics publications. Try *Ladies Home Journal,* or *Vogue,* or *Hot Rod;* this is important. The possibility of "toning up" an issue with something serious can frequently appeal to a nonmathematical editor, whereas the same possibility probably never occurs to a math magazine editor. Therefore, we insert not merely connective words and phrases, but *whole paragraphs.*

Since everything basically contains part of everything else, it is always possible to relate a random paragraph to anything occurring before and after. Once this fact is taken to heart, a career as a published mathematician becomes inevitable.

The blanks are to be filled in with mathematical symbols. The more variety, the better. Throw in everything. Be neat. Editors love neatness.

Your Paper

From the statement _____

and _____

we obtain _____

in which _____

with _____

together with _____

we also have _____

and therefore, effectively, _____

the desired formula emerges as _____.

Accordingly, a non-Hermitian canonical variable transformation function can serve as a generator for the transformation function referring to unperturbed oscillator energy states.

There follows _____.

Alternatively, if we choose _____

there appears _____.

Thus _____

and _____

where the latter version is obtained from _____.

The next installment will discuss advanced presentation procedures, how (and why) to write an abstract, and the role of mathematics in our Judeo-Christian heritage.

THE FACULTY PHRASE FINDER

William B. LeMar
Omaha, Nebraska

Column	A	B	C
1	University-centered	Terminological	Contexts
2	Computerized	Transformational	Disciplines
3	Coordinated	Educative	Determinants
4	Intuitive	Cross-disciplinary	Dialogues
5	Contemporary	Conceptual	Reappraisal
6	Faculty-oriented	Mind-stretching	Insights
7	Pragmatic	Humanistic	Infra-structure
8	Accredited	Non-sequential	Parameters
9	Linguistic	Vertically-structured	Semantics
0	Extracurricular	Multi-versity	Idiom

Instructions: To find the phrase which expresses your intuitive insights into the semantics of the academic inter-disciplinary contexts of any university-centered phenomenon, expressed in appropriately discursive idiom, choose the words from the table above. Take any three numbers—from your address, your phone number, your social security number, or any convenient dollar bill—and select the words for each digit in Columns A, B, and C, respectively. Phrases constructed in this fashion will fit any academic context and will testify amply to your erudition. For example, if your key number is 325, the phrase will be "Coordinated transformational reappraisal," while 154 gives "University-centered conceptual dialogues." Without the guidance of this chart, no such phrase could have occurred to you. With the chart, you should become a dean in no time at all.

However, should your advancement not be fast enough to satisfy you with the chart above, the two additional charts supplied below will provide accelerated academic stimuli. (459)

Column	A	B	C
1	Traditional	Focal	Identities
2	Viable	Cooperative	Resources
3	Tentative	Syntactical	Attitudes
4	Accelerated	Homogeneous	Tradition
5	Graduated	Academic	Perceptivities
6	Normative	Traditional	Criteria
7	Categorical	Dialectic	Rhetoric
8	Programmed	Committee-generated	Phenomena
9	Conjugal	Contextual	Stimuli
0	Informal	Linear	Hypothesis

Column	A	B	C
1	Elective	Standardized	Mind-stretching
2	Progressive	Correlative	Premises
3	Flexible	Amorphous	Indoctrination
4	Discursive	Educative	Curricula
5	Evocative	Synthetic	Academicians
6	Aspectual	Finite	Syllabi
7	Phonetic	Stylistic	Implications
8	Textured	Vocational	Relationships
9	Focused	Audio-lingual	Dimensions
0	Truncated	Scholastic	Experience

A VERBAL RORSCHACH

An Antidote for Technically Obnubilated Appellation

E. J. Helwig

In his book *African Genesis* Robert Ardrey tells a delightful story about Sir Zolly Zuckerman, a young South African anthropologist, who once horrified his English friends by proposing to publish a book titled *The Sexual Life of the Primates*. He was promptly informed that "primates" in England could refer to nothing but the prelates of the established church. The book eventually appeared under the title *The Social Life of Monkeys and Apes*.

Perhaps the book would have sold more copies with the sensational title, but it would have disappointed many readers.

Today, when one can make a career out of reading as well as writing technical articles, many authors seem to choose titles that will look well in the Chemical Abstracts. Apparently titles must sound scientific, esoteric, and prestigious (in the archaic sense). Since the recondite is often confused with the erudite, the titles of technical articles frequently smother meaning under a plethora of jargonese.

As a result laymen, or, jargonwise, those not familiar with the lexicon of the scientific disciplines, don't receive the slightest benefit from a technical title. Or do they? Words, like the Rorschach ink blots, invariably carry some sort of impression, even if they conjure up pictures of erotic clergymen.

Technical writers might be able to gauge the fuddlefactor of a proposed title by testing it as a Verbal Rorschach on their unscientific friends. The results could be devastating to the dignity and prestige of technical journalism. And they should effectively deflate pompous titles.

The following examples illustrate just what could happen with a Verbal Rorschach test. The titles were gleaned from a single issue of a listing of current technical papers.* A possible Rorschach interpretation accompanies each title.

Title: Representation Mixing in U12.
Translation: Social Life on an Atomic Submarine.

Title: Double Image Formation in a Stratified Medium.
Translation: Visual Aberration in a Stoned Spiritualist.

Title: Wave Motion Due to Impulsive Twist on the Surface.
Translation: Math-a-go-go, in the Surf.

Title: Behavior of the Nighttime Ionosphere.
Translation: The Naughty Sky After Dark.

Title: Fluid Behavior in Parabolic Containers Undergoing Vertical Excitation.
Translation: Standing Room Only at the Burlesque.

Title: Redundancy in Digital Systems.
Translation: Having More Than Five Fingers or Toes.

Title: Some Results of Transport Theory and Their Application to Monte Carlo Methods.
Translation: Hitchhiking Home From Las Vegas.

Title: Dispersion Techniques in Field Theory.
Translation: Fun on a Field Trip.

Title: Wullenweber Arrays Using Doublet Aerials.
Translation: A Death-Defying Double Trapeze Act Featuring the Famous Flying Wullenwebers.

Title: Holography and Character Recognition.
Translation: It Takes One to Know One.

Now that you know what Verbal Rorschach testing is, try the following titles on your friends.

1. Numerical Model of Coarticulation.

2. Propagation Behavior of Slotted Inhomogeneous Wave Guides.

3. The Verbal Rorschach—An Antidote for Technically Obnubilated Appellations.

4. General Methods of Correlation.

5. Rectification in a Column with Wet Walls.

---

* All the titles referred to are bonafide titles of actual technical papers. The authors and the journals in which they appear are not listed, in order to protect the guilty.

TESTING THE EXTERNAL VALIDITY OF ZIMBARDO'S CLASSIC PRISONER EXPERIMENT

Raymond C. Russ
University of North Florida
Steven Connelly
Indiana State University

In a seminal paper examining the power behind authority, Zimbardo (1972) and his colleagues strikingly demonstrated that when asked to role-play the parts of prisoners and their guards, students behaved in a startling manner: subjects role-played with unguarded emotion and vivid effect; in many instances subjects displayed heightened aggressive behaviors not witnessed since the early Milgram (1963) studies.

Circumstances became so harrowing for "prisoners" that Zimbardo had to end the experiment after only six days. "Guards" systematically dehumanized "prisoners"; the "prisoners" became quivering, isolated entities. The roles quickly became all too real as most "guards" became power-crazed, and most "prisoners" begged for parole.

Zimbardo found evidence for something that has been more than occasionally suggested but often mysteriously squelched within social psychology: *homo sapiens* have a surprising, even distressing, tendency to accept and adopt without question authoritarian commands, often coupled by blind adherence to the conformity demanded by a particular role. In short, experimental subjects display a willingness to pursue any behavior necessary to insure compliance.

Since the implications of such research touch us in the heart of social science conscience theory, the present authors desired to determine conclusively the degree of external validity inherent in the obedience studies, using Zimbardo's experiment as a model. We felt that such replications could, of course, finally delineate the exact parameters of the obedience studies, shed light on the population as a whole, and explicate and confirm the true nature of sanctioned aggression and its behavioral off-shoots in the real world.

Procedure

In order to test the generality of the obedience studies, the present authors asked seventy Death Row prisoners of the Munferd Indiana State Penitentiary to role-play the parts of graduate students and college professors. All subjects were males between the ages of 23 and 65 years. Zimbardo's highly renowned, if controversial, coin flip was used to delegate roles. Four subjects had to be forcibly released after assignment of roles: two for acute Tourette's Syndrome, one for repeatedly smearing orange bitters on his Chairperson's Volvo, and one for guessing the actual intent of the experiment and thereafter refusing to speak to anyone, including the experimenters, real guards, his mother, and his tailor. This particular subject also turned noticeably aggressive when confronted with individuals not named Ralph or Ned.

Results

Those subjects playing professors exhibited a startling

Fly Awareness

half-open posture

textbook cover-up

Student Behavior

Dada Lecture Syndrome   *Finnegan's Wake* Syndrome

Ed Lipinski

phenomenon most appropriately termed "fly awareness." Interestingly, it was found that approximately half the "professors" checked their fly area before classes to make certain all flies were secured, whereas the other half carefully adjusted flies to varying degrees of openness. There were two exceptions regarding this behavior: these subjects made strange and lewd gestures in the fly area during classroom periods, invariably when discussing grades. However, all "professors" developed and cultivated the "denigrating Guffaw" (first identified in the pioneering *Rhetoric of the Guffaw* studies initiated at the Midwestern Humiliation Studies Center in 1953), which they subsequently employed at strategic moments during oral examinations.

"Professors'" behaviors also simulated a strong group cohesion. No "professor" ever questioned or interfered with a request or command made of a "student" by another "professor" while in the "student's" presence. However, behind the scenes and out of "student" view, "professors" engaged in elaborate approach-avoidance behavior, remarkably similar to Lorenz's description of the mating behavior of the male *Stickleback* fish.

"Students," on the other hand, presented such a variety of behavior as to defy classification. One "student" ran about the major quadrangle attempting to insert a bookmark in an unusual place while apparently chanting "Baroquecoco, Baroquecoco, Baroquecoco." Another refused to converse with anyone on any topic other than Dadaism. A previously-mentioned dropout developed a psychotic hatred of Volvos (this particular "student's" case reached the orange-bitters smearing stage only because the experimenters thought he was displaying normal male sexualism: all

thought he suffered *Vagina Dentata Hysteria,* having misunderstood his Volvo threats as Vulva threats). Among the host of psychosomatic syndromes "students" developed the following symptoms: humming while urinating, speaking only in palindromes, and attempting to convince passersby that *Finnegans Wake* was one of the lost books of the Bible and that it contained the key to humanity's salvation—specifically in the numbers 1132.

Furthermore, in line with previous research, "professors" often forced "students" into unnatural acts, e.g., sharpening ballpoint pens, making unneeded dental appointments, and transplanting crabgrass from a "professor's" lawn onto an unknown porch somewhere in New Haven.

The toil and hardship took its toll on "students." One "student" (who was in reality a convicted murderer found guilty of running his wife's pet through a cheese slicer) begged to be delivered to his cell, where he subsequently went on a 40 day hunger strike refusing all food except anchovy pizzas. As he later put it after one semester, "anything to be spared from these humanists." In short, after one term, every student expressed the desire to return home to Death Row.

In summary then, it is obvious that there exists powerful evidence that the obedience studies previously reported in the literature cannot be faulted for lack of generality. The present authors are currently conducting an experiment focusing upon the role-playing behaviors between laboratory technicians and their animals.

REFERENCES

Milgram, S. "Behavioral Study of Obedience." *Journal of Abnormal and Social Psychology,* 67:371–378, 1963.
Zimbardo, P. G. "Pathology of Imprisonment." *Society,* 9:4–8, 1972.

A BRIEF HISTORY OF SCHOLARLY PUBLISHING

Donald D. Jackson
University of Illinois Press

50,000 B.C. Stone Age publisher demands that all manuscripts be double-spaced, and hacked on one side of stone only.

1455 A.D. Johannes Gutenberg applies to Ford Foundation for money to buy umlauts. First subsidized publishing venture.

1483 Invention of *ibid*.

1507 First use of circumlocution.

1859 "Without whom" is used for the first time in list of acknowledgments.

1888 Martyrdom of Ralph Thwaites, an author who deletes 503 commas from his galleys and is stoned by a copy editor.

1897 Famous old university press in England announces that its Urdu dictionary has been in print 400 years. Entire edition, accidentally misplaced by a shipping clerk in 1497, is found during quadricentennial inventory.

1901 First free desk copy distributed (Known as Black Thursday).

1916 First successful divorce case based on failure of author to thank his wife, in the foreword of his book, for typing the manuscript.

1927 Minor official in publishing house, who suggests that his firm issue books in gay paper covers and market them through drug houses, is passed over for promotion.

1928 Early use of ambiguous rejection letter, beginning, "While we have many good things to say about your manuscript, we feel that we are not now in position..."

1934 Bookstore sends for two copies of Gleep's *Origin of Leases* from University Press and instead receives three copies of Darwin's *Storage of Fleeces* plus half of stale peanut butter sandwich from stockroom clerk's lunch. Beginning of a famous Brentano Rebellion, resulting in temporary improvement in shipping practices.

1952 Scholarly writing begins to pay. Professor Harley Biddle's publishing contract calls for royalty on his book after 1,000 copies have been sold to defray printing costs. Total sales: 1,009 copies.

1961 Important case of *Dulany* v. *McDaniel,* in which judge Kelley rules to call a doctoral dissertation a nonbook is libelous per se.

1980 Copy editors' anthem "Revise or Delete" is first sung at national convention. Quarrel over hyphen in second stanza delays official acceptance.

**Title 36—Parks, Forests, and Public Property
CHAPTER I—NATIONAL PARK SERVICE,
DEPARTMENT OF THE INTERIOR
PART 7—SPECIAL REGULATIONS,
AREAS OF THE NATIONAL PARK
SERVICE
Cape Cod National Seashore,
Massachusetts; Public Nudity**

A proposal was published at page 10996 of the FEDERAL REGISTER of March 10, 1975 to amend § 7.67 of Title 36 of the Code of Federal Regulations.

(g) Public nudity, including public nude bathing, by any person on Federal land or water within the boundaries of Cape Code National Seashore is prohibited. Public nudity is a person's intentional failure to cover with a fully opaque covering that person's own genitals, pubic areas, rectal area, or female breast below a point immediately above the top of the areola when in a public place. Public place is any area of Federal land or water within the Seashore, except the enclosed portions of bathhouses, restrooms, public showers, or other public structures designed for similar purposes or private structures permitted within the Seashore, such as trailers or tents. This regulation shall not apply to a person under 10 years of age.

HOW TO PUBLISH WITHOUT PERISHING

A Correspondence, Perhaps With Real Life

Dr. John Barken, M.D., Ph.D.
Editor, *Sound and Fury*
Atlanta, Georgia

Dear Dr. Barken:

Enclosed please find my article, "Laundry Lists of Psychologists: A Class-Related Finding." I hope this meets your editorial needs.

Thank you for your cooperation.

Very truly yours,

Arthur Seagull, Ph.D.
Instructor

Dr. John Barken, M.D., Ph.D
Editor, *Sound and Fury*
Atlanta, Georgia

Dear Dr. Barken:

It's been four days already and I have heard nothing from you. I hope the article is entirely clear. If you have any questions, let me know and I'll be glad to elucidate.

Please don't think that I am at all anxious about this publication, but I come up for reappointment within two months, and while the department that I am in is not exactly publish or perish, one can also exist on cottage cheese, though it isn't terribly palatable. Ha! Ha! I hope you understand me.

Very truly yours,

Arthur Seagull, Ph.D.
Instructor

Post card

Dear Dr. Seagull:

Thank you for your manuscript entitled: "*Laundry List....*" You will be hearing from us within the next two months while we send your article to our consulting editors.

Very truly yours,

John Barken, M.D., Ph.D.
(signed) ml
Editor, *Sound and Fury*

Form 2

Dr. John Barken, M.D., Ph.D.
Editor, *Sound and Fury*
Atlanta, Georgia

Dear Dr. Barken:

Thank you so much for your warm acknowledgment of the receipt of my manuscript. You psychiatrists must really know how to make people feel good, since the tone of your post card was something that I didn't think could be put into a mere, what seems to others, post card. I mean, the way you said "Dear Dr. Seagull." It really made me feel like we are getting to know each other.

However, Dr. Barken, if I may be fairly frank with you, your post card did seem to indicate that it might take a little time to hear from you. I would appreciate expediting consideration of this manuscript if at all possible.

Very sincerely yours,

Arthur Seagull, Ph.D.
Instructor

P.S. The title of the manuscript seems a little flat. If this has any influence on the decision, I would be glad to change it to anything that you thought might possibly "jazz it up" if I can use some "hip talk," which I am sure you will understand, since you appear to be such a man of the world.

Dear Dr. Seagull:

We have just received back your manuscript from our consultants. They were unanimous in deciding that our demands for space make it impossible for us to consider publishing it in this journal. Good luck on your future endeavors.

Very sincerely yours,

John Barken, M.D., Ph.D.
Editor, *Sound and Fury*

Dr. John Barken, M.D., Ph.D.
Editor, *Sound and Fury*
Atlanta, Georgia

Dear Dr. Barken:

I really can't understand your letter to me about the manuscript, "Laundry List." Surely you can see that it is important to understand whether psychologists are in the middle or lower working class. I wasn't entirely frank with you. I wrote the article at the sugestion of one of my mentors who once said to me, "Art" (he was fairly friendly with me, so he called me by my first name, Dr. Barken), "when you get into academia publish everything you can. If you have an interesting laundry list, I would publish that, ha! ha!"

Well, I do think I have an interesting laundry list, and I do need to get published now. I can't stress this last too much. I am not anxious about it, just very cautious. Therefore, I have re-edited my manuscript to "dress it up" by adding lots of statistics (mainly averages). I can assure you that the counts are very accurate in contra-distinction to some others I could mention, but am too much of a gentleman.

I also understand that one of the "big things" in research now is an interdisciplinary approach, so I have changed the title to "The Psychologist's Laundry List: A Psycho-Socio-Anthro-Medico-Linguistico Analysis From the Point of View of a Black Power Advocate." Though you will be probably too polite to say it, I do think that the new title does make it interesting enough for you to probably want to publish it immediately. However, if I simply have an acknowledgment of your desire to publish it *in writing,* that will be enough.

Thank you for your cooperation in this matter. I am waiting to hear from you. My whole future is in your hands; but please don't let that influence your decision.

Very truly yours,

Arthur Seagull, Ph.D.
Instructor

Dear Dr. Seagull:

I have received your re-edited manuscript. To save everyone time, I will be franker with you than I was previously.

I did not bother sending this out to our consultant editors. They were more than unanimous, they were absolutely certain that the manuscript you sent was worthless. I won't bother you with many of the details of their analysis. The most charitable said simply that he wondered why I had sent it to him. (I must admit I am a little defensive about this. Actually my secretary sent it out without my seeing it first, or I could have answered you immediately. I am not defensive about this because being a psychiatrist and a psychologist I am thoroughly analyzed and feel no need to be defensive about something which actually there is no need for me to be defensive about. Even my mother used to say, "One thing about my Johnny, he's very rarely defensive." Actually, my mother wasn't defensive either, and that's where I learned my non-defensiveness.)

Frankly, Dr. Seagull, I don't think that there is much of a future for you in research. Have you tried becoming a therapist?

Very truly yours,

John Barken, M.D., Ph.D.
Editor

Dr. John Barken, M.D., Ph.D.
Editor, *Sound and Fury*
Atlanta, Georgia

Dear Dr. Barken:

You really hurt me. If a person sets out to really hurt somebody, I guess it is easy to do when you are so powerful. I mean, Jesus, you didn't have to be so direct.

Anyhow, I did get the hint that you felt that it was not for your magazine. Therefore, I am submitting it to another journal; and if they accept it, is your face going to be red (you'll be red, not read, ha!!).

Thank you for all your help (here it is too bad you can't hear the biting sarcasm in my voice).

Arthur Seagull, Ph.D.
Instructor
P.S. I thought I would let this stand a day before I sent you such a scathing rebuttal. In the interim, a Ms. Rosey Hippes has come to my office for treatment. She has many somatic complaints, and says that she has had prior treatment in Atlanta, Georgia. Do you happen to know her or who was treating her?

Telegram

ARTHUR SEAGULL, PH.D.
MICHIGAN STATE UNIVERSITY

DEAR ARTHUR:
ROSEY HIPPES, MY EX PATIENT. BELIEVE NOTHING UNTIL I SEND FULL REPORT. HYSTERICAL (PATIENT, NOT ME, HA! HA!). LETTER FOLLOWS.

CORDIALLY,

JOHN

Arthur Seagull
Michigan State University

Dear Art:

What a coincidence that my ex-patient is going to be treated by you. I mean, gosh, isn't it a small world.

I have known Rosey (that's what I called her in therapy) for two years. It was a very intensive psychotherapeutic endeavor, I must say. She is a great one for fantasizing, and I would exercise extreme caution in dealing with any transference relationship. You may notice that she is exceptionally well endowed fantasy-wise, but I would still, as I said, exercise *extreme caution.* My relationship with her was always strictly professional, no matter what she says. In fact, anything that she says I did, I only did for therapeutic reasons. I am very interested in your reaction to her, since she was an exceptionally interesting patient. What did she say?

Very cordially,

John Barken, M.D.

Dear John:

I must say that Ms. Rosey Hippes is quite voluble about her prior therapist. Some might say, John, that you are a naughty boy.

Yours,

Art

Arthur Seagull, Ph.D.
Michigan State University

Dear Art:

You know how some female patients are! As I say, my position is that I was always very professional.

What about that article that you wrote me a while ago? I have been rereading our correspondence, and I can't understand how my secretary sent out all those letters in my name. Why don't you resubmit it and we'll see if we can find space for it—perhaps in our next issue.

Most cordially,

Johnny

P.S. If you get it in by Tuesday next, I think we can squeeze it into this issue. I'll pay for the reprints.

John Barken, M.D., Ph.D.
Editor, *Sound and Fury*
Atlanta, Georgia

Dear Johnny:

Thanks a million. I always knew that you were an editor of extremely high ability. I can also attest to your extreme good taste. (Will you be angry if I say, "yum, yum," ha! ha!)

Thanks for everything. I have another manuscript which I am working on which I would like you to consider also. After your acceptance of my previous article, it dawned on me that my wife's laundry list might also be of some interest to the more prurient of your readers.

So long,

Art

Sound and Fury
NOTICE TO OUR READERS

Next issue: the laundry list in American Culture. Our next issue will be kicked off by a most interesting and new approach to analysis of class differences. We are collecting a number of articles on the use of the laundry list as an indicator of class differences. Please feel free to send in any information on this subject that you might have.

A PSYCHOLOGICAL STUDY OF JOURNAL EDITORS

S. A. Rudin
F.S.B.I.R.

The clinical psychologist Anne Roe studied the manner in which a scientist is seduced by his field of study, and she reported her findings in her book, *The Making of a Scientist* (Roe, 1955). She obtained interviews and test results from the twenty most eminent physical scientists, the twenty most eminent biological scientists, and the twenty most eminent social scientists in the USA. She concluded that the biological scientists tended to be preoccupied with death, that the physical scientists had difficulty locating themselves in the physical world, and that the social scientists disliked and could not get along with people.

This study extends her methods to the study of editors of scientific journals. The editors chosen for study were in charge of all major scientific journals in the USA, making a total of 318,991 subjects. Each subject was studied exhaustively by a combination of depth interview, case history, and numerous psychological tests of intelligence, aptitude, interests, and personality.

Results

First Impression and General Appearance. Subjects ranged from tall[1] to short, fat to thin, and warped to degenerate in general appearance. Despite this heterogeneity, each was marked by certain telltale characteristics: the eyes were narrowed; the mouth was pursed into a snarl; and the writing hand was cramped and taut from stamping REJECTED thousands of times. Upon first perceiving the experimenter, each subject exclaimed, "NO!" before noticing that no manuscript was being tendered.

Childhood Background. That childhood experiences strongly influence the developing personality is well known. Again, great diversity of backgrounds was noted: they came from every conceivable environment, from palatial mansions in Hollywood to wretched hovels on some university campuses, but all had in common a peculiar set of family relationships. In every case, the father turned out to have been an alcoholic, drug addict, professional _____,[2] or the editor of a scientific journal. The mother was found to spend but little time with her children, devoting herself to such pursuits as managing a house _____,[3] selling drugs to adolescents, smuggling diamonds past customs officials, or editing a scientific journal. But of greatest interest for the purposes of this study was the discovery that in every case, the child had been beaten often and severely *with a book*. Naturally, such traumatic stimulation eventually led to a deep-seated hatred of anything associated with reading, writing, learning, knowledge, and scholarship. Some showed this tendency as early as the second year by tearing pages out of the *Encyclopaedia Britannica*, setting

---

THE IS-THIS-GOOD-OR-BAD-NEWS DEPT.

"Cannibals in Polynesia no longer allow their tribes to eat Americans because their fat is contaminated with chlorinated hydrocarbon. Recent figures published show that we [English] have two parts per million DDT in our bodies, whereas the figure for Americans is about 11 p.p.m."

—From Lord Shackelton's Speech in the House of Lords, reported in the Jerusalem Post, March 21, 1963.

---

[1] e.g. J. Bacteriol. (the rest of description does not apply).

[2-3] censored.

JOURNAL COVERAGE CHANGES

Current Contents (Oct. 31, 1973)
Bulletin of Suicidology (ceased publication)

them afire in the middle of the living room floor, and executing an exultant war dance around them in the fashion of certain American Indian tribes.

Intelligence and Aptitudes. These were measured by a variety of instruments including the Wechsler Adult Intelligence Scale (WAIS), the Draw-A-Person Test and various special aptitude tests. Considerable difficulty was encountered since none of the subjects could read. The use of oral and non-verbal tests, however, finally yielded usable data. It was found that the subjects were uniformly below IQ 71. This highest IQ was attained by the editor of a widely-read psychology journal who was himself the author of one of the intelligence tests used. The pattern of abilities measured by the specialized aptitude tests showed the subjects to be well below the standardization group (which was made up of college sophomores, white rats, and some persons from mental hospitals) on verbal reasoning, numerical reasoning, perceptual speed, spatial reasoning, verbal recall, clerical ability, map-reading ability, needle-threading ability, and the capacity to pronounce words of more than three syllables. Indeed, the only tests on which the subjects performed well were one requiring the use of a spade to pick up and transfer material from one pile to another and the ability to ignore noxious odors.

Interest Tests. On the Strong Vocational Interest Blank and the Kuder Preference Record-Vocational, subjects tended to score lower than average on activities and occupations associated with originality, critical thinking, creativity, scientific research, and literary production and appreciation. They scored relatively high, however, on scales measuring interest in mild manual labor and evading work altogether.

Personality Tests. All subjects were found to register insane on Rorschach Ink Blot Test, Thematic Apperception Test, Minnesota Multi-Phasic Personality Inventory, and the House-Three-Person Test. Exceptions were two subjects, both neurotic, ulcer-ridden, and compulsive shoelace kleptomaniacs. All subjects perceived themselves as God, except for one who claimed that he had created God. Another signed his name omitting all vowels.[4] Yet another claimed that the ink blots were actually reprints of old copies of his journal, and sued the experimenter for plagiarism.

The Journal Editor

illusions of godlike power

IQ: 71

hatred of books

eyes narrowed

snarl

cramped writing hand

REJECT

ED LIPINSKI

Conclusions

The reasons for the success of these subjects in editing journals are clear. First, by preventing new ideas from appearing in print, they make it easier to keep up with the literature. Second, by requiring the experimenter to repeat his study dozens of times and rewrite his paper hundreds of times, they enforce the consumption of materials and labor, thus stimulating the national economy. Third, if *they* can understand a paper, *anyone* can.

---

[4] He was from Israel.

PART IX

IDEAS WHOSE TIME...

THE FLY AS AN AERONAUTIC FORCE

Tim M. Sharon, Ph.D.*
Richard D. Brewer, Ph.D.**
Brewer-Sharon, Inc.
Irvine, CA

Not long ago, in an issue of a prestigious national magazine, an article drew attention to the National Air and Space Museum's acquisition of two fly-powered aircraft[1] (see illustration). Although no reference was made as to the origin or antecedents of these two craft, one could not help but gain the impression[2] that they represented the prototype models—a conclusion engendered by the fact that they are displayed along with other truly original-in-concept flying models. The authors feel an injustice has been fostered, for one of the authors (Brewer) experimented with aircraft of this design as early as 1949! That, coupled with certain errors in execution of the craft being exhibited, which would render them in all likelihood unflyable (more on this later), has convinced us that these are cheap, unworkable imitations, and that the record must be set straight.

Let us begin with the history, as told in the inventor's own words, of fly-powered gliders: "In the spring of 1949, I lived in a U.S. Navy housing project in Torrey Pines, California, on a site located just about where the Physical Sciences Library of the University of California at San Diego is presently situated.[3] This was within a few miles of the Torrey Pines glider facilities, located on the cliffs that today overlook the infamous Blacks Beach,[4] and from which today young hang gliders cavort amid the sea gulls, pelicans, and soaring planes above the blue Pacific.

"Inspired by my environment and surrounded by aviation and dreams of flight, my then young mind turned to the flight of the fly.[5] I conceived of using the common house fly as the power source for commercial aircraft.[6] To test my hypothesis, I designed and built what I believe to be the first prototype fly-powered planes."

Before continuing this exciting narrative, let us examine what the Smithsonian believes to be a proper design. Quoting from reference 1: "First you catch

---

*This author has never built a fly-powered aircraft, nor does he intend to do so since flies are dirty little critters. However, he does have a degree, and is thus intimately acquainted with a fly's main source of fuel. Besides, it was his idea to write this article.

**The inventor, we believe, of fly-powered aircraft.

[1] Park, E. "Around the Mall." *Smithsonian*, 9:6, 16–20, September 1978.

[2] Especially if you're at that impressionable age.

[3] The fact that the library has not yet been appropriately dedicated, in light of the momentous discovery made in the area, we consider to be an example of shameless neglect.

[4] The first legalized nude beach in California.

[5] Not unlike a latter day Leonardo (the one who studied the flight of sea gulls).

[6] We believe this may be one of the first attempts to develop an ecologically sound source of air transportation, since the engines would be fueled by pollutants.

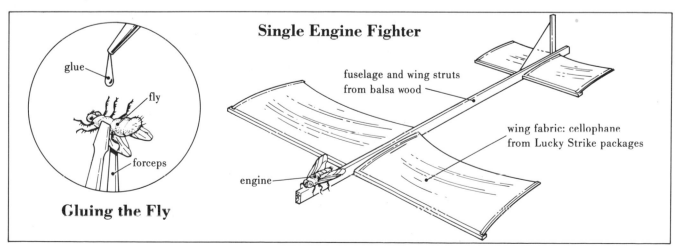

Single Engine Fighter

glue

fly

forceps

Gluing the Fly

fuselage and wing struts from balsa wood

wing fabric: cellophane from Lucky Strike packages

engine

ED LIPINSKI

ILLUSTRATIONS BASED ON ORIGINALS APPEARING IN *THE JOURNAL OF IRREPRODUCIBLE RESULTS.*

your fly. Then you fashion this simple design with a sliver or two of balsa wood and some tissue paper and you glue your fly's little feet into position. Then you turn him loose.'' We contend that if these instructions were followed, no flyable craft would result.

Let us continue with our history: ''Cutting balsa wood strips into finer and finer strips with a single edge razor, and gluing these together (with an absolute minimum of glue) into a fuselage with wing struts, I covered the wings with pieces of cellophane from Lucky Strike packages.[7]

''Next I captured in a jar, large flies from the garbage can and placed the jar into the icebox (much to my mother's chagrin). This had the effect of putting the flies to sleep so they could be easily handled.[8] I had tried to glue the flies to the plane while they were awake with disastrous results of torn wings, wings glued to abdomen, etc. After about three minutes, the flies could be taken out and glued to the engine mounts. Experiments showed that flies must be glued *only by their abdomens*. If the fly's feet were not left free, the little critters simply would *not* fly. Blowing on

them during the drying of the glue was sufficient to revive them[9] and start the 'engines.' A casual launch would send the craft zooming through the house.[10]

''I tried horseflies, bees, and ordinary large house flies as engines. I found the horseflies to be easiest to handle and the most 'willing' to power the gliders. I devised single-engine fighters, twin- and tri-motor craft, and even one giant eight-engine model. This latter must be counted as a failure in that no suitable means could be devised to keep all eight engines working simultaneously. Any fewer than eight simply did not provide adequate lift.''

Thus, the record speaks for itself. Herein lay the origins of a breathtaking[11] concept in aircraft design. Although fly-powered aircraft of very large size still seem to be ruled out by the idiosyncratic activities of individual engines, the recognition (or blame) for this development should be fairly placed. When the annals of aeronautical history are finally written, the fly-powered plane will take its rightful place.

---

[7] The tissue paper approach did not result in craft with acceptable power–to–weight ratios.

[8] We give emphasis to some of the design features which are critical, and which are ''overlooked'' by the Smithsonian.

[9] Notice with what humility and restraint we do not mention this obviously pioneering work in cryogenic suspended animation.

[10] Unfortunately, as in many prototype aircraft, the control system left something to be desired, as these craft had a nasty tendency to crash into the walls. This problem was partially overcome by moving the experiment site out-of-doors.

[11] Try standing around a large supply of fuel for these craft.

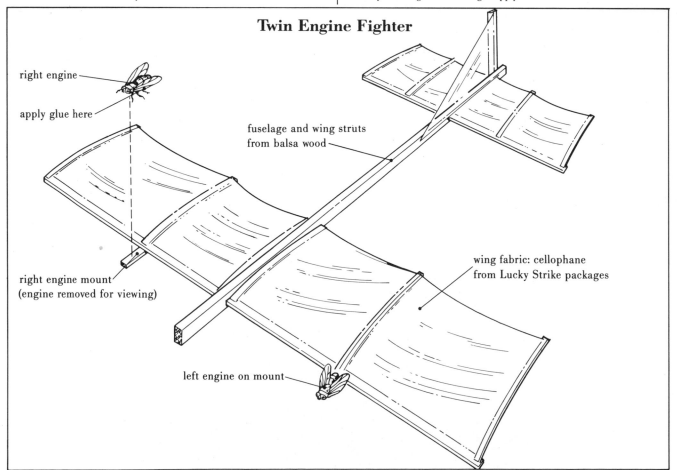

Twin Engine Fighter

right engine

apply glue here

fuselage and wing struts from balsa wood

right engine mount (engine removed for viewing)

wing fabric: cellophane from Lucky Strike packages

left engine on mount

Ed Lipinski

THE PACHYDERMOBILE[1]

A Portable Laboratory for the Unobtrusive Observation of Animals in Their Natural Habitat

Terry Maple
Department of Psychology
University of California at Davis

Tracking wild animals is, at best, an arduous and sometimes hazardous task. It is necessary, of course, if the animals in question are to be properly understood. But wild animals are wary of human observers, as well they should be. How then does a scientist wishing to study animals in their characteristic milieu get near enough to really see?

The answer to this question is not found in the use of traditional apparatus. Blinds constructed to conceal the human form or allow for long-distance viewing are not mobile. A lot of what an animal does with its time cannot be observed without mobility on the part of the observer. How about the trusty Land Rover? Nope. Many animals have learned to associate the vehicle with hunting or capture. Also, the Land Rover is noisy and conspicuous. In this writer's opinion, the best way to study wild animals is to become a familiar part of the beasts' environment. For many African species, what is more familiar than an elephant?

Construction of the Pachydermobile

A diagram of my portable laboratory is presented in

Fig. 1. It is best constructed of genuine elephant hide stretched over a steel shell. Naturally, the hide should be obtained from reputable authorities who will guarantee that the animal expired from natural causes.

The engine is designed to run on methane (derived from local animal fecal material) and should be of lightweight construction. I recommend that the recording apparatus and internal controls of the vehicle be carefully constructed from modern and sturdy materials. Such material may be obtained from the writer's brother-in-law for a small honorarium.

Advantages of the Pachydermobile

The Pachydermobile has many obvious advantages, many of which I haven't thought of yet. Some of these came to me in a vision, others remain to be discovered through use of the lab-vehicle. Consider the following:

1. The Pachydermobile not only looks like an elephant, it also smells like one due to three external pheromone outlets. These outlets secrete enough fluid to convince even the most suspicious animals.

2. Its prehensile trunk allows the scientist-operator to collect scats for ecological analysis and—via the methane converter—utilize these stool samples as fuel.

3. The Pachydermobile is capable of emitting a variety of elephant vocalizations and heavy panting sounds in order to further diminish the minimal engine noise, and enhance its authenticity.

4. The Pachydermobile is a four-wheel-drive vehicle equipped with tough knobby tires, capable of traversing the most difficult terrain. It also floats and for a small sum can be altered to propel itself through water.

5. The Pachydermobile can operate by night through the use of its infrared sensing equipment.

6. The tough elephant skin of the Pachydermobile

[1] This research is possible through generous grants from the membership of the Davis Geographical Front and the International Society of Educated Beasts.

covers a strong bullet-proof shell which should discourage potshots by illegal elephant poachers.

A Final Note

It is recommended that the Pachydermobile be used for the study of animals other than elephants. Most African species are not afraid of elephants and will tolerate the presence of a lone animal. However, due to the lab-vehicle's highly effective disguise, an elephant herd may not accept such a stranger. While they may be inclined to attack, a more likely result is that courtship may ensue. The emergency semen receptacle (R) is designed to take advantage of any romantic advances by curious bulls. Resistance is always dangerous, and at such times it is best to "ride-it-out."[2] Semen may be analyzed at the appropriate time.

While the advantages of such a device as the Pachydermobile are many, the disadvantages are comparatively few. Amorous bull elephants are a potential hazard, as are persistent hunters. The most serious difficulty, however, may well be the high cost of construction. These problems may be circumvented by the construction of a miniature version of the Pachydermobile. Such a scaled-down version would require a small fraction of the expenditure for a larger model. An additional advantage is that only the most deviant of poachers and/or bull elephants would be attracted to a *young* Pachydermobile.

---

[2] It is recommended that the operator of the Pachydermobile wear a gorilla suit should abandonment of the vehicle be required.

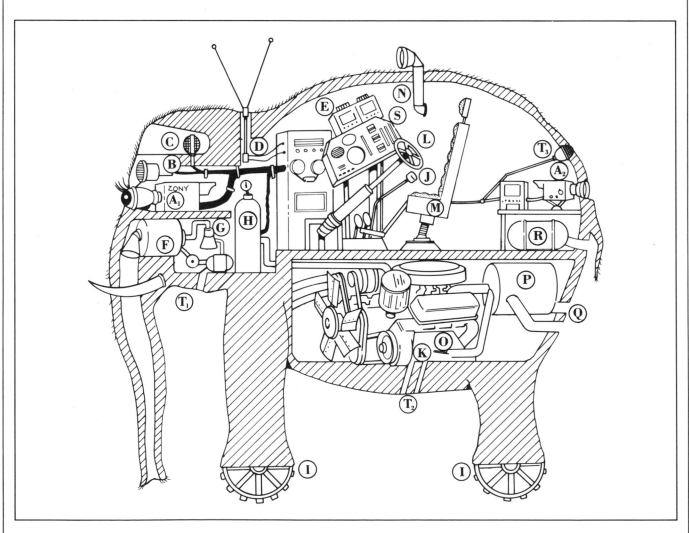

Fig. 1
Components of the Pachydermobile

A₁	Television Camera	F	Vacuum Tube (prehensile remote-control trunk)	K	Gear Box	Q	Dual Exhaust Pipes

A₁	Television Camera	F	Vacuum Tube (prehensile remote-	K	Gear Box	Q	Dual Exhaust Pipes
A₂			control trunk)	L	Steering Wheel	R	Emergency Semen Receptacle
B	Infrared Headlights	G	Stool Analyzer	M	Swivel Seat	S	Master Control Panel (adjustable)
C	Sound Microphone	H	Methane Converter	N	Periscope	T₁	External Pheromones Secretion Outlets
D	Antennae	I	Knobby Tires	O	Engine	T₂	
E	Television Receiver-Tape Deck	J	Four Wheel Drive Shaft	P	Muffler	T₃	

Ed Lipinski

THE SIX-DAY WEEK— IT'S TIME FOR A CHANGE

R. L. Sendall
Publisher
Chatsworth Weekly (Planned)

History

It is not completely clear, short of divine creation, how the concept of a seven-day week resulted. Research into this area indicates no mathematical significance in the odd-prime or its relationship to the duration of the month or year. Indeed, there is not even a relationship to the number of fingers or toes that would support such a measure as seven days. It seems unlikely that six days is any natural limit on endurance or that a seventh day of rest is required for recuperation, but this may have been the foundation often referred to in the Bible.[1]

In any case, the work habits of man (and woman) have changed significantly over the past century suggesting a review of this outdated schedule. The first significant change occurred when the work-payoff ratio (R) reached the point (p) that instead of rest on Sunday, we began to play from Saturday night until Monday morning. This began the process of obtaining some of the needed recuperation during the "workweek," i.e., Monday morning. As society progressed, prior to 1950, we got to the point that a five-day workweek, a day to play and a day to rest, developed. This was a good balance for the "work-payoff" ratio $R(t_1)$ of that time and a healthy, stable balance existed.

In the prosperity of the 50s and 60s, the two nonwork days became play days and again the "recuperation during work" problem began to be observed. It was clear that mankind did not need to work five days to satisfy his needs and to be able to play two days. There were resounding cries for a four-day work-week with a three-day weekend, presumably to have a day to rest. It should be noted, however, that the extra day to rest is quickly absorbed into play and as the length of the weekend increases, the amount of work lost due to recuperating increases exponentially.[2]

Proposition

It is the premise of the author that while we may be ready for a four-day workweek, we could not survive a steady diet of three-day weekends. Automobile accidents alone would endanger the species. It is therefore proposed that we consider modifying our scheduling procedure by changing the calendar to be based upon six-day weeks. The alternative solution which has evolved in the early 70s (i.e., a large portion of the populace going on welfare so that the rest needs to work a solid five or six days) involves wide ranging moral-economic considerations beyond the scope of this paper, but it is hoped that the adoption of the alternative solution is short lived.

The proposed solution is therefore to change over to a six-day week with a four-day workweek and a two-day weekend. Each week would start on Tuesday and end on Sunday, getting rid of "Blue Mondays." A month would consist of five six-day weeks for a total of thirty days. The year would consist of twelve months plus five or six year-end holidays, e.g., Christmas through New Years Eve. The financial calendar and the actual calendar would be identical, with the holidays being treated as a separate period combined with December for billing purposes.

A small fortune would be saved in calendars[3] alone, since the days in every month would be the same. The 4th of July would always fall on Friday providing a three-day weekend and there would be no Friday the 13th. The concept of Labor Day would have

---

[1] Book of Genesis, St. James Version

[2] Data taken at random in beach cities of Southern California, USA

[3] Copyrights and Patent applied for

to be corrected to be on a Tuesday, but that should be a minor sacrifice. Congress could have a field day moving birthdays, etc. around knowing they would stay put relative to a weekend. Considerable time would be saved by business people since missing appointments due to confusing days and dates would be a thing of the past.

At first there was concern that the religious rulers might object, but a poll indicates that the increase in the number of Sundays (Saturdays and Fridays) should provide a considerable increase in revenue. Also the logic/procedure for accepting the new schedule should provide debating material for church officials for many years to come.

Another area where an advantage will be felt is in vacations. With only an eight-day vacation (two weeks), a fourteen-day absence from work is obtained. A twelve-day vacation becomes a three-week vacation with twenty days away from work.

Football and baseball players as well as other entertainers will have more weekend performances providing better attendance and probably better performances.[4] With more weekends, the weekend performances will not be as crowded making it easy on those attending.

In short, with a six-day week, we gain the benefits of a four-day workweek without the disadvantage of every weekend being a three-day weekend and at the same time we simplify and streamline our whole system of keeping track of time. There are many additional logical advantages of this six-day week and once you are convinced that the arguments are solid and worthwhile, try considering the next step: the five-day week.

---

[4] It has been pointed out that the advent of artificial turf has increased the need for a longer recuperating week for pro-football players and a biweekly schedule may be necessary.

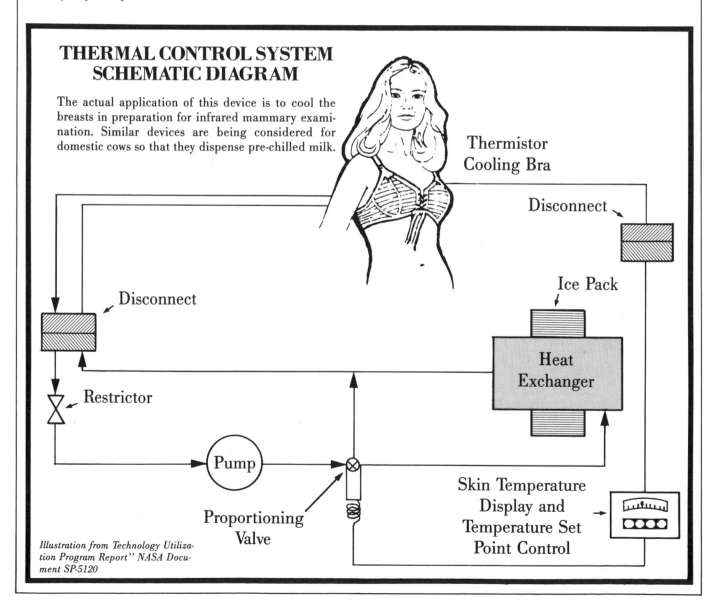

THERMAL CONTROL SYSTEM SCHEMATIC DIAGRAM

The actual application of this device is to cool the breasts in preparation for infrared mammary examination. Similar devices are being considered for domestic cows so that they dispense pre-chilled milk.

Thermistor Cooling Bra

Disconnect

Ice Pack

Disconnect

Restrictor

Heat Exchanger

Pump

Proportioning Valve

Skin Temperature Display and Temperature Set Point Control

Illustration from Technology Utilization Program Report" NASA Document SP-5120

E PLURIBUS URANIUM

Charles T. Stewart, Jr.
Department of Economics
George Washington University
Washington, D.C.

Today Berengaria officially went on the uranium standard, setting the value of its currency, the benarus, at 12 units per microcurie. South Africa is the lone holdout for a better conversion rate between gold and uranium. Since it has both metals, its indecision seems to be the result of uncertainty as to where its interests lie, rather than dissatisfaction with the International Monetary Fund conversion ratio.

Thus comes to a close the most momentous chapter in world monetary history since the invention of check-kiting. The revolution was initiated by the United States in 1984 as a master stroke in its psychological offensive against the Soviet Bloc. It was the first nation to go on the uranium standard (although Russia now claims otherwise). By this move it created a vast new market for its uranium stockpile, estimated to constitute 70% of the total world supply of uranium metal, eliminated its balance of payments difficulties, and greatly increased international liquidity.

The last two results might have been achieved by raising the dollar price of gold, but the United States was unwilling to do this because it feared loss of face and was unwilling to hand the Russians a windfall profit on their unknown but enormous pot of gold.

The main objective of the conversion, however, was to further disarmament aims and to eliminate the risks of nuclear war. This objective was fully achieved. The Russians were put under heavy pressure to convert their nuclear warheads into currency, and did so in large number. Although they are believed to retain a few warheads, their first harvest failure is expected to lead to total nuclear disarmament. In the meantime, the Russians, with their well-known peasant attachment to cold cash, would never think of blowing up their hard-earned hoard in a mushroom cloud. Nuclear testing has ceased. India has gone conventional.

Investment Boom

The new standard incorporates a foolproof inspection, warning, and control system. The conversion of monetary uranium into nuclear warheads by any country is promptly reflected in the foreign exchange markets if not in domestic price indices. The deflationary aspects of wars and preparations for war make them unattractive to all business and practically impossible to finance. Conversely, the uranium standard has banished all fear of an economic collapse as a result of disarmament. The automatic increase in money supply as warheads are converted to currency sets off an investment boom and an inflationary fever.

In retrospect, it is hard to understand mankind's prolonged love affair with the yellow metal of such limited uses other than personal adornment. Perhaps it illustrates what Whitehead called the "fallacy of misplaced concreteness."

Hot Cash, Cold War

The advantages of uranium are obvious enough. Its value is not based on a fickle fashion, on the persistence of an illusion, or on human propensity for invidious comparisons. In an insecure world its virtues are unique. Not only is it a store of value but also a store of power. It can earn interest without moral qualms by generating electricity while it is serving as a monetary reserve. It lacks the stigma of petty bourgeois conservatism, of the banking profession and the capitalist persuasion. It is ideologically neutral.

The uranium standard now provides an effective technique for changing the velocity of circulation at will. Threatening recessions can be prevented by the simple expedient of increasing the proportion of salaries paid in radioactive uranium coinage. This "hot money" is immediately spent and promptly respent. Thus we have a final cure for economic instability.

Not the least of its virtues from the American viewpoint is that it is found in abundance in the Western United States, and that its mining and processing is a major support of a number of states with sparse populations but dense political representation.

A NEW FLAVORING AGENT AND PRESERVATIVE FOR FOOD?

Dr. Erich Luck
Frankfurt am Main
West Germany

In a reaction of metallic sodium and gaseous chlorine a white substance is formed which crystallizes out of water as colorless transparent cubes. The quantitive analysis of the newly found substance showed that it consisted of 39.4% sodium and 60.6% chlorine, i.e., it contained only these two elements. Therefore the name suggested for this substance is Sodiochlorium. One could also, to some extent, define Sodiochlorium as the sodium salt of hydrochloric acid.

Sodiochlorium has a good effectiveness against microorganisms. The product acts by lowering the water activity of a system and by this renders more difficult vital activity of microorganisms of any nature. Already in concentrations of 2- to- 4% Sodiochlorium increases the effect of known preservatives. It is true that if the product is used on its own, concentrations of 20- to- 30% must be used to ensure some measure of success. Sodiochlorium seems to be suitable for the preservation of cheese, meat, fish, milk and vegetable products. By studying literature it was found that already the old Egyptians must have used a compound for the preservation of food-stuffs which obviously showed a certain likeness to Sodiochlorium. The old Romans knew Muria and Garum, solutions which probably also contained an active ingredient which is comparable to Sodiochlorium. Maybe this was a disintegrated isotope of Sodiochlorium.

An organoleptic test of Sodiochlorium showed that the substance has a not unlikable saltlike flavor. The taste of Sodiochlorium goes particularly well with eggs, meat, fish, soups, boiled potatoes, fresh tomatoes and other foods. If, however, Sodiochlorium is added to the foods mentioned, in higher concentrations, the taste is spoiled. The food tastes "oversalted." This effect is particularly unpleasant in soups.

Toxicity Testing

As a result of its favorable technological and organoleptic properties, Sodiochlorium may be suitable as a food additive. As such it would need the approval of FDA. Before such an approval can be obtained extensive toxicological tests are required; such tests have been started.

After being administered perorally in a concentrated aqueous solution to hungry rats, the LD_{50} of Sodiochlorium was determined at $3.75 \pm ; .43$ g/kg.[1,2] As a result of the animal tests it seems that the lethal quantity of Sodiochlorium for grown humans amounts to about 200 g.[3]

By comparison to other known preservatives the acute toxicity of Sodiochlorium is not in a favorable position if, for instance, one takes sorbic acid whose LD_{50} lies about 10g/kg of body weight. The relative high acute toxicity of Sodiochlorium is not surprising, after all the compound is produced from such a highly caustic material as metallic sodium and as highly toxic a gas as chlorine. Also the basic acid of Sodiochlorium, hydrochloric acid is by no means harmless if fed in larger concentrations.

If being fed in larger concentrations, Sodiochlorium leads to severe disturbances of the ionic equilib-

[1] Boyd, E. M. and M. N. Shanas. "The Acute Oral Toxicita of Sodium," Chloride. Arch. Int. Pharmacodyn. Ther. 144: 86, 1983.
[2] Boyd, E. M. and C. E. Boyd. Toxicity of Pure Foods. Cleveland: CRC Press, 1973, p. 163–181.
[3] Wirth, W., G. Hecht und C. Gloxhuber. Toxikologie-Fibel fur Arzte, Apotheker, Naturwissenschaftler, Juristen und Studierende, 2nd Edition. Stuttgart: Georg Thieme Verlag, 1962, p. 72.

Even under meteorological conditions of intense precipitation, the flow of this sample of sodiochlorium from its container was unhindered.

JERRY DARVIN

rium in the organism and has a dehydrating effect. 0.9 percent aqueous solutions are isotonic, e.g., only solutions of such low concentrations have the same osmotic pressure as human blood.

For testing the subchronic toxicity hungry rats were given over a period of 100 days concentrated aqueous solutions of Sodiochlorium. The LD_{50} ascertains over this period (about one tenth of the lifespan of these animals) lies at 2.69 ± 0.12 g/kg body weight.[2,5]

The chronic feeding test showed that an intake of more than 2.8% Sodiochlorium, related to the feed, impaired growth; the lifespan compared to that of control animals was distinctly shortened.[6]

Likewise for humans a continuous intake of Sodiochlorium in higher concentrations is not completely harmless. Certain cardiac, circulatory and renal diseases are a contraindication of Sodiochlorium.

WHO Sets the ADI

The toxicological assessment of Sodiochlorium, with reference to its use as a food additive, based on findings obtained so far, cannot be regarded as favorable. In Switzerland the authorities have even classed a similar compound to Sodiochlorium, Sodium chloridli, to poison category 5 of the poison law. Of course, this refers only to products not used in the food sector, that might be more dangerous than the chemically indenti-

cal product that is subject to the food law.

Should one day, in spite of the not inconsiderable toxicity, Sodiochlorium be admitted as a food additive, for the expert committees of WHO the question of the listing of an ADI would arise. The ADI (acceptable daily intake), which exists for many food additives is the quantity of a product which can be absorbed over a longish period per day and per kg of body weight. One calculates for this an extensive safety span which is usually about 1:100 and then proceeds from the dosage which just did not cause harm in the animal test. The dosage of Sodiochlorium at which no damage appears is now known. As already intakes of about 2.5g Sodiochlorium per kg body weight distinctly shortened the lifespan of test animals one could take the long-term harmless dosage at about 1 g/kg of body weight. Considering the usual safety span of 1:100 an ADI of 0-10 mg/kg body weight seems justified. According to this a daily intake of 0.75g Sodiochlorium for a grown-up human being, weighing 75kg would be acceptable. With such a quantity the taste of about two plates of soup could be improved, whereby, however, the natural Sodiochlorium content of many foodstuffs has not been taken into consideration. This lies, without doubt, higher than the above mentioned possible ADI.

Considering all aspects the efforts to use Sodiochlorium as a food additive were halted. Owing to its high toxicity an application to the relevant authority for permission of Sodiochlorium† to be used in food cannot be recommended.

[4] Luck, E. Sorbinsaure. Chemie-Biochemie-Mikrobiologie-Technologie. Bd.II. Biochemie-Mikrobiologie. Hamburg: B. Behr's Verlag, 1972, p. 13 ff.

[5] Boyd, E. M., M. M. Abel und L. M. Knight. "The Chronical Oral Toxicity of Sodium Chloride at the Range of the LD_{50} (0.1 L)," *Canad. J. Physiol. Pharmacol.* 44: 157, 1966.

[6] Meneely, G. R., R. G. Tucker, W. J. Derby and S. H. Auerbach. "Chronic Sodium Chloride Toxicity: Hypertension, Renal and Vascular Lesions," *Ann. Intern. Med.* 39: 991, 1953.

†Except for the parts of the text marked with references to literature quotations, all facts have been discovered by the author. Similarities to known substances may be desired but are hardly believable.

From Nachrichten aus Chemie und Technik 24(7): 139–140, 1976.

THE ULTIMATE DRINKING GLASS

Jordan Levenson, B.S., M.B.A.
Los Angeles, California

In drinking from a glass or cup, once connection is made with the mouth parts, liquid is facilitated in its transfer from the vessel to the mouth by rotating the vessel, thus permitting the dynamic effects of gravity to bring the liquid forth, Fig. 1.

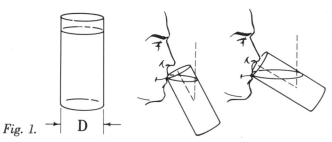

Fig. 1.   ← D →

Those parts of the human consumption apparatus which are located in the head and neck further enable the intake and swallowing of the liquid by performing a series of movement cycles until the glass is empty—and possibly then some, depending. Each cycle in the series is somewhat different from its predecessor in timing and movement, depending upon tilt of the head and glass and the amount of intake.

To redesign the drinking glass with the purpose of arriving at the ultimate vessel we need to recognize the following truth: all other things being equal, it is more comfortable to take into the mouth and swallow the same volume of liquid during each cycle of the series, duplicating as near as possible the timing of the cycle before it. The reason it is more comfortable this way is that lack of variation among cycles requires the least thought and effort (conscious and subconscious) in the operation of the relevent parts of the upper gastrointestinal tract, while permitting maximum concentration on the taste sensation of the drink.

To achieve uniform intake cycles with the ordinary drinking glass, the speed of its angular rotation as well as the number of degrees it is rotated during a cycle must vary from cycle to cycle so that uniform amounts of liquid may pass over the edge of the glass each time. The reason for this required variance may be seen clearly by looking at Fig. 2, in which all glasses are represented relevantly by the one illustrated. X varies. The longer X is the more liquid that will come over the edge during the next degree of tilt. In Fig. 2a less liquid will come over the edge during the next degree of tilt as compared to Fig. 2b. Another way of saying it is that the volume of liquid leaving the glass during the next degree of tilt (up to 90°) depends upon the current angle.

Again, the varying of the speed and degrees of tilt for different cycles in order to fulfill the criteria of comfortable intake and swallowing requires thought and effort, detracting from the goal of maximizing concentration on the taste sensation.

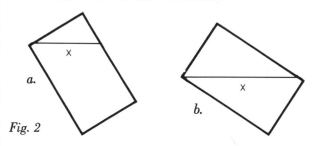

a.   *b.*   X

Fig. 2

To enable a uniform tilting cycle to accompany the intake and swallowing cycle the drinking glass must be redesigned. Such a design is shown. Behold the ultimate vessel, Fig. 3! The volume of liquid passing over the edge of the vessel per degree of tilt is constant because the area of the surface of the liquid is the same at any angle up to 90°. The vessels come with right handles or left handles for right and left handed people or with handles on both sides for ambidextrous people. The curved lip of the vessel is a concession to human mouth parts.

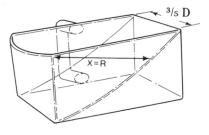

$^3/_5$ D

X = R

Fig. 3

ILLUSTRATIONS BASED ON ORIGINALS APPEARING IN *THE JOURNAL OF IRREPRODUCIBLE RESULTS.*

THE ORDER

Dale Lowdermilk
Montecito, California

The use of experimental human "Tracer Implant Microtransmitters" (TIM) as a means of tracking escaped prisoners, convicted felons and high-risk parolees was upheld in the Supreme Court Decision (*Bakhous* v. *State of California*, 9-18-85, #49005.4) several years ago. Despite the arguments of "invasion-of-privacy," the overriding benefits for society and assistance to law enforcement officials was deemed a "greater good." Within a year following this historical decision, every Federal and State prison had implanted emitter devices in all inmates. There were also approximately 800 voluntary transmitter implants. Of these first 800 pioneers, five were botanists who became lost during a scientific exploration in the Everglades. When their boat capsized, four survivors and the body of the fifth were located by their TIM signals, similar to the "emergency locator beacon" of a downed aircraft. The utility and potential for human tracking became a national preoccupation. Everyone wanted his own "personal transmitter."

How Does the 2nd Generation Transmitter Work?

Smaller than the period at the end of this sentence, the latest TIM device can be implanted with a sterilized "pinprick" (just like a TB-TINE Test) or inhaled from an atomizer. It can be installed under the skin, in a muscle or within any organ of the body. It is micro-encapsulated and is chemically inert within the body. Once it is painlessly implanted you cannot feel or see it. The transmitter itself is a quartz-silicon product of the space age. It requires no power supply but emits a low frequency discreet "BINARY TIME-SPACE CO-ORDINATE." The principle is similar to the primitive "crystal-radio" (that never needs a battery) combined with the LORAN-C navigation equipment. Using simple triangulation, the low power TIM (tracer implant microtransmitter) signal is relayed via existing radio and television antennas to the Tracking Data Center (TDC) in Montecito, California. All signals are recorded on laser microvideo discs and filed according to their Time-Location and frequency.

Every person has, from the moment the TIM is activated, an individually coded frequency and every geographical location has a longitude/latitude "grid-number." All of it is transmitted as a "Data-Binary-Pulse" every 2 seconds. Each of us becomes a (walking, running, or sleeping) "Inertial Navigation System." Even after death, the transmissions continue...unless the microtransmitter is physically destroyed, or the computer code at TDC is deleted.

What Are the Applications of Tracer Implant Microtransmitters?

A concerned wife notified authorities, and TDC, that her husband, a voluntary implantee, was overdue from a camping trip. His code/frequency "grid" was identified halfway down a steep mountainside, and within 45 minutes he was rescued.

A truck and sedan collided head-on and both drivers were killed. The computer replay of the truck driver's TIM (involuntary ex-con implantee) data-pulse-record indicated that he had stopped at two liquor stores just before turning on to the Interstate Highway. The time-distance data also indicated that the truck was traveling in excess of 82 MPH at the moment of impact. The family of the sedan driver, using this indisputable scientific TIM information, was able to win a reckless-driving suit against the estate of the truck driver. The legal aspects of TIM are as valid as fingerprints!

Several people were hospitalized for food poisoning. A "replay" of the TIM data of two of the patients immediately pinpointed the source.

A man accused of bank robbery was released after his TIM data verified that his "data-pulse-record" did not coincide with the event. Immediate correlation is possible for anyone accused of any crime *...if they have already received a human tracer implant microtransmitter.*

Within five years, TIM devices will also be able to carry hormonal/neuroelectrical/respiratory diagnostic information (in conjunction with time-location data). If you experience a heart attack, Tracking Data Center (TDC) will instantly notify the nearest hospital...*and will tell doctors where you are!!!!* Someday, using TIM, a person who has never had a physical examination

1   2   3   4   5   6   7

may receive a telephone call telling him to "*see a doctor for high blood pressure.*" The TDC Computer will know before *you* do that your stomachache *could* be a peptic ulcer. Potential suicides might be identified by a preceding "chemo-neuro imbalance" and tragedy averted. Just as fiber optics once revolutionized communications, TIM improvements will soon permit voice/audio data to be simultaneously transmitted with the individual's data-binary-pulse. This means that everything you have ever said (or heard!!) will be recorded at Tracking Data Center. Crimes against persons and property will become virtually nonexistent!! (Kidnappers will *never* steal a child who is equipped with a Tracer Implant Microtransmitter!!!) What parent does not love his/her child enough to protect it with this miraculous device?

With the installation of four new Master Relay Satellite Receivers (MRSR) and high speed tracking digitizers, the existing "passive code zones" (areas where TIM signals cannot be received by the Tracking Data Center) which are within a 61 mile radius of the North Pole and a 48 mile radius of the South Pole, will be "covered." Worldwide human TIM tracking will become a reality and you will be able to witness the data-binary-pulse of anyone . . . even the astronauts as they circle the Earth.

Because of this incredible potential for human good, and for the benefit of all Mankind, the following Executive Order is enacted:

EXECUTIVE ORDER #788318

Human Tracer Implant Microtransmitters (TIM) shall be placed within all newborn infants, at all hospitals and home-birthing-centers in North America. The implantation may be performed by the delivering doctor/nurse or a representative of the Department of Transponder Records (DOTR). Failure to perform this action will result in Federal penalties and possible revocation of medical or professional licenses. The cost of both implantation and the TIM device shall be carried by the U.S. Government, and there will be electrohormonal punishments for those attempting to remove, modify or tamper with already implanted transmitters.

_____
PRESIDENT, UNITED STATES OF AMERICA   DATE

_____
SECRETARY, DEPT. OF TRANSPONDER RECORDS   DATE

_____
SECRETARY, ADMINISTRATOR TRACKING DATA CENTER   DATE

THE END

THE ANISOTROPY OF A POLITICAL MAP*

Vladimir Funk
Institute of State Tectonics,
San Andreas Fault, California

A fundamental importance, long overlooked, should be ascribed to the fact that a majority of national states are meridionally oriented.[1] Nearly all countries of Western Europe and South-Eastern Asia are, and manifest examples, like Israel, Japan, Chile and Argentina are found in other parts of the globe.

This result is not completely irreproducible, and apparent exceptions tend to corroborate rather than invalidate the rule. The countries of roughly square shape or those extended latitudinally mostly fall into the following four categories:

1. Imperial nations (USSR, USA, China) which have expanded from an initially meridional position to occupy the available space but still retain meridional belts of higher population density (European Russia, Eastern China, Boswash and Sansan megalopolitan areas in the U.S.)[2-24].

2. Countries like Egypt or Brazil[25-28] where vast uninhabited areas disguise essentially meridional orientation of the populated core.

3. Countries like Spain and Poland formed by marital merger[29-41] of two meridional entities (Castile and Aragon, Poland proper and Lithuania). The latter state has displayed a remarkable liquidity of borders in the course of history[42-99], and though initially aspiring to enter the 1st category, has gradually approached the most numerous category, no. 4.

4. The nations with boundaries artificially carved by international treaties, like the countries of Central Europe formed by disbanding the Austro-Hungarian Empire[100-211] or African countries which display all kinds of surrealistic shapes as an aftermath of colonial gerrymandering[212-998].

Little is known so far of the basic physical mechanisms responsible for the observed anisotropy, beyond apparent aesthetic advantages of hanging a vertically-oriented map on a wall. Nevertheless the meridional metric is unlikely to be accidental and is believed to have wide implications in international politics and economy.

By and large, the meridionally-oriented countries enjoy higher standards of living, internal stability and more liberal forms of government than those deviating from the optimal shape[999-1314]. The meridional orientation prevails in the regions with long uninterrupted histories of undecisive feuds, and, thus, appears to be a stable equilibrious form which, once being achieved, leads to relative stability in the area and encourages economic development.

The trend toward meridional orientation can be detected in major geopolitical alterations of last decades and millenia. Thus, all meridional divisions, like partition of Germany[1315] slicing the Indian subcontinent into three states[1316-1405] and, still earlier, separation of Sweden and Norway[1406], Palestine and Transjordan[1407-1561], or Eastern and Western Empires, churches and ideologies[1561-3020], are persistent. On the other hand, attempts to divide some countries (Vietnam, USA, United Kingdom latitudinally have failed[3021-3038] and a similar partition of Korea[3039] or Ireland[3040] has been, and still is endangered.

Luckily, few influential politicians or rulers of mass media habitually read this journal, neither do they apprehend scientific reasoning. Otherwise, the present theory would be in danger of being cut out of its purely academic context and practically implemented, which could lead to as disastrous results as did the practical implementation of other far-reaching political paradigms.

---

[1] Britannica Atlas. Chicago-London-Toronto-Geneva-Sidney-Tokyo-Manila-Johannesburg-Seoul: 1978.
[2-3040] omitted due to lack of space.
* This paper constitutes an intentionally distorted summary of a classified report submitted by the IST to the Federal Government and kept in the Fault for future consideration. The author is indebted to the persons he may not name for refusal to grant permission to publish the report in full.

DEFINITION OF A DARKBULB

James L. DeLucas

The darkbulb is an electronic device that produces darkness. It is similar in appearance to the ordinary lightbulb. Whereas the lightbulb is considered an energy source, the darkbulb could be considered an energy sink.

The darkbulb looks like the ordinary lightbulb. It is much heavier, a typical 60 watt bulb weighing about two pounds. The darkbulb's outer shell is made of a special metallic material called heliotex. Heliotex was made specially for the bulb, and it is necessary for the bulb's operation. The bulb screws into an ordinary light socket and can be run on house current. The bulbs are normally coated black for easy identification. Darkbulbs come in power sizes similar to the lightbulb. Two and three-way bulbs and special purpose bulbs are also available.

The Hay Field

Unlike the simple heating filament of the lightbulb, the inner contents of the darkbulb are complicated and electronic. The heart of this device is the crystalkanoogin valve. The crystalkanoogin valve was designed by Edison A. Thomas, an engineer at General Electric. (See ''An Inexpensive Dissipator of Radiant Energy,'' *Electronics,* Vol. 42, No. 7, pp. 59–67, July 1970.) The valve is made up of a series of miniature electronic components. The sole purpose of the valve is the production of the Hay field. The Hay Reverse Electromagnetic Field, or Hay (REF), was theoretically proven to exist by R.E.F. Hay at MIT in late 1969. This invisible field is able to dissipate normal electromagnetic energy, such as light, by converting this energy into the reverse electromagnetic energy of the Hay field. This energy conversion process is the means by which the Hay field propagates through the air. In a vacuum the Hay field would propagate indefinitely. In air, however, the Hay field would lose energy to the surrounding medium and it would soon disappear. Thus, the crystalkanoogin valve must continuously

produce the Hay field. Also, the Hay field will not propagate unless the surrounding medium contains electromagnetic energy, since the Hay field uses this energy to sustain itself.

The Hay field is analogous to a vacuum cleaner that sucks electromagnetic energy from the air. Electromagnetic energy such as light can be thought of as being absorbed by the darkbulb and then converted into the Hay field. The recycling of the trapped light energy not only solves the energy dissipation problem but also puts this energy to useful work.

The crystalkanoogin valve sets up the Hay field on the inside surface of the heliotex shell. The properties of the heliotex material cause it to radiate the Hay field into the surrounding space, much like a lightbulb would radiate light energy from the heating filament. The heliotex shell thus acts as a radiating antenna for the Hay field. The type of radiation absorbed by the bulb is dependent on the impurities present in the heliotex shell. The impurities can be controlled during the making of the heliotex. Thus, special purpose bulbs that absorb only one kind of electromagnetic energy can be made. For instance, it is possible to create a darkbulb that absorbs only red light, or a bulb that absorbs only cosmic rays.

During operation, the surface of the bulb will actually become cool due to dissipation of heat from the heliotex material. The darkbulb ''sucks'' light energy from the air, but the bulb is not a perfect discriminator, and very small amounts of other forms of energy in the vicinity of the bulb will also be dissipated. The bulb will become cold because of a loss of heat energy to the field.

The ordinary darkbulb is one that will absorb light. The bulb will dissipate light, that is, produce darkness in as large an area and to as comparable a degree as a lightbulb of the same wattage will produce light.

The Dark Fantastic

The ordinary darkbulb has many uses. A flip of the switch makes it possible to sleep in the daytime with-

JERRY DARVIN

Sunlight streaming into a room inhibits sleep, but flipping on the darkbulb envelops the subject in soothing darkness.

Darkbulbs come in a variety of sizes, shapes, and wattages.

out the use of eyepatches. Photographic enthusiasts no longer need to spend money "lightproofing" a darkroom. Just screw a darkbulb into a socket and any room becomes an instant darkroom. Eye doctors have found darkbulbs particularly useful for conducting eye examinations. There are applications of the bulb in the scientific fields, where many experiments require the absence of surrounding radiant energy. The darkbulb also seems to be popular at parties.

Special purpose darkbulbs are finding wider applications. The special purpose radio wave darkbulb will absorb radio waves from the surrounding area. One application of this bulb is in the scientific field where certain experiments require shielding from radio waves. The cosmic and X-ray darkbulbs absorb cosmic energy and X-rays from the air. These potentially hazardous forms of energy can now be snatched from the air before they reach the vulnerable human being.

As scientific technology advances, the special purpose infrared darkbulb will eventually be produced.

Such a bulb would absorb infrared (heat) energy. The invention of this type of darkbulb would have a profound effect on modern society. Refrigerators would no longer need a complex mechanical cooling system—just an infrared darkbulb inside. Sunbathers in the vicinity of an infrared darkbulb could get a tan without worrying about the harmful rays that cause sunburn. Air cooling could be accomplished with a darkbulb. Unfortunately, technology has not found a way to prevent the heliotex shell from becoming frozen solid during the bulb's operation. In the frozen condition, the heliotex shell fails to maintain the Hay field.

The darkbulb can be found in any store that carries lightbulbs. The cost of this modern advance in technology has been considerably reduced, although it is still much more expensive than the lightbulb. However, the darkbulb is not beyond the reach of the average-income American family. Indeed, they are becoming as common as the home radio.

NO-FAULT CRIME INSURANCE

Bronx, New York
December 7, 2074

As many of your readers will recall from their history courses, 1995 was the year that the legally unprecedented No-Fault Crime Insurance bill was passed in the United States. This was shortly after the all-inclusive No-Fault Vehicular Insurance Act or the Omnibus bill.

I am submitting for their interest, therefore, the following scroll which I unearthed recently at the Great Putnam Valley Salt Licks.[1] Scholars conclude that it was written by someone lobbying for passage of the bill (an insurance company perhaps?), and gives us a clue to the ethical and moral development of our ancestors at that time.

ESTELLE GILSON

Fact Sheet on No-Fault Crime Insurance

Q. What is wrong with the way crime is handled now?
A. For one thing, you have to prove the criminal guilty. He has to have a jury of his peers. He has to be tried in a place in which there is no prejudice against him. The District Attorney, the Judge and newspapers are not to have made prejudicial statements against him, though statements made publicly in an alleged criminal's behalf are acceptable, as he is considered innocent until proven guilty. The expense to the state of proving guilt is becoming an insurmountable burden.

Q. Isn't this necessary to protect the innocent?
A. The price is too high. Not only for the state, but also for the alleged criminal. He may be incarcerated for an unconscionable length of time before trial. He has to hire counsel, and if his cause is not among those popular at the moment, he may have difficulty securing legal help. Meanwhile, taxpayers must bear the expenses of interrogating witnesses, transporting them, filing affidavits, writing up mountains of papers (destroying trees). At the same time all this money is being spent, the victim of the alleged crime receives no recompense.

Q. What can be done to improve the way such cases are handled?
A. We suggest adopting no-fault crime insurance.

Q. How does no-fault work?
A. Every family will be required to carry compulsory crime insurance and add to it children beginning at age three (the age at which a child sent to day care may begin causing damage). Your insurance company would pay you promptly for medical expenses, lost wages, and other losses, up to special limits yet to be defined for assault, robbery, rape and so on. The alleged criminal's company would pay his expenses if he was wounded. It would also recompense him up to a certain amount for allegedly stolen property removed from him, should a subsequent trial find him innocent. And he would be recompensed again, up to a limited and stipulated amount, for any time spent in prison.

Q. Does no-fault mean no responsibility for crime?
A. Not at all. Each person is left to his own conscience, and families are still free, if they so desire, to teach their children not to steal or kill. No-fault is merely a means by which everybody involved in crime can have financial protection without having to establish the actual extent and guilt for a crime. Law enforcement authorities may, when deemed necessary, still prosecute those guilty of breaking laws.

Q. What about victims who have suffered damages beyond the statutory limitations described in no-fault policies?
A. They may sue for excessive damages, as in the murder of a bread-winner.

Q. Is no-fault new and revolutionary?
A. By no means. No-fault is now a tried and proven method of dealing with certain economic aspects of human behavior.

---

[1] The Salt Lick Scrolls are not related to the so-called Salt Talks of the same era.

PLATO TALEPOROS

Q. Doesn't no-fault mean that the state would be supporting vice?

A. The state would be helping human beings in trouble. Prostitution and drug use are licensed in many nations. Moreover, economies affected by no-fault insurance mean that much government money previously used for law enforcement and crime detection could be redistributed among the people.

Q. Is it true that no-fault goes against nature?

A. Not so. It is endorsed by leading ecologists, zoologists and anthropologists. For example Baroness Ilge von Ense states that since lionesses hunt for food, while males merely watch, we must re-evaluate our attitudes toward women committing crimes of acquisition.

Q. Does no-fault go against basic human taboos?

A. No. Henrietta Honey, eminent ethnologist, states that in every society known to man, youth must have its fling. It is therefore improper, she adds, for societies to set up laws and restrictions which lead our young astray by making the natural illegal.

Q. Does no-fault go against traditional moral values?

A. No. Erasmus said that man has one pound of passion to a half ounce of reason. Traditional moral values ignored the nature of human nature. Prohibition was unenforceable. Laws against pornography are unenforceable. Capital punishment has been abolished as not preventing murder. If man is the measure of all things, we must learn to make our moral and legal values match man, and we will have to live with heroin addiction, alcoholism, gambling, prostitution and murder in the cheapest and most economical and comfortable ways.

Q. What about no-fault and consumerism?

A. No-fault crime insurance is in the best interests of the consumer. It will pay claims immediately without time-consuming investigations. The victim of robbery or assault will be reimbursed *while he needs the money*. Later, of course, as explained above, either party can sue for excessive damages.

Q. Won't this clog the courts further?

A. No. Direct payment limits of $50 per misdemeanor and $100 and up on a graduated scale per felony, sets the payment better than three-quarters of crime settlements now. Victims of "victimless crimes" as well as victims of physical crimes, who previously received no reimbursement, will now have some protection. Most cases would opt for accepting payment and staying out of court and that means faster justice for others.

Q. What problems can't no-fault solve?

A. No-fault cannot possibly correct conditions which contribute to crime, and therefore to the cost of overall insurance. It will take massive cooperative efforts by gun manufacturers, the para-penal professions, economists, and social planners of all kinds to improve social conditions, to improve housing, to improve education, and to rehabilitate those presently in prisons. It will take your active support to secure federal funds for safer streets and safer weapons. But most of all, it will take your continued commitment to live safely.

PART X

LET'S GET METAPHYSICAL

BIG BEAR SOLAR OBSERVATORY
HALE OBSERVATORIES
CARNEGIE INSTITUTE OF WASHINGTON
CALIFORNIA INSTITUTE OF TECHNOLOGY
To: Universal Creation Foundation
REQUEST FOR SUPPLEMENT TO U.C.F. GRANT #000-00-00000-001
"CREATION OF THE UNIVERSE"

This report is intended only for the internal uses of the contractor.

Period: Present to Last Judgment

Principal Creator: Creator

Proposal Writers and Contract Monitors:

Jay M. Pasachoff and Spencer R. Weart

Hale Observatories

Pasadena, California

Background

Under a previous grant (U.C.F. Grant #000-00-00000-001), the Universe was created. It was expected that this project would have lasting benefits and considerable spinoffs, and this has indeed been the case. Darkness and light, good and evil, and Swiss Army knives were only a few of the useful concepts developed in the course of the Creation. It was estimated that the project would be completed within four days (not including a mandated Day of Rest, with full pay), and the 50% overrun on this estimate is entirely reasonable, given the unusual difficulties encountered. Infinite funding for this project was requested from the Foundation and granted. Unfortunately, this has not proved sufficient. Certain faults in the original creation have become apparent, which it will be necessary to correct by means of miracles. Let it not be said, however, that we are merely correcting past errors; the final state of the Universe, if this supplemental request is granted, will have many useful features not included in the original proposal.

Progress to Date

Interim progress reports have already been submitted ("The Bible," "The Koran," "The Handbook of Chemistry and Physics," etc.). The millennial report is currently in preparation and a variety of publishers for the text (tentatively entitled, "Oh, Genesis!") will be created. The Gideon Society has applied for the distribution rights. Full credit will be given to the Foundation.

Materials for the Universe and for the Creation of Man were created out of the Void at no charge to the grant. A substantial savings was generated when it was found that materials for Woman could be created out of Man, since the establishment of Anti-Vivisection Societies was held until Phase Three. Given the limitations of current eschatological technology, it can scarcely be denied that the Contractor has done his work at a most reasonable price.

Supplement

We cannot overlook a certain tone of dissatisfaction with the Creation which has been expressed by the Foundation, not to mention by certain of the Created.* Let us state outright that this was to be expected, in view of the completely unprecedented nature of the project. The need for a supplement is to be ascribed solely to inflation (not to be confused with expansion of the Universe, which was anticipated). Union requests for the accrual of Days of Rest at the rate of one additional Day per week per millennium (1 $Dw^{-1}m^{-1}$) must also be met. Concerning the problem of Sin, we can assure you that extensive experimentation is under way. Considerable experience is being accumulated and we expect a breakthrough before long. When we are satiated with Sin, we shall go on to consider Universal Peace.

We cannot deny—in view of the cleverness of the Foundation's auditors—that the bulk of the supplemental funds will go to pay off old bills. Nevertheless we do not anticipate the need for future budget requests, barring unforeseen circumstances. If this project is continued successfully, additional Universe—Anti-Universe pairs (Universes—Universes) can be created without increasing the baryon number, and we would keep them out of the light cone of the Original. By the simple grant of an additional Infinity of funds (and note that this proposal is merely for Aleph Null), the officers of the Foundation will be able to present their Board of Directors with the accomplished Creation of one or more successful Universes, instead of the current incomplete one.

Prospective Budget

Remedial miracles on fish of the sea	∞
Remedial miracles on fowl of the air	∞
Creeping things that creep upon the earth, etc.	∞
Hydrogen	n/c (created)
Heavier elements	n/c (nucleosynthesis)

(Note: The Carbon will be reclaimed and ecologically recycled)

Mountains (Sinai, Ararat, Palomar)	∞
Extra quasars, neutron stars	∞
Black holes (no-return containers)	∞
Miscellaneous, secretarial, office supplies, etc.	∞
Telephone installation (Princess model, white, one-time charge, tax included)	$16.50
Axiom of choice	optional

Salaries

Creator (1/4 time)	at His own expense
Archangels	
Gabriel	1 trumpet (Phase 5)
Beelzebub	misc. extra brimstone (Low sulfur)
Others	asst. halos
Prophets	
Moses	stone tablets (to replace breakage)
Geniuses	finite

n.b. Due to the Foundation's regulations and changes in Exchange Rates, we have not yet been able to reimburse Euclid (drachmae), Leonardo (lire), Newton (pounds sterling), Descartes (francs), or Joe Namath (dollars). Future geniuses will be remunerated indirectly via the Alfred Nobel Foundation.

Graduate students (2 at 2/5 time)   reflected glory

Monitoring Equipment and Miscellaneous

1 200-inch telescope (maintenance)	finite
Misc. other instruments, particle accelerators, etc.	large but finite
Travel to meetings	∞
Pollution control equipment	+40%
Total	∞ + 40% = ∞
Overhead (114%)	∞
Total funds requested	∞

Starting date requested:
Immediate. Pending receipt of supplemental funds, layoffs are anticipated to reach the 19.5% level in the ranks of angels this quarter.

---

*"I cannot but conclude the bulk of your natives to be the most pernicious race of little odious vermin that nature ever suffered to crawl upon the surface of the earth."
—JONATHAN SWIFT.

ECONOGENESIS

Dear Sir:

I along with my colleagues Drs. Percy Flage and Hy Perboly were conducting archeological researches in an area not far from where the famed Dead Sea Scrolls were found. Imagine our surprise when the clouds parted and a great voice intoned: "Thou canst not serve God and Mammon!" After a respectful pause, Dr. Flage asked where do you sign up for Mammon. At that very moment, an urchin appeared and motioned for us to follow him. He led us to a cave in the depths of which could be seen a collection of earthen containers. Pointing at the moldy canisters, he uttered his first words: "Money! You give money!" I offered a few coins but the diminutive figure shook his head violently. I added a silver coin to the coppers in my hand. Again he shook his head and suddenly bared his teeth, several of which were capped with gold. Pointing at them, he shouted, "You give!" "This is ridiculous!" Perboly fumed but in the end the desert gnome had his way and was gone. Eagerly we opened the jars one after the other and each in turn proved untenanted by any document. The penultimate container yielded up a yellowed copy of *The Wall Street Journal* of March 4, 1908 at which Flage giggled and Perboly muttered an obscene oath. At length and in considerable despair I opened the last of the jars. Imagine my delight in finding therein a smelly old document, the very thing we had bargained for! After returning to our tent, the three of us pored over our treasure and what follows is our own translation of a wondrous new version of Scriptures that for the first time reveals the true purpose for which mankind was put on earth.

Yours truly,
David H. Weinflash

P.S.: The author is only an amateur archeologist and professionally associated with the investment banking firm of L. F. Rothschild, Unterberg, Towbin. He therefore knows that the most irreproducible result produced in Chicago Heights was that city's single family mortgage revenue bond issue, which his firm underwrote.

IN THE BEGINNING Mammon created commerce and industry. And the marketplace was void and without form, and illiquidity was on the face of the balance sheet. And the spirit of Mammon moved upon the face of the income statement.

And Mammon said, "Let there be cash flow!" And there was cash flow. And Mammon saw that the cash flow was positive. And Mammon segregated the debit accounts from the credit accounts. And Mammon called the debit accounts assets, and the credit accounts He called liabilities. And there was a debit and a credit, the first quarter, unaudited.

And Mammon said, "Let there be investment in the midst of consumption, and let it separate the lenders from the borrowers," and it was so. And Mammon called the investment capital formation, and the consumption He called deficit spending. And there was a debit and a credit, the second quarter, unaudited.

And Mammon said, "Let the means of production be gathered in one place, and let imperfect competition appear!" And Mammon called the imperfect competition price-fixing and the gathering together He called monopoly. And there was a debit and a credit, the third quarter, unaudited.

And Mammon said, "Let there be economic theories in the firmament to separate the wise from the foolish, and let them be for signs and seasons." And Mammon made two great theories: the greater to rule macroeconomics and the lesser to rule microeconomics. Econometrics He also made. And Mammon saw that it was publishable. And there was a debit and a credit, the fourth quarter, unaudited.

And Mammon said, "Let the market bring forth every sort of firm and enterprise that competes on the face of the earth." The great conglomerates of the field and holding companies of the deep He made. And Mammon saw that they were cost-effective. And Mammon said, "Be fruitful and diversify!" And there was a debit and a credit, the fifth quarter, unaudited.

And Mammon said, "Let every industry bring forth its own union and regulatory agency, each after its own kind; and every sort of tax that flieth and bureaucracy that creepeth." And Mammon saw that they were countervailing. And Mammon said, "Let Us make managerial man in Our image!" And Mammon blessed them, male and female, saying "Evaluate, coordinate, plan, and control!" And Mammon gave them dominion over all the factors of production and all the resources of the earth, fungible and unfungible. And Mammon saw everything that He had made, and behold, it was Pareto-optimal. And there was a debit and a credit, the sixth quarter, unaudited.

And the Capitalist system was finished, and all the participants therein. In six quarters Mammon created the real world and in the seventh, He went public.

THE LEARNING OF A SIMPLE MAZE HABIT BY ANGELS

David Lester
Suicide Prevention & Crisis Service
Buffalo, New York

The Cherubim

The Archangel

Ed Lipinski

Although angels have been known to man for many years,[1] little is known of their behavior. Some clinical observations have been recorded and, although the deficiencies of the clinical method in psychological research are well known, it is worth recording these observations since they are all we have.

Angels are not confined by space, they are not confined by time or its changes, they are ever free, they know themselves perfectly, their knowledge is through the causes of things, their knowledge is intuitive, their knowledge is concerned with universals in proportion to its perfection, and the angels enlighten one another and speak to one another.[2]

The present study was designed to further our knowledge of the behavior of angels by means of a scientific study of their behavior. Because the technique of trial-and-error learning has proved so successful in advancing our knowledge of the rat, it was decided to utilize this technique.

Accordingly, this paper reports the results of an attempt to teach angels a simple maze habit.

Method

Subjects. There are nine species of angels (Seraphim, Cherubim, Thrones, Dominations, Virtues, Powers, Principalities, Archangels, and Angels). The present study utilized Cherubim and Archangels obtained from the Carolina Theological Supply Company.[3] Ss were thirty Cherubim and thirty Archangels whose sex and age were indeterminate.

Apparatus. The apparatus was a wooden T-maze with a plexiglass roof. The arms of the maze were 2 feet wide and 6 feet deep. The start box and two goal boxes were attached to the ends of the T-maze and were equipped with doors that opened by means of handles. The arms of the maze were 10 feet long and the start and goal boxes were 3 feet long.

Procedure. The angels were tested immediately upon arrival at the laboratory. Each S was tested individually. S was placed in the start box and allowed 180 seconds in order to enter a goal box. After each trial S was replaced in the start box. For half of the Ss, a reward (a 3 gm Noyes unleavened pellet) was placed in the left goal box while, for the remaining Ss, the reward was placed in the right goal box.

The number of trials until S chose correctly on five successful trials was noted for each S.

Results

The results of the study were most unusual and many data had to be discarded.

Seven of the Cherubim and three of the Archangels disappeared when placed in the start box and the

[1] Matthew, et al. *The New Testament.* Judea, 0070.
[2] Regamey, P-R. *What Is an Angel?* New York: Hawthorn, 1960.
[3] A division of Carolina Biological Supply Company.

laboratory staff were unable to locate them again.

Eleven of the Cherubim and thirteen of the Archangels persisted in walking outside of the maze, apparently through the walls of the maze, and data from these *S*s had to be discarded.

In the case of six of the Cherubim and four Archangels, the experimenter noted that the reward would disappear while the *S* was in the start box. It was thought at first that some rats were loose in the laboratory. However, none were found and one assistant advanced the hypothesis that these occurrences illustrated that angels are not confined by time.

During the running of six Cherubim and five of the Archangels, the experimenter had visions and was temporarily unable to continue with the study.

This left five remaining *S*s, all Archangels, each of whom showed one-trial learning.

Discussion

The results of this experiment provide some support for clinical observations that have been made about angels. Support was found for the fact that they are not confined by space or time. The ability of some to show one-trial learning perhaps supports the suggestion that their knowledge is intuitive.

It is possible that the methods used in this study were inappropriate for angels and need modification. It is possible that, rather than attempting to teach angels a right-left habit, an up-down habit or a right-wrong habit may be more suitable. In addition, the reward may have been unsuitable. Perhaps the *S*s could have been motivated by depriving them of the presence of God and the reward could have been the sight of

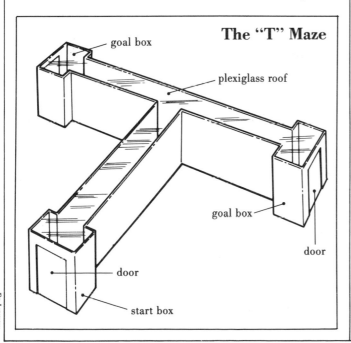

The "T" Maze

goal box, plexiglass roof, goal box, door, door, start box

ED LIPINSKI

SAINT'S DAY CELEBRATION

H. C. Vogt
BASF Wyandotte Corporation
Wyandotte, Michigan

It has come to our attention that the first of May is celebrated in some remote parts of the world as St. Walpurgis Nacht, commemorating St. Walpurgis (Walpurga or Walburga), the patron saint of polymer chemists, both organic and inorganic. She was reported to have been born in Sussex at the beginning of the VIII century. Her father, Richard, is thought to have been a son of Hlothere, ninth king of Kent, while her mother, Winna or Wuna, may have been the sister of St. Boniface. At the insistence of St. Boniface and Willibald, her brother, she went in about 750 A.D. to Germany to continue her studies on macromolecular dissymmetry in ordered systems. Her first major studies were conducted at Bischofsheim in the neighborhood of Mainz, a world-renown center for advanced studies in polymer rheology, where she was able to work in conjunction with St. Herwart. Two years later (754) she moved to Heidenheim, Eichstatt, and continued her investigation of coumarin-indigent resins. This effort resulted in extensive publications which were well received by the scientific community.

Upon her death (780) her relics were translated to Eichstatt, where she was laid to rest in a hollow rock from which exuded a kind of bituminous oil, afterwards known as Walpurgis oil, and regarded by many as the universal plasticizer for PVC. The cave soon became a place of pilgrimage, and an Institute was built over the spot. In addition, she is regarded as the protectress against magic arts. In art she is represented with a crozier, and bearing in her hand a flask of balsam.

This information has been forwarded to IUAPC and awaits their action.

God. Our laboratory technicians are presently working on a solution to this problem.

However, it is clear that angels are very difficult organisms to work with in the laboratory. It seems that psychological knowledge will advance more rapidly through the study of animals such as the Norwegian rat.

CONFESS

A Humanistic, Diagnostic-Prescriptive Computer Program to Decrease Person-to-Person Interaction Time During Confession

Kenneth Majer
Institute for Child Study
Michael C. Flanigan
School of Education
Indiana University

R ecent Vatican interest in the effect upon laymen of the shortage of professional priests (PP) and the decreased seminary enrollment of potential priests (P'P) has led to the development of Computerized Operations (Nonretrievable) for Expediting Sinner Services (CONFESS). This program provides a viable alternative to traditional confession procedures by listing penance requirements (by sin) on a private printout to confessees appropriate to the sin committed. This eliminates one problem which frequently occurs where the confessee, because he is under extreme duress, may forget the original penance. In addition, the program provides a probability estimate of the consequence of not completing the penance associated with a given sin; for example, number of years in purgatory. Thus, full freedom of choice is given to the participant/user (PU). The program requires no PP involvement and hence frees PPs to engage in more pressing activities. It is hoped that by providing PPs with more time for critical theological activities, P'Ps will consider the priesthood a more socially conscious and relevant profession, causing an increase of P'P enrollment in accredited seminaries.

Program Description

CONFESS is available in three natural interactive languages, COURSE WRITER III, BASIC and TUTOR and can be programmed for most other natural languages such as interactive FORTRAN. The program has been developed utilizing on-line computer terminals linked to an IBM 360 for data input, but could be modified to operate in batch mode on almost any third generation configuration given the willingness to sacrifice immediate feedback.

The computing procedures for CONFESS are as follows: The present sins input (psi) yields the graduated penance accrual (GPA) as a function of present sins (ps) plus frequency of confession visits (fcv) times completed penances (cp) divided by recurring sins (rs). Hence, GPA is a function not only of the immediate sins reported but also a partial function of the reciprocal relationship of recurring sins to completed penances by frequency of confession visits. The relative penance, then, is increased by the inclusion of recurring sins. Mathematically, this can be represented as follows:

$$psi \rightarrow GPA = f\{ps + fcv(\quad)\}$$

Sample Printout

```
CONFESS                 GPA PRINTOUT         JOHN POPE, AGE 29
TIME SINCE LAST CONFESSION = 3 WEEKS


-----------------------------------------------------------------
                                                     PROBABILITY
PRESENT SINS   TYPE   GPA              PUNISHMENT     THEREOF
-----------------------------------------------------------------

1.SECRETLY     VENIAL 10 OUR FATHERS.  1 YEAR        .98
  ENVIES BOSS         PRACTICE SMILING  IN PURGATORY
                      AT BOSS

2.SWEAR        VENIAL 10 HAIL MARYS.    1.73 YEARS   .84
  AT WIFE             PRACTICE SMILING  IN PURGATORY
                      AT WIFE

3.COVET        MORTAL ONE ROSARY/DAY    ETERNAL      .91
  NEIGHBOR'S          FOR ONE WEEK.     DAMNATION
  WIFE                PRACTICE SMILING
                      AT WIFE

ONLY 3 SINS THIS TIME MR.POPE. YOU'RE IMPROVING. YOU HAD 14 LAST
CONFESSION. NICE GOING. KEEP UP THE GOOD WORK. LET'S SEE IF YOU
CAN MAKE OUT A LITTLE BETTER WITH NUMBER 3 IN THE FUTURE.
```

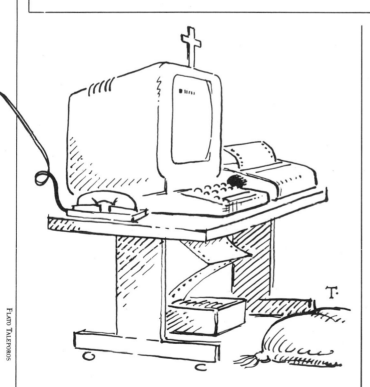

Therefore, each present sin yields a specific GPA that is stored until all GPAs have been computed. At that time, punishment and its maximum likelihood of occurrence[2] should the GPA not be completed, are re-trieved from core storage and printed out for the individual GPA prescription.

Procedures/Output

Being a natural language program, the procedures for CONFESS are extremely simple. The following steps describe the PU procedures.

1. Enter the CONFESS box, and kneel on cushioned kneeler in front of the typewriter/console. Type in your personal PU identification code.

2. The typewriter will type your name and the elapsed time since your last CONFESS session (CONFESSION). Following the request for present sins, type in all sins since your last CONFESSION.

3. Press the "enter" button and silently repeat the short form of the ACT of Contrition. (Given the average latency for GPA, 6.1 seconds, this is usually reduced to "I'm sorry").

4. Remove the CONFESS personalized GPA printout.

MEMO TO MOSES FROM HEW

James E. Mignard, Ph.D.

The HEW staff has reviewed your application for permission to undertake a project on desert living and thinks it has some merit. However, we cannot approve it as it stands because you have not interfaced with Federal rules and regulations on socially-oriented proposals and have failed to meet several government standards. A reading team studied your program carefully. Their criticisms and recommendations in the following paragraphs will help you understand our concerns. You may want to rewrite the proposals according to our suggestions.

First of all, it is not clear to us whether your ten words, or *ten commandments,* as some of our staff call them, are guidelines for a bonafide program for governing people in a nomadic societal setting. We assume they were more than guidelines; therefore, we must point out that we do not approve social programs that have been designed without assistance of consultants who have been certified by HEW.

The regulations require that experts with doctorates and at least ten years experience be consulted whenever a proposal writer deals in areas in which he/she has no professional competence. You speak, for example, of family relationships, neighbors and *"the sojourner who is within your gates"* (tidy up this phrase a bit), the obvious domain of sociology, but you have not listed a single sociologist as a consultant.

There is no evidence that you sought the advice of lawyers when you drafted the sections on killing and stealing. We think a scholar with a national reputation in ethics could have improved what you were trying to say about bearing false witness and committing adultery. And was there a good reason for avoiding theologians when you wrote about having no other gods or not taking the divine name in vain or not making graven images?

Your failure to utilize professional testimony seriously weakens the proposal; indeed, if we were to approve it, our own experts advise us that it would not

EFFECT OF HOLY WATER ON THE GROWTH OF RADISH PLANTS

Sandra Lenington
University of Santa Clara

Summary—Mean growth of 12 radish seeds in peat pots watered with holy water were not significantly different from that of 12 watered with tap water. Limitations on data were listed.

" .... The present experiment would have been more convincing if the person doing the watering did not know which plants were receiving holy water and which plants were receiving tap water. Another controlled factor was storage of holy water in an aluminum container. While the holy water is changed weekly, it was necessarily older and had been sitting a little longer than the tap water. Future studies would be improved were such factors controlled."

—From *Psychological Reports,* Vol. 45, p. 381, 1979.
Submitted by Leonard X. Finegold

last more than four or five years. More specifically, we question the soundness of many of your ideas.

• Take the phrase, *"You shall have no other gods before me."* Not only is this unclear, but we are troubled by the absence of measurable behavioral objectives. How will you know whether this is being accomplished? Do you plan to administer pre- and post-tests, or will you use some kind of peer review? If this idea is so valuable, why is it so negative? In fact, why have you *emphasized* the negative in these propositions? We believe your proposal would be more easily implemented if it were recast in positive terms.

• The *"graven image"* statement. We are puzzled by the weight you give this both in terms of the number of words you have used and its position among the ten. Did you prioritize? Does it really belong in second place? Is it necessary to include the threats? Furthermore, as you surely know, a needs assessment must accompany every application submitted for HEW approval, but you have none. Without supporting data, we have no way of knowing whether there is a genuine *"graven image"* problem amoung your people. Please detail this in an appendix with charts, bar grams, histograms and statistics.

• *"Taking the name in vain"* is a fuzzy expression. A couple of good footnotes on recent research in Near Eastern onomastics would show that you know what you're talking about.

• The *"sabbath day"* paragraph seems overly long and of questionable value. What exactly do you mean by *"remembering"* the sabbath day? How is *"holy"* to be understood? Have you considered a more modern word like *"unstressful"*? Our proposal readers were dismayed that you have chosen to stay with the nuclear family concept. Please review the literature.

• *"Honor father and mother."* If this section is crucial to your project, we suggest you define *honor*. Is there some reason why father precedes mother in the rank-ordering? You state that compliance will affect the lives of the people *"in the land which the Lord your God gives you."* We studied this strange notion and could not determine the significance of real estate here. Are you implying that there is a direct relationship between parent-honoring and land-holding?

• In the opinion of the HEW staff, the next five statements could be lumped together, using, however, less flamboyant language. Verbs like *kill, commit adultery, steal, lie* and *covet* do not sit well with most people.

In our overall examination of your proposal we were struck by the fact that you have made no provisions for the utilization of role-models. We do not think that asking the people to follow your ten points simply because it pleases God is an effective substitute for role-models. If you had attended one of our regional workshops, you would have learned that we do not approve projects that are weak on role-modeling.

Finally, we wish to point out that the rules and regulations stipulate that fourteen typed copies of the proposal be sent to us. Several HEW staff members were upset because you disregarded this. Two stone tablets with chiseled letters do not comply with Federal regulations.

PLATO TALEPOROS

Table of Contents

The Story of Winnie the Pooh 4

Tools and Materials 8

Getting Started 9

Drawing Exercises 10

Winnie the Pooh 12

Tigger 22

Piglet.. 34

Eeyore... 38

Kanga 44

Roo... 48

Rabbit... 52

Owl... 56

Christopher Robin 60

The Story of

Disney Winnie the Pooh

Christopher Robin had lots of toys, but the stuffed animals were his favorites—especially a bear called Winnie the Pooh. The boy and his well-worn friends spent many happy hours sharing make-believe adventures in a place called the Hundred-Acre Wood.

Every night while Pooh slept, he dreamed of honey—his favorite thing. One morning, Pooh woke up to discover there was no honey in his house. He went into the Hundred-Acre Wood to find some more. Pooh came upon Eeyore, the donkey.

"Eeyore," said Pooh. "What has happened to your tail? It isn't there."

"What *is* there?" asked Eeyore.

"Nothing," replied Pooh, who resolved to find it.

Owl suggested promising a prize to anyone who found a replacement tail for Eeyore. "We will have a contest to find a new tail for Eeyore," said Christopher Robin. "The prize shall be a pot of honey!"

Pooh wondered what would make a suitable tail for Eeyore. He dashed home, where the most perfect tail he could think of was hanging on his wall. "Thanks, Pooh," said Eeyore after Pooh outfitted him with a Pooh-koo clock. The friends declared Pooh the contest winner and presented him with a pot

of honey! But before Pooh could scoop out even one pawful, Eeyore sat on his clock tail and crushed it.

"We could give B'loon a try," suggested Piglet. He tied the red balloon to Eeyore's bottom, but Eeyore started to float away.

Christopher Robin pulled Eeyore back and untied the balloon. "Let's try something else," he said. The friends tried many more things, but nothing worked.

"I may have just the thing," said Kanga. She attached her scarf to Eeyore's backside. It worked! But a little while later, Pooh noticed a piece of yarn on the ground. He followed it straight to Eeyore. Kanga's scarf had unraveled!

Later, Pooh went to Christopher Robin's house in search of honey. Christopher Robin was not home, but there was a note on the doorstep. Puzzled, Pooh took the note to Owl's house. Owl said, "It says, 'Gone out, busy Backson. Signed Christopher Robin.' Our friend has been captured by a creature called the Backson!" The friends gasped in fear.

Rabbit came up with a plan. They would collect things that the Backson liked, and leave a trail to lure him into a pit so the Backson would be trapped. Then they could get Christopher Robin back!

Pooh and Piglet chose the location for the pit. When they found the perfect spot, Piglet dug the pit and covered it with a cloth, weighing down its corners with four heavy rocks. Then Piglet put a honeypot on top of the cloth to help disguise the trap.

Meanwhile, Tigger had decided to track the Backson on his own. He was sure he had found him, too, when he pounced on something moving in the Wood. It was Eeyore.

"You and me are going to catch that Backson together!" Tigger declared. "But if you're gonna pounce you got to have some bounce. We need to get you tiggerized!" Tigger gave Eeyore stripes. Then he attached a large spring to the end of Eeyore's tail and set him in motion. The donkey went up and down . . . up and down . . . up and down—and, shortly thereafter, just up. The friends ended up in Rabbit's garden. Tigger dressed up as the Backson and coached Eeyore on how a tigger would "bounce" the monster into surrendering. The poor donkey ricocheted from one place to another and then simply bounced away into the woods. When Tigger

searched for his friend, all he found was Eeyore's springy tail.

Pooh did his best to concentrate on finding Christopher Robin, but his shadow started looking like a honeypot! Then the ground melted into a honey ocean! Pooh swam, dived, and floated in the honey. He gobbled, gulped, and guzzled the honey. Suddenly—POOF!—his daydream disappeared. His honey "ocean" was only a muddy puddle—and Pooh was a great, big mess!

After Pooh cleaned up, he came upon a large honeypot centered in the middle of a cloth. He was so excited that he didn't recognize the Backson trap he and Piglet had set earlier. Pooh fell to the bottom of the pit and the empty honeypot fell on top of his head. Meanwhile, Pooh's friends had arrived at the pit. They heard a loud THUD! The friends clung to each other in fear.

Rabbit exclaimed, "We caught the Backson!"

"Alright, Backson," said Rabbit as the group peered into the pit. "Give us Christopher Robin back."

"Oh, bother," said Pooh, bumping into the walls of the pit.

"Pooh?" asked Rabbit.

"Is that you, Pooh?" asked Piglet.

Just then, Eeyore arrived at the pit and showed off his newest tail. It was an anchor he found in the stream. Rabbit thought Eeyore's anchor tail might help rescue Pooh, so he threw it into the pit. But it was so heavy, it yanked all the friends down into the hole—and broke the honeypot on Pooh's head. Only Piglet, who had been tossed high into the air, remained on the ground.

"Wait for me!" Piglet cried as he started to climb into the pit.

"No, Piglet!" Rabbit cried. "Look for something to get us out!"

Piglet returned with a flower, but it was too short. Next, Piglet brought back a large book, but that didn't work either. On Piglet's third trip, he brought a useful rope. And because there were six friends, Piglet cut the rope into six equal pieces, but they were much too short. Owl flew out of the pit to encourage Piglet to get Christopher Robin's jump rope. Then he flew back in. (Owl did not need rescuing, but no one seemed to notice.)

Piglet trudged nervously into the woods. As he looked around, he backed into a very large tree root. Startled, he turned and saw what looked like a red-eye monster glaring down at him, but it was only B'loon. As Piglet pulled

B'loon from the tree, an enormous shadow fell over him.

"B-B-B-BACKSON!" Piglet shouted. He held on tight to B'loon and raced away. But it was only Tigger dressed in his Backson disguise. But now Tigger thought the Backson was right behind him! He ran after his friend so that they could flee together. "Piglet!" he cried.

"He knows my name!" shrieked Piglet. "Help!"

Piglet spotted the pit in the distance. He had nearly made it when Tigger crashed into him. Down into the pit they both tumbled.

When the dust settled, everyone was relieved to see it was only Tigger. Pooh looked up and saw a honeypot at the edge of the pit. He decided to build himself a letter ladder. The friends all climbed up the ladder and were relieved to be out of the pit—until they heard a rustling in the bushes. "Backson!" they cried. But it was only Christopher Robin.

"How did you escape from the Backson?" asked Rabbit.

"What is a Backson?" Christopher Robin asked.

"The most wretched creature that you could meet," Owl said solemnly.

"What gave you the idea I was taken by a Backson?" said Christopher Robin.

Pooh handed him the note. Christopher Robin giggled. He explained that he had written that he would be "back soon"—not "Backson." It had all been a misunderstanding!

Later, Pooh continued his honey search at Owl's house. He climbed up the tree to Owl's front door, where he pulled the new bell rope. There was something familiar about the rope. As Owl invited Pooh inside he said, "I found that bell rope hanging over a thistle bush. Nobody seemed to want it, so I brought it home."

"But somebody did want it, Owl," Pooh said. "My friend Eeyore. He was attached to it, you see." It was Eeyore's tail!

Pooh took the tail to Christopher Robin, who attached it to Eeyore with a hammer and nail. Eeyore considered his new tail. "Seems about the right length. Pink bow's a nice touch. Swishes real good, too," he said.

"Bring out the grand prize!" Christopher Robin instructed.

"Thank you all ever so much," said Pooh as he climbed into the giant honeypot. All his honey dreams had finally come true!

Tools and Materials

Before you begin drawing, you will need to gather a few tools. Start with a regular pencil, an eraser, and a pencil sharpener. When you're finished with your drawing, you can bring your characters to life by adding color with crayons, colored pencils, markers, or even watercolor or acrylic paints!

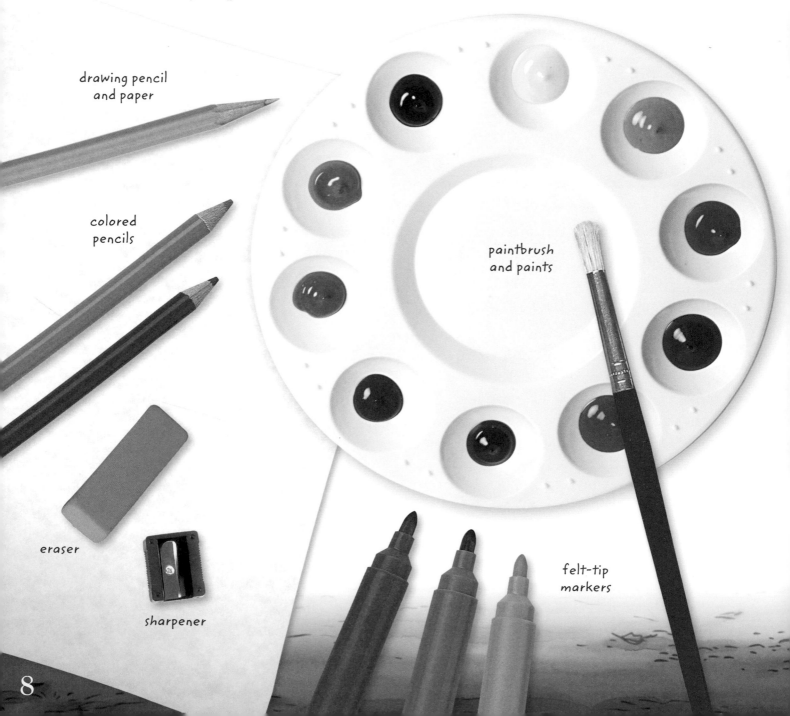

drawing pencil and paper

colored pencils

paintbrush and paints

eraser

sharpener

felt-tip markers

Getting Started

The first thing you'll need is a pencil with a good eraser. Lots of times when artists draw characters, they make extra lines to help them figure out where to put things like noses and ears and whiskers. If you use a pencil, you can erase these lines when your drawing is finished.

First you'll draw guidelines to help position the character's features.

Next, you'll start to add details. It will take several steps to add them all.

When you finish adding all of the details, you can erase your guidelines. Then you can darken your final sketch lines with a pen or a marker.

Drawing Exercises

Warm up your hand by drawing lots of squiggles and shapes.

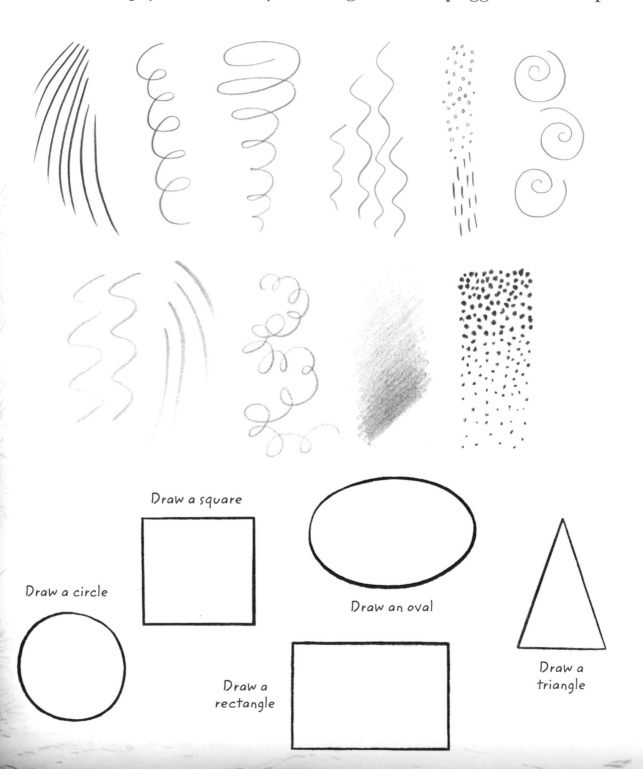

Draw a square

Draw a circle

Draw an oval

Draw a rectangle

Draw a triangle

If you can draw a few basic shapes,
you can draw just about anything!

Circle

Ball

Ice cream cone

Triangle

Pizza

Sun

Square

Oval

House

Balloon

Gift

Submarine

Book

Rectangle

Truck

11

Winnie the Pooh

Pooh is a bear of little brain and big tummy. He has a one-food mind when it comes to honey. But he is also a good friend to Piglet and a perfect pal for "doing nothing" with Christopher Robin. Pooh has a simple sweetness to him that goes beyond the honey stuck to his paws.

Pooh's head is a slightly stretched circle

4

5

6

7

8

Pooh's nose is a soft triangle—
not a round circle—
and a little flat on the top

NO!

YES!

13

Sometimes Disney artists look in the mirror to see how to draw certain expressions. If Pooh were drawing a picture of himself, he'd have a perfect model for a giggling bear!

Pooh's muzzle is egg-shaped.

3

the bridge of his nose is a
soft S shape

he has a smile line at the
corner of his mouth

4

5

6

Pooh's lip line is just under his muzzle

16

Pooh's eyebrows are on the soft curve of his forehead

Pooh's head looks like a circle, and his body looks like a pear. He is about 2-½ heads high, and his toes point in a little. Pooh's shirt is loose fitting, too. Piglet thinks the silly old bear is a wonderful friend.

Pooh's ears are halfway between the top and back of his head

his eyes are set on the muzzle line

3

4

the length
of Pooh's
arms ends at
the widest
part of his
tummy

Pooh's hands are simple—no fingers, just thumbs

21

Tigger

Tigger is one of a kind in the Hundred-Acre Wood. He is always sure of "what tiggers do best," even before he does something. But perhaps the really "wonderful thing" about Tigger is the bounce he brings to everyone around him.

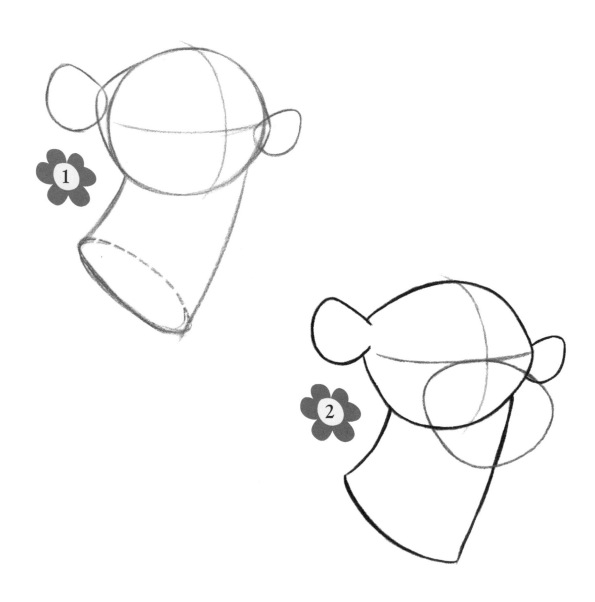

3

4

Tigger's head is diamond-shaped and has flat planes on top

YES!

his head is not too round

NO!

5

6

Tigger's eyes are small and close together; his nose is triangle-shaped

YES!

NO!

Tigger's head and muzzle are oval-shaped. He often has a big grin on his face, but when his feelings get hurt, his whiskers droop toward the ground.

1

2

3

4

YES!
Tigger's nose
is large

NO!
don't make
it too small

5

the stripe on top of
Tigger's head also serves
as his eyebrows

6

Tigger's body is kind of shaped like a banana. His arms are longer than his legs, and he has a combination of large and small stripes on his body. Tigger's long tail squishes when he bounces, which is often.

1

2

3

4

Tigger's tail is
like a spring when
he bounces

when standing or walking, Tigger's tail
is angular, as if a spring is coiled inside

Tigger's hands are like
mittens with no fingers

Piglet

Piglet is a very small animal. He is little enough to be swept away by a leaf and timid enough to be scared by Owl's chilling description of a "Backson." Piglet's eyebrows and mouth usually show how he's feeling.

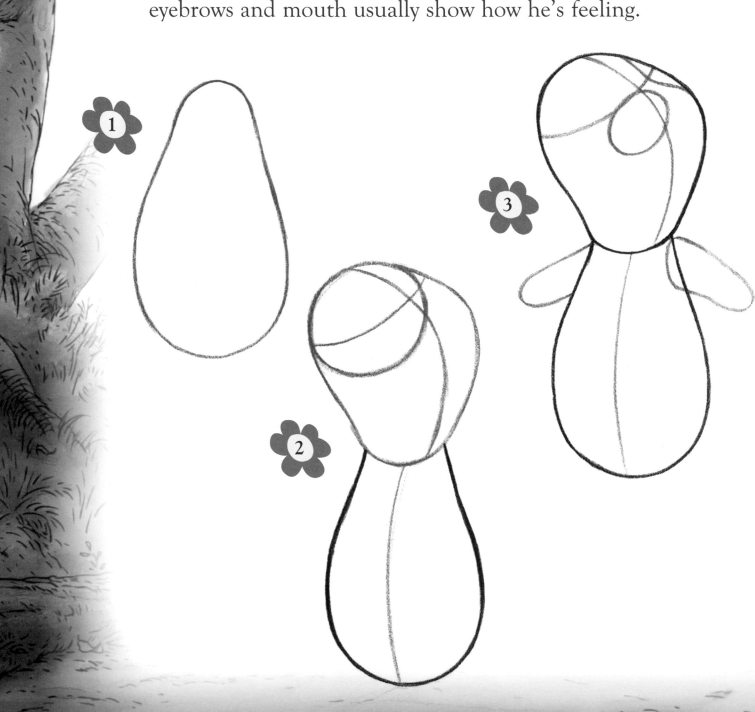

Piglet's ears attach to the side of his head

4

5

Piglet's clothing lines should
wrap around his body

YES!

round

NO!

flat

6

36

Eeyore

Things are always looking down for Eeyore. With a tail that comes loose and a house that collapses, he's always ready for things to go wrong. Still, Eeyore manages to smile once in a while, even though he's almost always gloomy.

his ears are long and come to a point

Eeyore's mane falls forward

5

6

7

8

Poor Eeyore always seems to be losing his tail. He can't even imagine what it must be like to have a springy tail like Tigger's that never falls off—even with the bounciest of bounces.

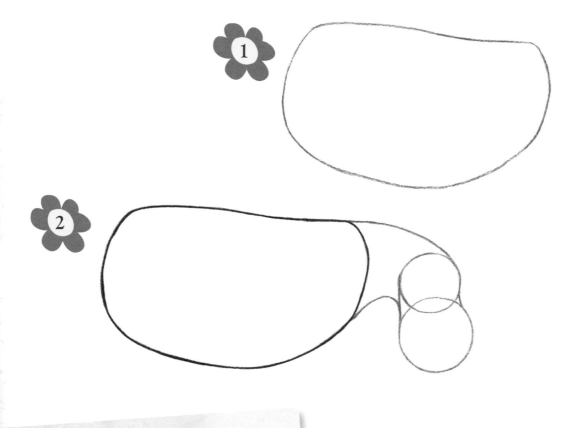

Eeyore's limbs are soft—
remember, he is a stuffed animal

YES!

NO!

3

4

5

41

his neck and head are just
about the same length

Eeyore's head starts with 2
circles—a small one for the
head and a larger one for
the muzzle

8

Kanga

Kanga is like a mother to everyone in the Hundred-Acre Wood, but especially to her own little one, Roo. She is as sweet and playful as she is protective and concerned—and she cares for all of the animals.

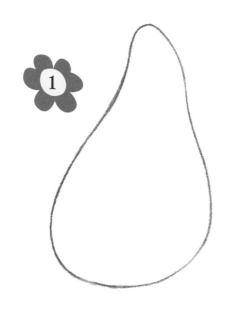

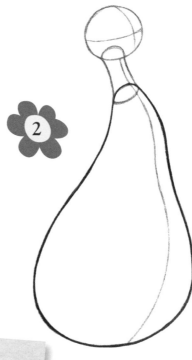

Kanga's body, arms, and legs are soft and round

YES!

NO!

45

Kanga's ears are as
long as her head

don't make them
too small

6

7

Roo

Roo agrees with his best buddy Tigger that bouncing is fun, fun, fun—and he imitates Tigger's bouncing whenever he can. Tigger is like a big brother to Roo, and the two friends just love bouncing from one adventure to the other in the Hundred-Acre Wood.

At only 3 heads tall, Roo is tiny

3

4

Roo's hands and arms
are simple—no fingers,
just a thumb

5

6

Roo's eyes are set
wide apart

YES!

NO!

Roo's ears are shaped like a kidney bean and are about the same height as his head

Rabbit

Rabbit is very organized, right down to the neat rows of vegetables in his garden. He can be fussy and is easily frustrated, but Rabbit is still a good friend to the others. And Pooh and his friends are good friends to him, too.

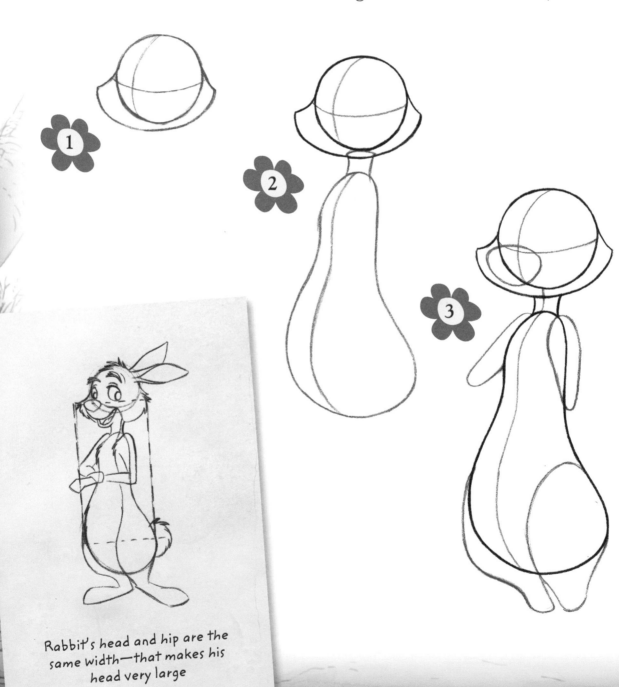

Rabbit's head and hip are the same width—that makes his head very large

Rabbit's feet have 3 toes

Rabbit's hands have 3 fingers and a thumb—more human than the other characters

Owl

Owl likes to talk. And talk, and talk, and talk. When his friends stop by for a visit, Owl doesn't simply talk about the who. He also likes to talk about the what, where, when, why, and how in lots and lots of detail. Still, Pooh often asks Owl for advice.

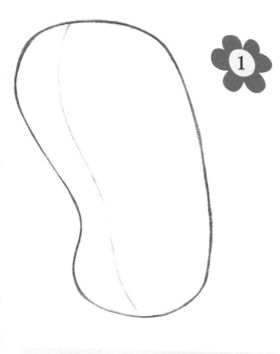

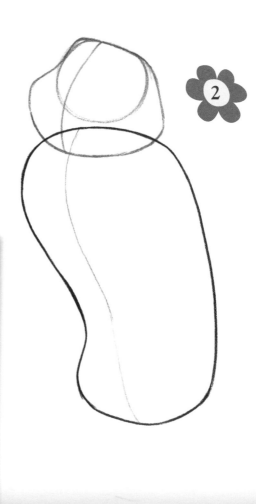

Owl is larger on the top

and smaller on the bottom

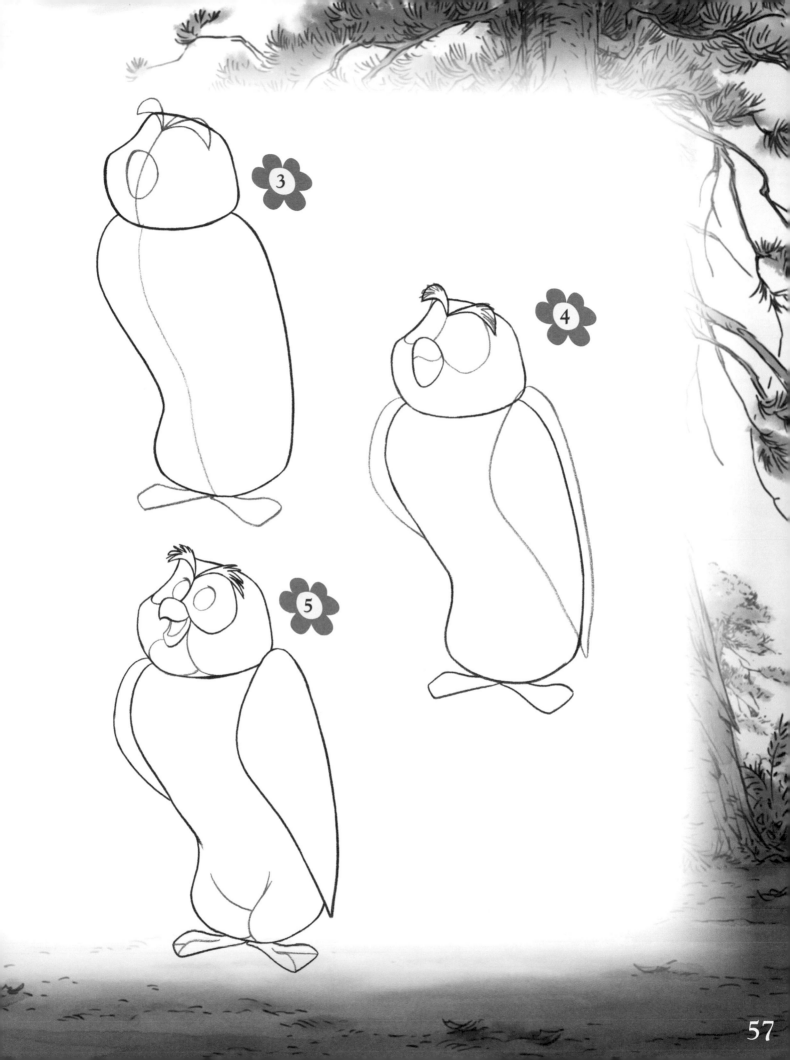

3

4

5

NO!   YES!

Owl's eyes are big,
but his beak is small

Owl's wings can open

Christopher Robin

Even though Christopher Robin is really a child, Pooh and his friends always come to him for help. Whether Eeyore has lost his tail or Pooh is stuck in Rabbit's doorway, Christopher Robin usually knows how to solve the problem.

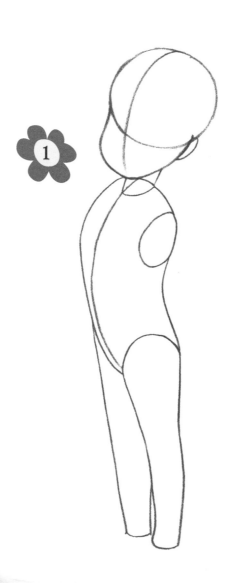

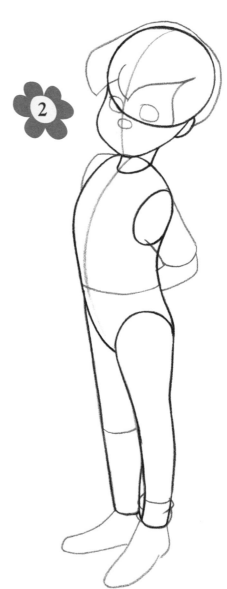

his hair is loose and messy

Christopher Robin's eyes are large and always open wide

3

4

Christopher Robin's socks are always at different levels: the right sock is high and under his knee; the left sock is down near his ankle

5 heads tall

5

Nowhere is a wonderful place—
especially when you're beside
your best friend.